D0089601

Modismos

Americanos

Esenciales

Essential American Idioms
for Spanish Speakers

Richard A. Spears, Ph.D.
Deborah Skolnik, M.A., Spanish Editor

Printed on recyclable paper

NTC Publishing Group
Lincolnwood, Illinois USA

Library of Congress Cataloging-in-Publication Data

Spears, Richard A.
    Modismos Americanos esenciales = Essential American idioms for
Spanish speakers / Richard A. Spears ; Deborah Skolnik, Spanish
editor.
      p.   cm.
    Includes index.
    ISBN 0-8442-7100-4 (alk. Paper)
    1. English language--Conversation and phrase books--Spanish.
2. English language--United States--Idioms--Dictionaries--Spanish.
3. Americanisms--Dictionaries--Spanish.   I. Skolnik, Deborah, 1969-
. II. Title.
PE1129.S8S67   1995
428.2'461--dc20   95-18984
                                      CIP

5 6 7 8 9 VP 0 9 8 7 6 5 4 3 2 1

CONTENTS

AL USUARIO

Cada idioma tiene locuciones que no pueden comprenderse a pie de la letra. Aun si usted conociera los significados de todas las palabras que figuran en dicha locución y comprendiera la gramática completamente, el significado global de la locución todavía podría ser desconcertante. El inglés tiene miles de tales modismos. Este diccionario representa una colección escogida de los que se encuentran con mayor frecuencia en el inglés norteamericano cotidiano. Esta colección es lo suficientemente pequeña como para servir de guía útil de estudios para los principiantes y lo suficientemente grande como para sevir de libro de consulta para el uso diario.

Las locuciones de este diccionario provienen de muchas fuentes. Se han recogido algunas de los periódicos y las revistas. Otras han originado en los diccionarios y los libros de consulta ya existentes. Los estudiantes que estudian el inglés como segundo idioma o como idioma extranjero en la Universidad Northwestern también han proporcionado muchos de los artículos, y sus listas y preguntas han sido de valiosa ayuda en escoger los modismos específicos que figuran en este libro.

Modismos Americanos Esenciales: Essential American Idioms for Spanish Speakers debe resultar de gran utilidad para los que aprenden a comprender el inglés idiomático, para los que tienen una incapacidad de audición, y para todos los hablantes de inglés que desean saber más del idioma.

Cómo usar este diccionario

1. Las expresiones se dan en un orden alfabético que hace caso omiso de los guiones, los espacios y otra puntuación. Se da cada expresión en su forma y sintaxis normales. Los artículos que comienzan con palabras funcionales breves, tales como *a, an, as, at, be, by, do, for,*

from, have, in, off, on, out, under, y *up* figuran tanto en su sintaxis normal como en una sintaxis invertida, de referencia recíproca al artículo normativo; por ejemplo, bajo el artículo **active duty, on,** se remite al lector al artículo **on active duty.**

2. Un artículo principal puede tener una forma variante o más. El artículo principal y sus formas variantes están impresos en **letra negrita,** y a las formas variantes las precede el término "AND". Dos formas variantes o más las separan un punto y coma. Las palabras encerradas entre parenteses bajo cualquier artículo son de uso optativo. Por ejemplo, **break (out) into tears** representa a **break out into tears** y **break into tears.** Cuando se refieren a las locuciones principales de un artículo en el diccionario, están impresas en letra inclinada.

3. Algunas de las locuciones de un artículo pueden tener más de un sentido principal. Estos significados están dotados de un número impreso en letra negrita. Los significados numerados también pueden tener otras variantes que se enseñan con letra negrita después del numeral. Véase, por ejemplo, **get something sewed up.**

4. Algunos de los artículos tienen una forma equivalente en español, a la cual le precede una flecha y está impresa en **letra negrita.**

5. Algunos artículos tienen más formas afines dentro del mismo artículo. Estas formas las presenta el término "ALSO," y las referencias recíprocas llevan al usuario a cada uno de estos artículos encajados en el principal. Véase, por ejemplo, **get a black eye.**

6. Las formas variantes de una definición las separan dos puntos, y a algunas definiciones las siguen ciertos comentarios o explicaciones entre parenteses. Véase, por ejemplo, **add fuel to the fire.**

7. En algunos casos donde la locución del artículo se refiere o a las personas o a las cosas—tal como lo ejemplifica **"someone or something"** —los sentidos numerados pueden utilizarse sólo con las personas o sólo con las cosas. En dichos casos, el sentido numerado comienza con "[con *alguien*]" o "[con *algo*]." Véase, por ejemplo, **cut someone or something to the bone.**

8. Cada artículo o sentido tiene por lo menos dos ejemplos impresos en *letra itáltica.*

9. Un índice de las locuciones es español comienza en la página 243 y le permite al usuario localizar las locuciones en español que son equivalentes a los modismos en inglés.

LOS TÉRMINOS Y LOS SÍMBOLOS

☐   señala el comienzo de un ejemplo.

ALSO/TAMBIÉN   presenta otra forma variante dentro de un artículo, la cual tiene afinidad con el artículo principal, pero con un significado o forma que es levemente distinto. Véase el punto cinco bajo "Cómo usar este diccionario."

AND/Y   señala que la locución del artículo tiene formas variantes que significan lo mismo o casi lo mismo como la locución del artículo. Una forma variante o más a las cuales precede el término **AND/Y.** Véase el punto dos bajo "Cómo usar este diccionario."

cliché/cliché   describe una expresión que es trillada y se utiliza con demasiada frecuencia.

Compare to/Comparar a   significa consultar el artículo señalado y repasar su forma o significado con relación a la locución del artículo en el cual figuran las instrucciones de "comparar a".

informal/coloquial   describe una expresión muy coloquial que probablemente se emplea más en el lenguaje hablado que en el escrito.

proverb/proverbio   describe un dicho de forma fija que se cita a menudo y que ofrece un buen consejo o un pensamiento de la sabiduría popular.

rude/grosero   describe una expresión que es insultante o cruel.

See/Ver significa remitirse al artículo sañalado.

See also/Ver también significa consultar el artículo señalado para mayor información o para encontrar expresiones afines de forma o de significado a la locución del artículo en el cual figuran las instrucciones de "ver también".

See under/Ver en significa remitirse a la locución del artículo señalado y localizar la locución que usted está buscando dentro del artículo señalado.

slang/jerga; argot describe una expresión que se reconoce como coloquial o juguetona. Se piensa que tales términos no convienen a la escritura formal.

TO THE USER

Every language has phrases that cannot be understood literally. Even if you know the meanings of all the words in such a phrase and you understand the grammar completely, the total meaning of the phrase may still be confusing. English has many thousands of such idiomatic expressions. This dictionary is a selection of the most frequently encountered idiomatic expressions found in everyday American English. The collection is small enough to serve as a useful study guide for learners, and large enough to serve as a reference for daily use.

The phrases in the dictionary come from many sources. Many have been collected from newspapers and magazines. Others have come from existing dictionaries and reference books. Students studying English as a second or foreign language at Northwestern University have also provided many of the entries, and their lists and questions have helped in selecting the particular idiomatic expressions that appear in this book.

Modismos Americanos Esenciales: Essential American Idioms for Spanish Speakers should prove useful for people who are learning how to understand idiomatic English, the hearing impaired, and for all speakers of English who want to know more about the language.

How to Use This Dictionary

1. Expressions are entered in an alphabetical order that ignores hyphens, spaces, and other punctuation. Each expression is entered in its normal form and word order. Entries that begin with short function words such as *a, an, as, at, be, by, do, for, from, have, in, off, on, out, under,* and *up* appear both in normal word order and in inverted word order, cross-referenced to the normal entry; for example, at the entry **active duty, on** the reader is referred to the entry **on active duty.**

2. A main entry may have one or more alternate forms. The main entry and its alternate forms are printed in **boldface type,** and the alternate forms are preceded by "AND." Two or more alternate forms are separated by a semicolon. Words enclosed in parentheses in any entry form are optional. For example: **break (out) into tears** stands for **break out into tears** and **break into tears.** When entry phrases are referred to in the dictionary, they are printed in *slanted type.*

3. Some of the entry phrases have more than one major sense. These meanings are numbered with boldface numerals. Numbered senses may also have additional forms that are shown in boldface type after the numeral. See, for example, **get something sewed up.**

4. Some of the entries have a Spanish equivalent. This is introduced by an arrow and given in **boldface type.**

5. Some entries have additional related forms within the entry. These forms are introduced by "ALSO," and cross-referencing leads the user to each of these embedded entries. See, for example, **get a black eye.**

6. Alternate forms of the definitions are separated by semicolons, and some definitions are followed by comments or explanations in parentheses. See, for example, **add fuel to the fire.**

7. In some cases where the entry phrase refers to either people or things—as expressed by **"someone or something"**—the numbered senses can be used with people only or things only. In such cases the numbered sense begins with "[with *someone*]" or "[with *something*]." See, for example, **cut someone or something to the bone.**

8. Each entry or sense has at least two examples printed in *italics.*

9. An Index of Spanish Phrases begins on page 243 and enables the user to locate Spanish phrases that are equivalent to the English idioms.

TERMS AND SYMBOLS

☐ (a box) marks the beginning of an example.

ALSO introduces an additional variant form within an entry, which is related to the main entry, but has a slightly different meaning or form. See point five in "How to Use This Dictionary."

AND indicates that an entry phrase has variant forms that are the same or almost the same in meaning as the entry phrase. One or more variant forms are preceded by AND. See point two in "How to Use this Dictionary."

cliché describes an expression that is used too frequently and too casually.

Compare to means to consult the entry indicated and examine its form or meaning in relation to the entry phrase containing the "Compare to" instruction.

informal describes a very casual expression that is most likely to be spoken and not written.

proverb describes a frequently quoted fixed saying that gives advice or makes a philosophical observation.

rude describes an expression that is insulting or harsh.

See means to turn to the entry indicated.

See also means to consult the entry indicated for additional information or to find expressions similar in form or meaning to the entry phrase containing the "See also" instruction.

See under   means to turn to the entry phrase indicated and look for the phrase you are seeking within the entry indicated.

slang   describes an expression that is recognized as casual or playful. Such terms are not considered appropriate for formal writing.

A

A bird in the hand is worth two in the bush. un refrán significando que la cosa ya poseída es mejor que la cosa que posiblemente se vaya a poseer. → **Más vale pájaro en mano que ciento [o buitre] volando.** □ *Bill has offered to buy my car for $3,000. Someone else might pay more, but Bill made a good offer, and a bird in the hand is worth two in the bush.* □ *I might be able to find a better offer, but a bird in the hand is worth two in the bush.*

according to Hoyle conforme a las reglas; de acuerdo con la manera típica de hacer algo. (Se refiere a las reglas de los juegos. Edmond Hoyle escribió un libro de juegos. Se usa esta expresión normalmente para las cosas, en general, en vez de los juegos.) → **como Dios manda.** □ *That's wrong. According to Hoyle, this is the way to do it.* □ *The carpenter said, "This is the way to drive a nail, according to Hoyle."*

a chip off the old block una persona (normalmente varón) que se comporta igual que su padre. También se refiere a una persona que se asemeja físicamente a su padre. (El padre es el "bloque viejo.") → **de tal palo, tal astilla.** □ *John looks like his father—a real chip off the old block.* □ *Bill Jones, Jr., is a chip off the old block. He's a banker just like his father.*

act high-and-mighty comportarse con orgullo y poderío; comportarse con altanería. → **tener mucho copete.** □ *Why does the doctor always have to act so high-and-mighty?* □ *If Sally wouldn't act so high-and-mighty, she'd have more friends.*

Actions speak louder than words. un refrán significando que es mejor combatir un problema en vez de sólo hablar sobre él. → **Obras son amores y no buenas razones; El movimiento se demuestra andando.** □ *Mary kept promising to get a job. John finally looked her in the eye and said, "Actions speak louder than* *words!"* □ *After listening to the senator promising to cut federal spending, Ann wrote a simple note saying, "Actions speak louder than words."*

active duty, on   Véase *on active duty.*

act of God   un acontecimiento (normalmente un accidente) para lo cual ninguna persona es responsable; una perturbación de la naturaleza, como una tormenta, un terremoto, o un vendaval. □ *My insurance company wouldn't pay for the damage because it was an act of God.* □ *The thief tried to convince the judge that the diamonds were in his pocket due to an act of God.*

act one's age   comportarse con más madurez; comportarse más adulta de lo que es. (Se dice mucho a niños o adolescentes.) □ *Come on, John, act your age. Stop throwing rocks.* □ *Mary! Stop picking on your little brother. Act your age!*

add fuel to the fire AND **add fuel to the flame**   empeorar un problema; decir o hacer algo que empeora una situación mala; hacer que una persona enojada se ponga más enojada. → **echar leña al fuego.** □ *To spank a crying child just adds fuel to the fire.* □ *Bill was shouting angrily, and Bob tried to get him to stop by laughing at him. Of course, that was just adding fuel to the flame.*

add fuel to the flame   Véase la entrada previa.

add insult to injury   empeorar una situación mala; ofenderle a una persona ya ofendida. (Un cliché.) → **para colmo; para más inri.** □ *First, the basement flooded, and then, to add insult to injury, a pipe burst in the kitchen.* □ *My car barely started this morning, and to add insult to injury, I got a flat tire in the driveway.*

A fool and his money are soon parted.   un refrán significando que una persona que se comporta con ignorancia en asuntos de dinero lo pierde pronto. (Muchas veces referente a una persona que acaba de perder una cantidad de dinero a causa de su juicio malo.) → **A los tontos no les dura el dinero.** □ *When Bill lost a $400 bet on a horse race, Mary said, "A fool and his money are soon parted."* □ *When John bought a cheap used car that fell apart the next day, he said, "Oh, well, a fool and his money are soon parted."*

afraid of one's own shadow una persona que se asusta fácilmente; una persona siempre asustada, tímida, or sospechosa. (Nunca se usa literalmente.) □ *After Tom was robbed, he was even afraid of his own shadow.* □ *Jane has always been a shy child. She has been afraid of her own shadow since she was three.*

A friend in need is a friend indeed. un refrán significando que un amigo verdadero es una persona que ayuda a sus amigos cuando se encuentran en situaciones difíciles. → **En las malas se conoce a los amigos.** □ *When Bill helped me with geometry, I really learned the meaning of "A friend in need is a friend indeed."* □ *"A friend in need is a friend indeed" sounds silly until you need someone very badly.*

against the clock compitiendo contra el reloj; con mucha prisa para hacer algo antes de una hora específica. □ *Bill set a new track record, running against the clock. He lost the actual race, however.* □ *In a race against the clock, they rushed the special medicine to the hospital.*

air, in the Véase *in the air.*

air, off the Véase *off the air.*

air, on the Véase *on the air.*

air someone's dirty linen in public hablar de asuntos privados o vergonzosos en público, especialmente durante una riña. *Linen* se refiere a problemas como si fueran sábanas y manteles o otro lino sucio.) □ *John's mother had asked him repeatedly not to air the family's dirty linen in public.* □ *Mr. and Mrs. Johnson are arguing again. Why must they always air their dirty linen in public?*

air, up in the Véase *up in the air.*

A little bird told me. aprendido de una fuente misteriosa o secreta. (Muchas veces se usa como respuesta evasiva a una persona buscando la fuente de alguna información. Esta frase es descortés en algunas circunstancias.) □ *"All right," said Mary, "where did you get that information?" John replied, "A little bird told me."* □ *A little bird told me where I might find you.*

A little knowledge is a dangerous thing. un refrán significando que el conocimiento incompleto puede avergonzar o dañar a alguien o algo. □ *The doctor said, "Just because you've had a course in first aid, you shouldn't have treated your own illness. A little knowledge is a dangerous thing."* □ *John thought he knew how to take care of the garden, but he killed all the flowers. A little knowledge is a dangerous thing.*

all fours, on Véase *on all fours.*

all in a day's work parte de las tareas esperadas; típico o normal. □ *I don't particularly like to cook, but it's all in a day's work.* □ *Putting up with rude customers isn't pleasant, but it's all in a day's work.* □ *Cleaning up after other people is all in a day's work for a chambermaid.*

all over but the shouting decidido y concluído; terminado salvo la celebración. (La frase es elaboración de *all over,* significando "finished.") □ *The last goal was made just as the final whistle sounded. Tom said, "Well, it's all over but the shouting."* □ *Tom worked hard in college and graduated last month. When he got his diploma, he said, "It's all over but the shouting."*

All roads lead to Rome. un refrán significando que hay muchas rutas posibles para llegar a la misma meta. → **Por todas partes se va a Roma; Todos los caminos llevan a Roma.** □ *Mary was criticizing the way Jane was planting the flowers. John said, "Never mind, Mary, all roads lead to Rome."* □ *Some people learn by doing. Others have to be taught. In the long run, all roads lead to Rome.*

all skin and bones Véase en *nothing but skin and bones.*

All's well that ends well. un refrán significando que un suceso con resultado bueno es bueno aunque algunas cosas salieron mal en el camino. (La frase también es título de una obra de Shakespeare. Ahora se usa como cliché.) □ *I'm glad you finally got here, even though your car had a flat tire on the way. Oh, well. All's well that ends well.* □ *The groom was late for the wedding, but everything worked out all right. All's well that ends well.*

All that glitters is not gold. un refrán significando que muchas cosas atrayentes y fascinantes no tienen valor. → **No es oro todo lo que reluce.** □ *The used car looked fine but didn't run well at all. "Ah, yes," thought Bill, "all that glitters is not gold."* □ *When Mary was disappointed about losing Tom, Jane reminded her, "All that glitters is not gold."*

all thumbs muy desmañado y torpe, especialmente con las manos. (La frase significa que las manos de alguien sólo tienen pulgares.) □ *Poor Bob can't play the piano at all. He's all thumbs.* □ *Mary is all thumbs when it comes to gardening.*

all walks of life todos los grupos sociales, económicos, y étnicos; todo tipo de gente. (Una frase fija. No ocurre en el singular o sin *all*.) □ *We saw people there from all walks of life.* □ *The people who came to the art exhibit represented all walks of life.*

All work and no play makes Jack a dull boy. un refrán significando que una persona debe divertirse así como trabajar. (*Jack* no es referente a una persona específica. Se puede usar la frase para referirse a mujeres y hombres.) □ *Stop reading that book and go out and play! All work and no play makes Jack a dull boy.* □ *The doctor told Mr. Jones to stop working on weekends and start playing golf, because all work and no play makes Jack a dull boy.*

An eye for an eye, a tooth for a tooth. un tema bíblico indicando que la pena debe igualar a la transgresión. (Ahora la frase es usada como refrán. No es literal.) □ *Little John pulled Jane's hair, so the teacher pulled John's hair as punishment, saying, "An eye for an eye, a tooth for a tooth."* □ *He kicked me in the leg, so I kicked him in the leg. After all, an eye for an eye, a tooth for a tooth.*

An ounce of prevention is worth a pound of cure. un refrán significando que es más fácil y mejor evitar algo malo que tener que hacer frente a los resultados. □ *When you ride in a car, buckle your seat belt. An ounce of prevention is worth a pound of cure.* □ *Every child should be vaccinated against polio. An ounce of prevention is worth a pound of cure.*

A penny saved is a penny earned. un refrán significando que el dinero que una persona ahorra por frugalidad es igual al dinero que gana en el trabajo. (Algunas veces se usa la frase para explicar la tacañería.) □ *"I didn't want to pay that much for the book," said Mary. "After all, a penny saved is a penny earned."* □ *Bob put his money in a new bank that pays more interest than his old bank, saying, "A penny saved is a penny earned."*

apple of someone's eye la persona o la cosa preferida de alguien; un novio o una novia; la persona o la cosa que alguien quiere. (Una persona o una cosa que ha atraído el ojo o la atención de alguien.) □ *Tom is the apple of Mary's eye. She thinks he's great.* □ *John's new stereo is the apple of his eye.*

armed to the teeth armado con muchas armas mortales. (Como si toda clase de armamentos fuera usadas, hasta e incluso los dientes.) □ *The bank robber was armed to the teeth when he was caught.* □ *There are too many guns around. The entire country is armed to the teeth.*

arm-in-arm personas unidas o enganchadas con los brazos. → **tomados del brazo; de bracete.** □ *The two lovers walked arm-in-arm down the street.* □ *Arm-in-arm, the line of dancers kicked high, and the audience roared its approval.*

arms, up in Véase *up in arms.*

A rolling stone gathers no moss. un refrán que describe a la persona que cambia mucho de trabajo o residencia, y entonces no acumula ni posesiones ni responsabilidades. (Normalmente se usa esta frase como crítica.) □ *"John just can't seem to stay in one place," said Sally. "Oh, well, a rolling stone gathers no moss."* □ *Bill has no furniture to bother with because he keeps on the move. He keeps saying that a rolling stone gathers no moss.*

as a duck takes to water fácil y naturalmente. (Referente a los patitos, quienes parecen poder nadar la primera vez que entran en el agua.) → **encontrarse en seguida en su salsa con algo.** □ *She took to singing, just as a duck takes to water.* □ *The baby adapted to bottle-feeding as a duck takes to water.*

as an aside   como comentario; como comentario que todo el mundo no debe oír. □ *At the wedding, Tom said as an aside, "The bride doesn't look well."* □ *At the ballet, Billy said as an aside to his mother, "I hope the dancers fall off the stage!"*

(as) bad as all that   tan mal como contado; tan mal como parece. (Normalmente la frase es usada como negación.) □ *Come on! Nothing could be as bad as all that.* □ *Stop crying. It can't be bad as all that.*

(as) blind as a bat   con vista imperfecta; ciego. (Sin embargo, típicamente los murciélagos no son ciegos. La frase sobrevive a causa de la aliteración.) → **ciego como un topo.** □ *My grandmother is as blind as a bat.* □ *I'm getting blind as a bat. I can hardly read this page.*

(as) busy as a beaver AND **(as) busy as a bee**   muy ocupado. (La frase sobrevive a causa de la aliteración.) □ *I don't have time to talk to you. I'm as busy as a beaver.* □ *You don't look busy as a beaver to me.* □ *Whenever there is a holiday, we are all as busy as bees.*

(as) busy as a bee   Véase la entrada previa.

(as) busy as Grand Central Station   muy ocupado; lleno de clientes o otras personas. (Esta frase se refiere a Grand Central Station, una estacíon de trenes en la ciudad de Nueva York.) □ *This house is as busy as Grand Central Station.* □ *When the tourist season starts, this store is busy as Grand Central Station.*

(as) clear as mud   algo que no es comprensible. (La frase es familiar o usada de broma.) □ *Your explanation is as clear as mud.* □ *This doesn't make sense. It's clear as mud.*

(as) comfortable as an old shoe   muy cómodo; muy confortable y familiar. (Referente a un zapato que una persona ha llevado durante mucho tiempo, así que es muy cómodo.) □ *This old house is fine. It's as comfortable as an old shoe.* □ *That's a great tradition—comfortable as an old shoe.*

(as) cool as a cucumber tranquilo; alguien que mantiene la calma. (Sin embargo, los pepinos no son frescos necesariamente. La frase sobrevive a causa de la aliteración.) → **más fresco que una lechuga.** □ *The captain remained as cool as a cucumber as the passengers boarded the lifeboats.* □ *During the fire the homeowner was cool as a cucumber.*

(as) crazy as a loon muy bobo; completamente loco. (*Loon* significa somorgujo en español, que es ave acúatica con una llamada que suena como risa boba. □ *If you think you can get away with that, you're as crazy as a loon.* □ *Poor old John is crazy as a loon.*

(as) dead as a dodo muerto; ya no existe. (El dodo, un pájaro antiguo de Mauritius, es extinto. La frase sobrevive a causa de la aliteración.) □ *Yes, Adolf Hitler is really dead—as dead as a dodo.* □ *That silly old idea is dead as a dodo.*

(as) dead as a doornail muerto. (Claro, *doornails,* no están vivos. La frase sobrevive a causa de la aliteración.) □ *This fish is as dead as a doornail.* □ *John kept twisting the chicken's neck even though it was dead as a doornail.*

(as) different as night and day completamente diferente. □ *Although Bobby and Billy are twins, they are as different as night and day.* □ *Birds and bats appears to be similar, but they are different as night and day.*

(as) easy as (apple) pie muy fácil. (En esta frase, se considera fácil la cocina de los pasteles.) □ *Mountain climbing is as easy as pie.* □ *Making a simple dress out of cotton cloth is easy as apple pie.*

(as) easy as duck soup muy fácil; no necesitando esfuerzo. (El pato da mucha grasa y mucho jugo cuando se cuece, así que sale una sopa sin esfuerzo.) □ *Finding your way to the shopping center is easy as duck soup.* □ *Getting Bob to eat fried chicken is as easy as duck soup.*

as far as it goes tanto como algo haga, cubra, o logre. (Normalmente se dice de algo que es insuficiente.) □ *Your plan is fine as far as it goes. It doesn't seem to take care of everything, though.* □

As far as it goes, this law is a good one. It should require stiffer penalties, however.

(as) fit as a fiddle   sano y de buena forma físicamente. (La frase no tiene sentido, y sólo sobrevive a causa de la aliteración.) → **sano como una manzana.** □ *Mary is as fit as a fiddle.* □ *Tom used to be fit as a fiddle. Look at him now!*

(as) flat as a pancake   muy llano. □ *The punctured tire was as flat as a pancake.* □ *Bobby squashed the ant flat as a pancake.*

(as) free as a bird   libre de cuidados; completamente libre. □ *Jane is always happy and free as a bird.* □ *The convict escaped from jail and was as free as a bird for two days.* □ *In the summer I feel free as a bird.*

(as) full as a tick AND **(as) tight as a tick**   muy lleno de comida o bebida. (Referente a una garrapata que se ha llenado de sangre.) □ *Little Billy ate and ate until he was as full as a tick.* □ *Our cat drank the cream until he became tight as a tick.*

(as) funny as a crutch   sin gracia. □ *Your trick is about as funny as a crutch. Nobody thought it was funny.* □ *The well-dressed lady slipped and fell in the gutter, which was funny as a crutch.*

(as) good as done   igual a ser terminado; casi terminado. (Se puede sustituir muchos participios por *done* en esta frase: *cooked, dead, finished, painted, typed,* etc.) □ *This job is as good as done. It'll just take another second.* □ *Yes, sir, if you hire me to paint your house, it's as good as painted.* □ *When I hand my secretary a letter to be typed, I know that it's as good as typed right then and there.*

(as) good as gold   genuino; auténtico. (Es cliché.) La frase sobrevive a causa de la aliteración.) → **más bueno que el pan.** □ *Mary's promise is as good as gold.* □ *Yes, this diamond is genuine—good as gold.*

(as) happy as a clam   feliz y contento. (Observe las variaciones en los ejemplos. No están necesariamente felices ni tristes las almejas.) □ *Tom sat there smiling, as happy as a clam.* □ *There they all sat, eating corn on the cob and looking happy as clams.*

(as) happy as a lark feliz y alegre. (Observe las variaciones en los ejemplos.) → **como unas pascuas.** □ *Sally walked along whistling, as happy as a lark.* □ *The children danced and sang, happy as larks.*

(as) hard as nails muy duro; frío y cruel. (Referente a los clavos que se usan con un martillo.) → **ser muy duro (de corazón).** □ *The old loaf of bread was dried out and became as hard as nails.* □ *Ann was unpleasant and hard as nails.*

(as) high as a kite AND **(as) high as the sky** 1. muy alto. □ *The tree grew as high as a kite.* □ *Our pet bird got outside and flew up high as the sky.* 2. borracho o drogado. → **estar totalmente colocado; estar totalmente drogado; estar hasta atrás.** □ *Bill drank beer until he got as high as a kite.* □ *The thieves were high as the sky on drugs.*

(as) high as the sky Véase la entrada previa.

(as) hungry as a bear con mucha hambre. □ *I'm as hungry as a bear. I could eat anything!* □ *Whenever I jog, I get hungry as a bear.*

aside, as an Véase *as an aside.*

(as) innocent as a lamb sin culpabilidad; ingenuo. (Es cliché.) □ *"Hey! You can't throw me in jail,"* cried the robber. *"I'm innocent as a lamb."* □ *Look at the baby, as innocent as a lamb.*

as it were se puede decir. (A veces se usa para dar autorización a una idea que no parece razonable.) □ *He carefully constructed, as it were, a huge sandwich.* □ *The Franklins live in a small, as it were, exquisite house.*

ask for the moon pedir demasiado; exigir mucho; pedir algo que es difícil o imposible de obtener. (No es literal.) → **pedir el moro y el oro.** □ *When you're trying to get a job, it's unwise to ask for the moon.* □ *Please lend me the money. I'm not asking for the moon!*

ask for trouble   hacer o decir algo que lleva a la desgracia. →
buscarse problemas; tener ganas de meterse en líos. □ *Stop
talking to me that way, John. You're just asking for trouble.* □
Anybody who threatens a police officer is just asking for trouble.

asleep at the switch   no desempeñando un trabajo; no cumpliendo
con las obligaciones a la hora oportuna. (No tiene que referirse a
conmutador verdadero.) □ *The guard was asleep at the switch when
the robber broke in.* □ *If I hadn't been asleep at the switch, I'd have
seen the stolen car.*

(as) light as a feather   sin mucho peso. → **ligero como una
pluma; liviano como una pluma.** □ *Sally dieted until she was as
light as a feather.* □ *Of course I can lift the box. It's light as a
feather.*

(as) likely as not   probablemente; con igual posibilidad para
cualquiera de dos opciones. (La frase es fija; no hay otras formas.)
□ *He will as likely as not arrive without warning.* □ *Likely as not,
the game will be cancelled.*

as luck would have it   por buena o mala suerte; como salió; por
casualidad. (La frase es fija; no hay otras formas.) → **quiso la suerte
que.** □ *As luck would have it, we had a flat tire.* □ *As luck would
have it, the check came in the mail today.*

(as) mad as a hatter   1. loco. (Del personaje llamado Mad Hatter
en *Alice's Adventures in Wonderland,* una obra de Lewis Carroll.)
→ **estar como una cabra.** □ *Poor old John is as mad as a hatter.*
□ *All these screaming children are driving me mad as a hatter.* 2.
enfadado. (Este sentido de la frase viene de la interpretación incorrecta
de *mad* en su primer sentido.) □ *You make me so angry! I'm as mad
as a hatter.* □ *John can't control his temper. He's always mad as
a hatter.*

(as) mad as a hornet   enfadado. (Los avispones tienen un
temperamento terrible.) □ *You make me so angry. I'm as mad as
a hornet.* □ *Jane can get mad as a hornet when somebody criticizes
her.*

(as) mad as a March hare   enfadado. (De un personaje en *Alice's Adventures in Wonderland,* una obra de Lewis Carroll.) □ *Sally is getting as mad as a March hare.* □ *My Uncle Bill is mad as a March hare.*

(as) mad as a wet hen   enfadado. (Se puede asumir que una gallina quisquillosa se pondría enfadada si estuviera mojada.) □ *Bob was screaming and shouting—as mad as a wet hen.* □ *What you said made Mary mad as a wet hen.*

as one   como si un grupo fuera una persona. (Especialmente con los verbos *act, move,* or *speak.*) □ *All the dancers moved as one.* □ *The chorus spoke as one.*

(as) plain as day   **1.** muy ordinario y sencillo. □ *Although his face was as plain as day, his smile made him look interesting and friendly.* □ *Our house is plain as day, but it's comfortable.* **2.** claro y comprensible. (Tan transparente como la luz natural.) □ *The lecture was as plain as day. No one had to ask questions.* □ *His statement was plain as day.*

(as) plain as the nose on one's face   obvio; evidente. □ *What do you mean you don't understand? It's as plain as the nose on your face.* □ *Your guilt is plain as the nose on your face.*

(as) poor as a church mouse   muy pobre. (Es cliché. Si uno asumiera que los devotos normalmente son pobres, el ratón sería el miembro más pobre de la iglesia.) → **más pobre que las ratas.** □ *My aunt is as poor as a church mouse.* □ *The Browns are poor as church mice.*

(as) pretty as a picture   muy bonito. (Es cliché. La frase sobrevive a causa de la aliteración.) → **ser de postal; ser precioso.** □ *Sweet little Mary is as pretty as a picture.* □ *Their new house is pretty as a picture.*

(as) proud as a peacock   muy orgulloso; altanero. (Es cliché. Referente a las plumas bonitas de la cola del pavo real. La frase sobrevive a causa de la aliteración.) □ *John is so arrogant. He's as proud as a peacock.* □ *The new father was proud as a peacock.*

(as) quick as a wink   muy rápidamente. (Es cliché. Referente a la rapidez del guiño.) → **en un abrir y cerrar de ojos.** □ *As quick as a wink, the thief took the lady's purse.* □ *I'll finish this work quick as a wink.*

(as) quiet as a mouse   muy callado; tímido y silencioso. (Se usa muchas veces con los niños.) → **sin decir ni pío.** □ *Don't yell; whisper. Be as quiet as a mouse.* □ *Mary hardly ever says anything. She's quiet as a mouse.*

(as) regular as clockwork   regular y seguro. → **como un reloj.** □ *She comes into this store every day, as regular as clockwork.* □ *Our tulips come up every year, regular as clockwork.*

(as) scarce as hens' teeth AND **scarcer than hens' teeth** muy escaso o inexistente. (Es cliché. Las gallinas no tienen dientes.) □ *I've never seen one of those. They're as scarce as hens' teeth.* □ *I was told that the part needed for my car is scarcer than hens' teeth, and it would take a long time to find one.*

(as) sick as a dog   muy enfermo; enfermo y vomitivo. (Referente al vómito agonizado del perro.) □ *We've never been so ill. The whole family was sick as dogs.* □ *Sally was as sick as a dog and couldn't go to the party.*

(as) slippery as an eel   tortuoso; no digno de confianza. (También se usa literalmente.) → **escurridizo como una anguila.** □ *Tom can't be trusted. He's as slippery as an eel.* □ *It's hard to catch Joe in his office because he's slippery as an eel.*

(as) smart as a fox   inteligente y listo. □ *My nephew is as smart as a fox.* □ *You have to be smart as a fox to outwit me.*

(as) snug as a bug in a rug   cómodo y a gusto. (Una frase que el adulto dice al niño cuando lo acuesta. La frase sobrevive a causa de la rima.) → **estar en la gloria.** □ *Let's pull up the covers. There you are, Bobby, as snug as a bug in a rug.* □ *What a lovely little house! I know I'll be snug as a bug in a rug.*

(as) sober as a judge (Es cliché.) **1.** muy formal, sombrío, o remilgado. □ *You certainly look gloomy, Bill. You're sober as a judge.* □ *Tom's as sober as a judge. I think he's angry.* **2.** no borracho; alerta y completamente sobrio (Este sentido de la frase viene de la interpretación incorrecta del primer sentido.) □ *John's drunk? No, he's as sober as a judge.* □ *You should be sober as a judge when you drive a car.*

(as) soft as a baby's bottom muy blando y suave al toque. □ *This cloth is as soft as a baby's bottom.* □ *No, Bob doesn't shave yet. His cheeks are soft as a baby's bottom.*

(as) soon as possible al momento más pronto. → **cuanto antes; lo más pronto posible.** □ *I'm leaving now. I'll be there as soon as possible.* □ *Please pay me as soon as possible.*

(as) strong as an ox muy fuerte. → **fuerte como un toro; fuerte como un roble.** □ *Tom lifts weights and is as strong as an ox.* □ *Now that Ann has recovered from her illness, she's strong as an ox.*

(as) stubborn as a mule muy testarudo. → **más terco que una mula.** □ *My husband is as stubborn as a mule.* □ *Our cat is stubborn as a mule.*

as the crow flies distancia calculada en línea recta a través de la tierra, en vez de las distancias calculadas por caminos, ríos, etc. (Esta frase asume que los cuervos vuelan en línea recta.) → **a vuelo de pájaro.** □ *It's twenty miles to town on the highway, but only ten miles as the crow flies.* □ *Our house is only a few miles from the lake as the crow flies.*

(as) thick as pea soup muy espeso. (Normalmente referente a niebla.) □ *This fog is as thick as pea soup.* □ *Wow, this coffee is strong! It's thick as pea soup.*

(as) thick as thieves muy unidos; amistosos; aliados. (Es cliché. La frase sobrevive a causa de la aliteración.) → **beben agua del mismo jarrito; estar a partir un piñon; estar uña y carne.** □ *Mary, Tom, and Sally are as thick as thieves. They go everywhere together.* □ *Those two families are thick as thieves.*

(as) tight as a tick   Véase en *(as) full as a tick.*

(as) tight as Dick's hatband   muy apretado. (La frase es muy anticuada.) □ *I've got to lose some weight. My belt is as tight as Dick's hatband.* □ *This window is stuck tight as Dick's hatband.*

a stone's throw away   a poca distancia; a poca distancia comparativamente. (La frase puede referirse a distancias en pies o millas.) → **a un paso; a tiro de piedra.** □ *John saw Mary across the street, just a stone's throw away.* □ *Philadelphia is just a stone's throw away from New York City.*

(as) weak as a kitten   débil; enclenque. (Referente al gatito recién nacido.) □ *John is as weak as a kitten because he doesn't eat well.* □ *Oh! Suddenly I feel weak as a kitten.*

(as) white as the driven snow   muy blanco. (Es cliché.) □ *I like my bed sheets to be as white as the driven snow.* □ *We have a new kitten whose fur is white as the driven snow.*

(as) wise as an owl   muy sabio. □ *Grandfather is as wise as an owl.* □ *My goal is to be wise as an owl.*

at a premium   a precio caro; a precio caro a causa de una calidad o circunstancia especial. → **estar muy cotizado.** □ *Sally bought the shoes at a premium because they were of very high quality.* □ *This model of car is selling at a premium because so many people want to buy it.*

at a snail's pace   muy despacio. → **a paso de tortuga.** □ *When you watch a clock, time seems to move at a snail's pace.* □ *You always eat at a snail's pace. I'm tired of waiting for you.*

at death's door   a la muerte. (Eufemística y literaria.) → **a las puertas de la muerte.** □ *I was so ill that I was at death's door.* □ *The family dog was at death's door for three days, and then it finally died.*

at half-mast   medio puesto o bajado. (Referente principalmente a las banderas. Se puede usar como chiste para las cosas además de las banderas.) → **a media asta.** □ *The flag was flying at half-mast* *because the general had died.* □ *Americans fly flags at half-mast on Memorial Day.* □ *The little boy ran out of the house with his pants at half-mast.*

at loggerheads   en contra de; en un atolladero; debatido. → **estar en desacuerdo; estar en pugna con.** □ *Mr. and Mrs. Franklin have been at loggerheads for years.* □ *The two political parties were at loggerheads during the entire legislative session.*

at loose ends   inquieto e inestable; desempleado. □ *Just before school starts, all the children are at loose ends.* □ *When Tom is home on the weekends, he's always at loose ends.* □ *Jane has been at loose ends ever since she lost her job.*

at one fell swoop AND **in one fell swoop**   un acontecimiento único, como suceso singular. (Esta frase conserva la vieja palabra inglesa, *fell,* significando "terrible" o "mortal." Ahora es cliché, algunas veces con sugestión humorística.) → **de una sola vez; de un tirón.** □ *The party guests ate up all the snacks at one fell swoop.* □ *When the stock market crashed, many large fortunes were wiped out in one fell swoop.*

at one's wit's end   a los límites de los recursos mentales de uno. → **estar desesperado; no saber más qué hacer.** □ *I'm at my wit's end with this problem. I cannot figure it out.* □ *Tom could do no more. He was at his wit's end.*

at sea (about something)   confuso; perdido y aturdido. (Como si uno estuviera perdido en el mar.) □ *Mary is all at sea about getting married.* □ *When it comes to higher math, John is totally at sea.*

at sixes and sevens   desordenado; perdido y aturdido. (Apropriada de los dados.) → **estar hecho un lío; estar muy embrollado.** □ *Mrs. Smith is at sixes and sevens since the death of her husband.* □ *Bill is always at sixes and sevens when he's home by himself.*

at someone's doorstep AND **on someone's doorstep**   al cargo de alguien; como la responsabilidad de alguien. (No es literal.) □ *Why do you always have to lay your problems at my*

doorstep? □ *I shall put this issue on someone else's doorstep.* □
I don't want it on my doorstep.

at the bottom of the ladder　al nivel más bajo de paga y
estado. → **desde abajo.** □ *Most people start work at the bottom of
the ladder.* □ *When Ann got fired, she had to start all over again
at the bottom of the ladder.*

at the drop of a hat　inmediatamente y sin exhortación. → **en
cualquier momento.** □ *John was always ready to go fishing at the
drop of a hat.* □ *If you need help, just call on me. I can come at
the drop of a hat.*

at the eleventh hour　en el último momento posible. → **a última
hora.** □ *She always turned her term papers in at the eleventh hour.*
□ *We don't worry about death until the eleventh hour.*

at the end of one's rope AND **at the end of one's
tether**　a los límites de la capacidad de uno. → **en las últimas.**
□ *I'm at the end of my rope! I just can't go on this way!* □ *These
kids are driving me out of my mind. I'm at the end of my tether.*

at the end of one's tether　Véase la entrada previa.

at the last minute　en la última oportunidad posible. → **a última
hora.** □ *Please don't make reservations at the last minute.* □ *Why
do you ask all your questions at the last minute?*

at the outside　al máximo. → **a lo sumo.** □ *The car repairs will
cost $300 at the outside.* □ *I'll be there in three weeks at the outside.*

at the top of one's lungs　Véase la entrada siguiente.

at the top of one's voice AND **at the top of one's lungs**
en voz muy alta; en voz tan alta como posible para hablar o gritar.
→ **a voz en cuello; a voz en grito; a grito pelado.** □ *Bill called
to Mary at the top of his voice.* □ *How can I work when you're all
talking at the top of your lungs?*

at this stage (of the game)　en el momento actual de algún
suceso; actualmente. → **a estas alturas.** □ *We'll have to wait and*

see. There isn't much we can do at this stage of the game. □ *At this stage, we are better off not calling the doctor.*

average, on the   Véase *on the average.*

A watched pot never boils.   un refrán significando que los problemas no se resuelven sólo por pensar mucho en ellos. (Referente a la idea de que si uno está esperando a que el agua hierva, puede pasar mucho tiempo esperando. Se dice del problema a que una persona está prestando mucha atención.) → **el que espera, desespera.** □ *John was looking out the window, waiting eagerly for the mail to be delivered. Ann said, "Be patient. A watched pot never boils."* □ *Billy weighed himself four times a day while he was trying to lose weight. His mother said, "Relax. A watched pot never boils."*

away from one's desk   no disponible para hablar por teléfono; no disponible para ser visto. (A veces dicho por las recepcionistas de oficina. La frase significa que la persona a quien uno ha llamado no está disponible por razones personales o de negocios. Muchas veces la persona ha ido al servicio.) □ *I'm sorry, but Ann is away from her desk just now. Can you come back later?* □ *Tom is away from his desk, but if you leave your number, he will call you right back.*

ax to grind, have an   Véase *have an ax to grind.*

B

babe in the woods una persona ingenua o inocente; una persona inexperta. → **estar totalmente perdido.** □ *Bill is a babe in the woods when it comes to dealing with plumbers.* □ *As a painter, Mary is fine, but she's a babe in the woods as a musician.*

back in circulation 1. [algo] disponible al público de nuevo. (Se dice especialmente de las cosas que circulan, como el dinero, los libros de biblioteca, y las revistas.) □ *I've heard that gold coins are back in circulation in Europe.* □ *I would like to read* War and Peace. *Is it back in circulation, or is it still checked out?* 2. saliendo socialmente de nuevo; saliendo de nuevo después de un divorcio o una ruptura. → **estar en circulación.** □ *Now that Bill is a free man, he's back in circulation.* □ *Tom was in the hospital for a month, but now he's back in circulation.*

back-to-back 1. con las espaldas que se tocan. → **espalda con espalda.** □ *They started the duel by standing back-to-back.* □ *Two people who stand back-to-back can manage to see in all directions.* 2. siguiendo inmediatamente. (Se dice de las cosas o los sucesos. En este caso, los sucesos son "back-to-front," desde el fin de uno al comienzo de otro.) → **en sesión continua.** □ *The doctor had appointments set up back-to-back all day long.* □ *I have three lecture courses back-to-back every day of the week.*

back to the drawing board hora de empezar algo de nuevo; hora de empezar a planear algo de nuevo. (Observe las variaciones en los ejemplos. Referente al tablero de delineante donde están diseñados máquinas o edificios.) → **a empezar de nuevo; vuelta a empezar.** □ *It didn't work. Back to the drawing board.* □ *I flunked English this semester. Well, back to the old drawing board.*

back to the salt mines   hora de volver al trabajo, a la escuela, o a otra cosa que posiblemente sea desagradable. (La frase implica que la persona que habla es esclavo que trabaja en las minas de sal.) → **cada mochuelo a su olivo.** □ *It's eight o'clock. Time to go to work! Back to the salt mines.* □ *School starts again in the fall, and then it's back to the salt mines again.*

back to the wall, have one's   Véase *have one's back to the wall.*

bad as all that, (as)   Véase *(as) bad as all that.*

bad faith, in   Véase *in bad faith.*

bad sorts, in   Véase *in bad sorts.*

bad taste, in   Véase *in bad taste.*

bag and baggage AND **part and parcel**   con el equipaje; con todos los efectos. (Es frase fija.) □ *Sally showed up at our door bag and baggage one Sunday morning.* □ *All right, if you won't pay the rent, out with you, bag and baggage!* □ *Get all your stuff—part and parcel—out of here!*

bag of tricks   una colección de técnicas o métodos especiales para hacer algo. □ *What have you got in your bag of tricks that could help me with this problem?* □ *Here comes Mother with her bag of tricks. I'm sure she can help us.*

bang, go over with a   Véase *go over with a bang.*

bang one's head against a brick wall   Véase en *beat one's head against the wall.*

bank on something   contar con algo. (Tener confianza en algo de la misma manera que una persona tendría confianza en el banco.) → **confiarse en algo.** □ *The weather service said it wouldn't rain, but I wouldn't bank on it.* □ *My word is to be trusted. You can bank on it.*

bargain, in the   Véase *in the bargain.*

bark up the wrong tree   hacer una decisión equivocada; pedir algo de la persona errónea; seguir el camino erróneo. (Referente al perro de caza que sigue un animal hasta que éste suba un árbol, pero el perro ladra o aúlla debajo del árbol equivocado.) → **equivocarse de medio a medio; a buen santo te encomiendas.** □ *If you think I'm the guilty person, you're barking up the wrong tree.* □ *The baseball players blamed their bad record on the pitcher, but they were barking up the wrong tree.*

base, off   Véase *off base.*

bat for someone, go to   Véase *go to bat for someone.*

bat out of hell, like a   Véase *like a bat out of hell.*

bats in one's belfry, have   Véase *have bats in one's belfry.*

batting an eye, without   Véase *without batting an eye.*

be a copycat   ser una persona que copia o imita las acciones de otra persona. (La persona que copia o imita normalmente es considerada inmadura.) → **ser copión.** □ *Sally wore a pink dress just like Mary's. Mary called Sally a copycat.* □ *Bill is such a copycat. He bought a coat just like mine.*

be a fan of someone   ser aficionado a alguien; idolatrar a alguien. (La palabra *fan* viene de *fanatic.*) □ *My mother is still a fan of the Beatles.* □ *I'm a great fan of the mayor of the town.*

beard the lion in his den   enfrentarse a un adversario en su territorio. (Amenezar como si uno estuviera agarrando la barba de una criatura aterradora, como el león.) → **agarrar al toro por las astas; coger al toro por los cuernos.** □ *I went to the tax collector's office to beard the lion in his den.* □ *He said he hadn't wanted to come to my home, but it was better to beard the lion in his den.*

bear one's cross AND **carry one's cross**   llevar o aguantar la carga; aguantar las dificultades de la vida. (El tema de esta frase es bíblico. Siempre se usa figuradamente excepto en un contexto bíblico.) → **cada pago aguante su vela.** □ *It's a very bad disease, but I'll bear my cross.* □ *I can't help you with it. You'll just have to carry your cross.*

bear someone or something in mind   Véase en *keep someone or something in mind.*

bear the brunt (of something)   resistir o aguantar la parte peor o la parte más fuerte de algo, como un ataque. □ *I had to bear the brunt of her screaming and yelling.* □ *Why don't you talk with her the next time? I'm tired of bearing the brunt.*

bear watching   requerir observación; merecer observación. □ *This problem will bear watching.* □ *This is a very serious disease, and it will bear watching for further developments.*

beat about the bush   Véase en *beat around the bush.*

beat a dead horse   seguir luchando en una batalla que ya ha sido ganado; seguir defendiendo una postura después de que la cuestión que ha sido resuelta. (La frase significa que un caballo muerto no correrá a pesar de las palizas.) → **como arar en el mar; como machacar en hierro frío.** □ *Stop arguing! You have won your point. You are just beating a dead horse.* □ *Oh, be quiet. Stop beating a dead horse.*

beat a path to someone's door   venir en multidudes a ver a alguna persona. (La frase significa que tantas personas querrán ver a esa persona que harán un camino a la puerta de su casa.) → **asediar a alguien.** □ *I have a product so good that everyone is beating a path to my door.* □ *If you really become famous, people will beat a path to your door.*

beat around the bush AND **beat about the bush**   evitar la respuesta a una pregunta; andar con evasivas; perder tiempo. → **andarse con rodeos; andarse por las ramas.** □ *Stop beating around the bush and answer my question.* □ *Let's stop beating about the bush and discuss this matter.*

be a thorn in someone's side   siempre causar molestia. → **ser una espina que alguien tiene clavada.** □ *This problem is a thorn in my side. I wish I had a solution to it.* □ *John was a thorn in my side for years before I finally got rid of him.*

beat one's head against the wall AND **bang one's head against a brick wall** perder tiempo intentando alcanzar algo inalcanzable. (No es literal.) □ *You're wasting your time trying to fix up this house. You're just beating your head against the wall.* □ *You're banging your head against a brick wall trying to get that dog to behave properly.*

beat the gun conseguir hacer algo antes de la señal final. (La frase se origina en los deportes, y se refiere a marcar un gol en los últimos segundos del partido.) □ *The ball beat the gun and dropped through the hoop just in time.* □ *Tom tried to beat the gun, but he was one second too slow.*

Beauty is only skin deep. un refrán significando que las apariencias son superficiales. (Muchas veces la frase implica que una persona bella puede ser muy cruel adentro.) □ BOB: *Isn't Jane lovely?* TOM: *Yes, but beauty is only skin deep.* □ *I know that she looks like a million dollars, but beauty is only skin deep.*

bee in one's bonnet, have a Véase *have a bee in one's bonnet.*

been through the mill una persona o cosa maltratada o agotada. (Como cereales pulverizados en un molino.) → **vérselas negras; pasarlas duras.** □ *This has been a rough day. I've really been through the mill.* □ *This old car is banged up, and it hardly runs. It's been through the mill.*

before you can say Jack Robinson casi inmediatamente. (Muchas veces se encuentra esta frase en los cuentos de niños.) □ *And before you could say Jack Robinson, the bird flew away.* □ *I'll catch a plane and be there before you can say Jack Robinson.*

be from Missouri requerir una prueba; requerir la muestra de algo. (La frase viene del apodo del estado de Missouri, the "Show Me State".) □ *You'll have to prove it to me. I'm from Missouri.* □ *She's from Missouri and has to be shown.*

Beggars can't be choosers. un refrán significando que una persona no debe criticar algo que recibe gratis; si alguien pide o mendiga algo, no tiene el derecho de elección. → **A caballo regalado**

no hay que mirarle el diente. □ *I don't like the old hat that you gave me, but beggars can't be choosers.* □ *It doesn't matter whether people like the free food or not. Beggars can't be choosers.*

begin to see daylight empezar a ver el fin de una tarea larga o dura. (Como si uno estuviera viendo el alba después de una noche larga de trabajo.) → **vislumbrar el final.** □ *I've been working on my thesis for two years, and at last I'm beginning to see daylight.* □ *I've been so busy. Only in the last week have I begun to see daylight.*

begin to see the light empezar a comprender (algo). → **abrir los ojos; comprender las cosas.** □ *My algebra class is hard for me, but I'm beginning to see the light.* □ *I was totally confused, but I began to see the light after your explanation.*

be halfhearted (about someone or something) no tener entusiasmo para alguien o algo. □ *Ann was halfhearted about the choice of Sally for president.* □ *She didn't look halfhearted to me. She looked angry.*

believe it or not decidir creer algo o decidir no creer algo. □ *Believe it or not, I just got home from work.* □ *I'm over fifty years old, believe it or not.*

bench, on the Véase *on the bench.*

bend, go (a)round the Véase *go (a)round the bend.*

bend someone's ear hablar con alguien, posiblemente hasta ser una molestia. (No es literal. No se toca la oreja de la persona.) → **darle la lata a alguien.** □ *Tom is over there, bending Jane's ear about something.* □ *I'm sorry. I didn't mean to bend your ear for an hour.*

be old hat ser pasado de moda o anticuado. → **estar más visto que el tebeo.** □ *That's a silly idea. It's old hat.* □ *Nobody does that anymore. That's just old hat.*

be poles apart ser muy diferentes; estar lejos de llegar a un acuerdo. (Referente al Polo Norte y al Polo Sur, que se piensa estar tan lejos como dos puntos cualesquiera de la tierra.) → **ser polos**

opuestos. □ *Mr. and Mrs. Jones don't get along well. They are poles apart.* □ *They'll never sign the contract because they are poles apart.*

be the spit and image of someone AND **be the spitting image of someone** parcccrse mucho a alguien; asemejarse mucho a alguien. → **ser el vivo retrato de alguien; ser la viva imagen de alguien.** □ *John is the spit and image of his father.* □ *I'm not the spit and image of anyone.* □ *At first, I thought you were saying I'm the spitting image of Mother.*

be the spitting image of someone Véase la entrada previa.

be the teacher's pet ser el esudiante preferido del profesor. (Como si el profesor tratara al estudianto como un gato, un perro, o otro animal doméstico.) → **ser el favorito del profesor.** □ *Sally is the teacher's pet. She always gets special treatment.* □ *The other students don't like the teacher's pet.*

between a rock and a hard place AND **between the devil and the deep blue sea** en una posición muy difícil; enfrentando una decisión muy difícil. → **entre la espada y la pared.** □ *I couldn't make up my mind. I was caught between a rock and a hard place.* □ *He had a dilemma on his hands. He was clearly between the devil and the deep blue sea.*

between the devil and the deep blue sea Véase la entrada previa.

beyond one's depth **1.** en aguas demasiado profundas. (Este sentido de la frase es literal.) → **no hacer pie; no tocar el fondo.** □ *Sally swam out until she was beyond her depth.* □ *Jane swam out to get her even though it was beyond her depth, too.* **2.** más allá del entendimiento o de la capacidad de uno. □ *I'm beyond my depth in algebra class.* □ *Poor John was involved in a problem that was really beyond his depth.*

beyond one's means más que uno puede pagar. → **un tren de vida que no se puede costear; un tren de vida que sus ingresos no se lo permiten.** □ *I'm sorry, but this house is beyond our means. Please show us a cheaper one.* □ *Mr. and Mrs. Brown are living beyond their means.*

beyond the pale   inaceptable; proscrito. □ *Your behavior is simply beyond the pale.* □ *Because of Tom's rudeness, he's considered beyond the pale and is never asked to parties anymore.*

big frog in a small pond   ser una persona importante en medio de las personas de menor importancia. □ *I'd rather be a big frog in a small pond than the opposite.* □ *The trouble with Tom is that he's a big frog in a small pond. He needs more competition.*

big mouth, have a   Véase *have a big mouth.*

bird in the hand is worth two in the bush, A.   Véase *A bird in the hand is worth two in the bush.*

birds and the bees   la reproducción humana (Una manera eufemística de referirse al sexo y la reproducción.) □ *My father tried to teach me about the birds and the bees.* □ *He's twenty years old and doesn't understand about the birds and the bees.*

Birds of a feather flock together.   un refrán significando que personas similares quieren pasar tiempo juntas. → **Dios los cría y ellos se juntan.** □ *Bob and Tom are just alike. They like each other's company because birds of a feather flock together.* □ *When Mary joined a club for redheaded people, she said, "Birds of a feather flock together."*

birthday suit, in one's   Véase *in one's birthday suit.*

bite off more than one can chew   abarcar más que puede hacer uno; tener demasiada confianza. (Se usa la frase literalmente para la comida y figuradamente para otras cosas, especialmente los proyectos difíciles.) → **Quien mucho abarca poco aprieta; Juan Palomo: yo me lo guiso y yo me lo como.** □ *Billy, stopping biting off more than you can chew. You're going to choke on your food someday.* □ *Ann is exhausted again. She's always biting off more than she can chew.*

bite one's nails   estar nervioso o preocupado; morder las uñas a causa del nerviosismo o la ansiedad. (Se usa literalmente y figuradamente.) □ *I spent all afternoon biting my nails, worrying about you.* □ *We've all been biting our nails from worry.*

bite one's tongue   luchar por no decir algo que uno quiere decir. (Se usa literalmente sólo para referirse a la mordedura accidental de la lengua.) □ *I had to bite my tongue to keep from telling her what I really thought.* □ *I sat through that whole conversation biting my tongue.*

bite the dust   caerse a la derrota; morirse. (Típicamente se oye en las películas que tratan de la frontera del oeste de los Estados Unidos.) → **morder el polvo [persona]; irse a pique [cosa].** □ *A bullet hit the sheriff in the chest, and he bit the dust.* □ *Poor old Bill bit the dust while mowing the lawn. They buried him yesterday.*

bite the hand that feeds one   dañar a alguien que le ha ayudado a alguien. (No es literal. Referente a la mordedura de un perro ingrato.) □ *I'm your mother! How can you bite the hand that feeds you?* □ *She can hardly expect much when she bites the hand that feeds her.*

black and white, in   Véase *in black and white.*

black, in the   Véase *in the black.*

black sheep of the family   el miembro peor o más marginado de la familia. (Una manada de ovejas blancas no quieren tener una cría negra.) □ *Mary is the black sheep of the family. She's always in trouble with the police.* □ *He keeps making a nuisance of himself. What do you expect from the black sheep of the family?*

blind alley, up a   Véase *up a blind alley.*

blind as a bat, (as)   Véase *(as) blind as a bat.*

blind leading the blind   una situación en que personas que no saben hacer algo intentan explicárselo a otras personas. □ *Tom doesn't know anything about cars, but he's trying to teach Sally how to change the oil. It's a case of the blind leading the blind.* □ *When I tried to show Mary how to use a computer, it was the blind leading the blind.*

block, on the   Véase *on the block.*

blood, in the Véase *in the blood.*

blow off steam Véase en *let off steam.*

blow one's own horn Véase en *toot one's own horn.*

blow someone's cover revelar la identidad o la intención verdadera de alguien (La frase es familiar o de jerga.) □ *The spy was very careful not to blow her cover.* □ *I tried to disguise myself, but my dog recognized me and blew my cover.*

blow something out of all proportion Véase *out of all proportion.*

blow the whistle (on someone) informar de los males de alguien a otras personas (por ejemplo, la policía) que pueden poner fin a estos males. (Como si uno estuviera soplando el silbato de la policía.) □ *The citizens' group blew the whistle on the street gangs by calling the police.* □ *The gangs were getting very bad. It was definitely time to blow the whistle.*

blue, out of the Véase *out of the blue.*

boggle someone's mind abrumar a alguien; confundir los pensamientos de alguien; asombrar a alguien. → **dar vueltas de cabeza.** □ *The size of the house boggles my mind.* □ *She said that his arrogance boggled her mind.*

bolt out of the blue, like a Véase *like a bolt out of the blue.*

bone of contention el tema o la idea fundamental de una discusión; el asunto pendiente de un desacuerdo. (Se pelean los perros para obtener el hueso.) → **manzana de la discordia.** □ *We've fought for so long that we've forgotten what the bone of contention is.* □ *The question of a fence between the houses has become quite a bone of contention.*

bone to pick (with someone), have a Véase *have a bone to pick (with someone).*

born with a silver spoon in one's mouth   nacido a muchas ventajas familiares; nacido a una familia rica; mostrando las señales de una riqueza familiar. □ *Sally was born with a silver spoon in her mouth.* □ *I'm glad I was not born with a silver spoon in my mouth.*

born yesterday, not   Véase *not born yesterday.*

both hands tied behind one's back, with   Véase *with both hands tied behind one's back.*

bottom of one's heart, from the   Véase *from the bottom of one's heart.*

bottom of the ladder, at the   Véase *at the bottom of the ladder.*

bound hand and foot   con las manos y los pies atados. □ *The robbers left us bound hand and foot.* □ *We remained bound hand and foot until the maid found us and untied us.*

bow and scrape   ser muy humilde y servil. (Inclinarse ante alguien hasta tocar la tierra. Normalmente no se usa literalmente.) □ *Please don't bow and scrape. We are all equal here.* □ *The salesclerk came in, bowing and scraping, and asked if he could help us.*

bread and butter   el sustento o los ingresos de alguien. (La fuente del dinero con que se compran pan y mantequilla, u otra comida, para la casa.) □ *Selling cars is a lot of hard work, but it's my bread and butter.* □ *It was hard to give up my bread and butter, but I felt it was time to retire.*

break camp   desmontar el equipo de campamento; hacer las mochilas y reanudar la excursión. → **levantar el campo.** □ *Early this morning we broke camp and moved on northward.* □ *Okay, everyone. It's time to break camp. Take those tents down and fold them neatly.*

break new ground   empezar a hacer algo que nadie ha hecho antes; ser innovador en alguna empresa. → **abrir nuevas fronteras.** □ *Dr. Anderson was breaking new ground in cancer research.* □ *They were breaking new ground in consumer electronics.*

break one's back (to do something)   Véase la entrada siguiente.

break one's neck (to do something) AND **break one's back (to do something)**   trabajar muy duro para hacer algo. (Nunca se usa literalmente.) → **deslomarse.** □ *I broke my neck to get here on time.* □ *That's the last time I'll break my neck to help you.* □ *There is no point in breaking your back. Take your time.*

break out in a cold sweat   sudar a causa de la fiebre, el miedo, o la ansiedad; empezar a sudar profusamente y de repente. □ *I was so frightened I broke out in a cold sweat.* □ *The patient broke out in a cold sweat.*

break (out) into tears AND **break out in tears**   empezar a llorar de repente. □ *I was so sad that I broke out into tears.* □ *I always break into tears at a funeral.* □ *It's hard not to break out in tears under those circumstances.*

break someone's fall   agarrar a una persona que se está cayendo; aminorar el impacto de una persona que se está cayendo. □ *When the little boy fell out of the window, the bushes broke his fall.* □ *The old lady slipped on the ice, but a snowbank broke her fall.*

break someone's heart   causar pena emocional. (La frase no es literal.) → **romper (partir) el corazón a alguien.** □ *It just broke my heart when Tom ran away from home.* □ *Sally broke John's heart when she refused to marry him.*

break the ice   iniciar la conversación y los intercambios sociales; hacer que se empiece algo. (A veces *the ice* se refiere a frialdad social. También se usa literalmente.) → **romper el hielo; dar el primer paso.** □ *Tom is so outgoing. He's always the first one to break the ice at parties.* □ *It's hard to break the ice at formal events.* □ *Sally broke the ice by bidding $20,000 for the painting.*

break the news (to someone)   contar noticias importantes y normalmente malas. → **dar la noticia.** □ *The doctor had to break the news to Jane about her husband's cancer.* □ *I hope that the doctor broke the news gently.*

breathe down someone's neck   **1.** vigilar a alguien; vigilar las actividades de una persona. Referente a una persona que está de pie detrás de otra persona. Se puede usar literalmente.) → **estar encima de alguien.** □ *I can't work with you breathing down my neck all the time. Go away.* □ *I will get through my life without your help. Stop breathing down my neck.* **2.** intentar apresurar a alguien; hacer que alguien haga algo a tiempo. (El sujeto no tiene que ser una persona. Véase el segundo ejemplo.) → **estar encima de alguien.** □ *I have to finish my taxes today. The tax collector is breathing down my neck.* □ *I have a deadline breathing down my neck.*

breathe one's last   morir; respirar por la última vez antes de morir. → **exhalar el último suspiro.** □ *Mrs. Smith breathed her last this morning.* □ *I'll keep running every day until I breathe my last.*

bring something to light   revelar algo; descubrir algo. (Como si alguien estuviera revelando algo que era escondido antes de la luz del día.) → **sacar a luz.** □ *The scientists brought their findings to light.* □ *We must bring this new evidence to light.*

bring the house down AND **bring down the house**   emocionar al público del teatro hasta la risa o los aplausos o los dos. (No es literal.) → **ser un exitazo; ser muy aplaudido.** □ *This is a great joke. The last time I told it, it brought the house down.* □ *It didn't bring down the house; it emptied it.*

bring up the rear   moverse detrás de otras personas; estar colocado al fin de una cola. (La frase se refirió originalmente a la marcha de soldados.) → **cerrar la marcha.** □ *Here comes John, bringing up the rear.* □ *Hurry up, Tom! Why are you always bringing up the rear?*

broad daylight, in   Véase *in broad daylight.*

brush with something, have a   Véase *have a brush with something.*

build castles in Spain   Véase la entrada siguiente.

build castles in the air AND **build castles in Spain**   soñar despierto; hacer planes que nunca se pueden realizar. (No se usa ninguna de las dos frases literalmente.) □ *Ann spends most of her time building castles in Spain.* □ *I really like to sit on the porch in the evening, just building castles in the air.*

bull in a china shop   una persona que es muy torpe, especialmente cerca de las cosas frágiles; una persona desconsiderada o indiscreta. (*China* es loza buena.) □ *Look at Bill, as awkward as a bull in a china shop.* □ *Get that big dog out of my garden. It's like a bull in a china shop.* □ *Bob is so rude, a regular bull in a china shop.*

bullpen, in the   Véase *in the bullpen.*

bump on a log, like a   Véase *like a bump on a log.*

burn one's bridges (behind one)   **1.** tomar decisiones que no se pueden cambiar más tarde. □ *If you drop out of school now, you'll be burning your bridges behind you.* □ *You're too young to burn your bridges that way.* **2.** estar en alguna situación (como un puesto) desagradable de que va a marchar, asegurándose que no le van a dar la bienvenida al volver. □ *If you get mad and quit your job, you'll be burning your bridges behind you.* □ *No sense burning your bridges. Be polite and leave quietly.* **3.** destruir la ruta por la que ha viajado o seguido, así que la retirada es imposible. □ *The army, which had burned its bridges behind it, couldn't go back.* □ *By blowing up the road, the spies had burned their bridges behind them.* → **quemar las naves.**

burn someone at the stake   **1.** prender fuego a alguien que está atado a un poste (como una forma de ejecución). □ *They used to burn witches at the stake.* □ *Look, officer, I only ran a stop sign. What are you going to do, burn me at the stake?* **2.** reprender o denunciar a alguien con severidad, pero sin violencia. □ *Stop yelling. I made a simple mistake, and you're burning me at the stake for it.* □ *Sally only spilled her milk. There is no need to shout. Don't burn her at the stake for it.*

burn someone or something to a crisp   quemar a alguien o algo total o muy gravemente. □ *The flames burned him to a crisp.* □ *The cook burned the meat to a crisp.*

burn the candle at both ends   trabajar muy duro y quedarse levantado hasta muy tarde por la noche. (Un modo de hacer que una vela dé mucha luz, o figuradamente un modo de hacer que una persona trabaje mucho.) → **vivir una vida muy agitada.** □ *No wonder Mary is ill. She has been burning the candle at both ends for a long time.* □ *You can't keep on burning the candle at both ends.*

burn the midnight oil   quedarse levantado para trabajar, especialmente para estudiar, hasta muy tarde por la noche. (Referente a usar una lámpara de aceite para trabajar.) → **quemarse las pestañas; quemarse las cejas.** □ *I have to go home and burn the midnight oil tonight.* □ *If you burn the midnight oil night after night, you'll probably become ill.*

burn with a low blue flame   estar muy enojado. (Referente al calor imaginario que la furia causa. Una llama baja y azul es muy caliente a pesar de su puequeñez y calma.) □ *By the time she showed up three hours late, I was burning with a low blue flame.* □ *Whenever Ann gets mad, she just presses her lips together and burns with a low blue flame.*

burst at the seams   **1.** reventarse (figuradamente) con orgullo o risa. □ *Tom nearly burst at the seams with pride.* □ *We laughed so hard we just about burst at the seams.* **2.** reventarse (figuradamente) a causa de la plenitud. → **estar a tope.** □ *The room was so crowded that it almost burst at the seams.* □ *I ate so much I almost burst at the seams.*

burst with joy   casi reventarse (figuradamente) de alegría. □ *When I got my grades, I could have burst with joy.* □ *Joe was not exactly bursting with joy when he got the news.*

bury one's head in the sand AND **hide one's head in the sand**   no hacer caso de o no esconder de indicios obvios de peligro. (Referente al avestruz.) □ *Stop burying your head in the sand. Look at the statistics on smoking and cancer.* □ *And stop hiding your head in the sand. All of us will die somehow, whether we smoke or not.*

bury the hatchet dejar de pelearse o discutir; poner fin a resentimientos viejos. (El acto de enterrar la hacha es símbolo del fin de una guerra o una batalla.) → **hacer las paces; envainar la espada.** □ *All right, you two. Calm down and bury the hatchet.* □ *I wish Mr. and Mrs. Franklin would bury the hatchet. They argue all the time.*

business, go about one's Véase *go about one's business.*

busy as a beaver, (as) Véase *(as) busy as a beaver.*

busy as a bee, (as) Véase *(as) busy as a bee.*

busy as Grand Central Station, (as) Véase *(as) busy as Grand Central Station.*

button one's lip ponerse y quedarse callado. (Muchas veces se usa con los niños.) □ *All right now, let's button our lips and listen to the story.* □ *Button your lip, Tom! I'll tell you when you can talk.*

button, on the Véase *on the button.*

buy a pig in a poke comprar o aceptar algo sin verlo o examinarlo. (*Poke* significa "bolsa" or "saco.") □ *Buying a car without test-driving it is like buying a pig in a poke.* □ *He bought a pig in a poke when he ordered a diamond ring by mail.*

buy something creer lo que dice una persona; aceptar algo como hecho. (También se usa literalmente.) □ *It may be true, but I don't buy it.* □ *I just don't buy the idea that you can swim that far.*

buy something for a song comprar algo por muy barato. → **comprar algo por cuatro cuartos; comprar algo por poca cosa.** □ *No one else wanted it, so I bought it for a song.* □ *I could buy this house for a song, because it's so ugly.*

buy something sight unseen comprar algo sin haberlo visto primero. □ *I bought this land sight unseen. I didn't know it was so rocky.* □ *It isn't usually safe to buy something sight unseen.*

by a hair's breadth AND **by a whisker**   apenas; por distancia muy corta. → **por un pelo.** □ *I just missed getting on the plane by a hair's breadth.* □ *The arrow missed the deer by a whisker.*

by a whisker   Véase la entrada previa.

by leaps and bounds   rápidamente; por movimientos grandes hacia adelante. (No se usa mucho literalmente, pero es posible usarlo así.) → **a grandes pasos.** □ *Our garden is growing by leaps and bounds.* □ *The profits of my company are increasing by leaps and bounds.*

by return mail   por correo de vuelta al remitente. (Una frase indicando que el remitente espera pronto una respuesta a su carta por correo.) → **a vuelta de correo.** □ *Since this bill is overdue, would you kindly send us your check by return mail?* □ *I answered your request by return mail over a year ago. Please check your records.*

by the nape of the neck   por la nuca del cuello. (Se dice normalmente como amenaza en serio o en broma. Referente al modo en que uno recoge un perrito.) □ *He grabbed me by the nape of the neck and told me not to turn around if I valued my life. I stood very still.* □ *If you do that again, I'll pick you up by the nape of the neck and throw you out the door.*

by the same token   del mismo modo; igualmente. □ *Tom must be good when he comes here, and, by the same token, I expect you to behave properly when you go to his house.* □ *The mayor votes for his friend's causes. By the same token, the friend votes for the mayor's causes.*

by the seat of one's pants   por suerte y sin mucha habilidad; apenas. (Se usa especialmente con *to fly.*) □ *I got through school by the seat of my pants.* □ *The jungle pilot spent most of his days flying by the seat of his pants.*

by the skin of one's teeth   apenas; por una cantidad igual a la anchura de la piel (imaginaria) de los dientes.) → **por los pelos.** □ *I got through that class by the skin of my teeth.* □ *I got to the airport late and missed the plane by the skin of my teeth.*

by the sweat of one's brow   por los esfuerzos de uno; por el trabajo duro de uno. → **con el sudor de la frente.** □ *Tom raised these vegetables by the sweat of his brow.* □ *Sally polished the car by the sweat of her brow.*

by virtue of something   a causa de algo; debido a algo. → **en virtud de algo.** □ *She's permitted to vote by virtue of her age.* □ *They are members of the club by virtue of their great wealth.*

by word of mouth   verbalmente en vez de por escrito. (Una frase fija.) → **de palabra; de viva voz.** □ *I learned about it by word of mouth.* □ *I need it in writing. I don't trust things I hear about by word of mouth.*

C

cake and eat it too, have one's Véase *have one's cake and eat it too.*

call a spade a spade llamar a alguien o algo por su nombre correcto; hablar francamente de algo, aún desagradable. → **llamar al pan pan y al vino vino; al pan, pan y al vino, vino.** □ *Well, I believe it's time to call a spade a spade. We are just avoiding the issue.* □ *Let's call a spade a spade. The man is a liar.*

call it a day dejar de trabajar y volver a casa; decir que el día de trabajo ha terminado. → **dar por acabado.** □ *I'm tired. Let's call it a day.* □ *The boss was mad because Tom called it a day at noon and went home.*

call it quits dejar de trabajar; dimitir de algo; anunciar que uno va a dimitir de su puesto. □ *Okay! I've had enough! I'm calling it quits.* □ *Time to go home, John. Let's call it quits.*

call someone on the carpet reprender a una persona. (Referente a la imagen del despacho del jefe, cubierto de alfombras, a que está llamado el empleado para recibir una reprensión. □ *One more error like that and the boss will call you on the carpet.* □ *I'm sorry it went wrong. I really hope he doesn't call me on the carpet again.*

call the dogs off AND **call off the dogs** dejar de amenazar, perseguir, o acosar a alguien; (literalmente) ordenar que los perros dejen de la caza. (Observe las variaciones en los ejemplos.) □ *All right, I surrender. You can call your dogs off.* □ *Tell the sheriff to call off the dogs. We caught the robber.* □ *Please call off your dogs!*

can't carry a tune   sin la capacidad de cantar una melodía sencilla; falta de capacidad musical. (Casi siempre se usa en el sentido negativo. Se usa también con *cannot*.) → **no poder cantar afinado**. □ *I wish that Tom wouldn't try to sing. He can't carry a tune.* □ *Listen to poor old John. He really cannot carry a tune.*

can't hold a candle to someone   no ser igual a alguien; no ser digno de a asociarse con alguien; no poder estar a la altura de alguien. (Se usa también con *cannot*. Referente a no ser digno aún de alzar una vela a iluminar el camino de alguien.) → **no llegar ni a la suela del zapato de alguien**. □ *Mary can't hold a candle to Ann when it comes to auto racing.* □ *As for singing, John can't hold a candle to Jane.*

can't make heads or tails (out) of someone or something   no poder comprender a alguien o algo; no poder distinguir un lado de alguien o algo del otro lado. (Porque está oscuro o porque algo es confuso. También se usa con *cannot*.) → **no encontrar ni pies ni cabeza a alguien o algo**. □ *John is so strange. I can't make heads or tails of him.* □ *Do this report again. I can't make heads or tails out of it.*

can't see beyond the end of one's nose   no ser consciente de cosas que pueden pasar en el futuro; sin una visión del futuro; egocéntrico. (También se usa con *cannot*.) □ *John is a very poor planner. He can't see beyond the end of his nose.* □ *Ann can't see beyond the end of her nose. She is very self-centered.*

can't see one's hand in front of one's face   no poder ver muy lejos, normalmente a causa de la oscuridad o la niebla. (También se usa con *cannot*.) □ *It was so dark that I couldn't see my hand in front of my face.* □ *Bob said that the fog was so thick he couldn't see his hand in front of his face.*

cards, in the   Véase *in the cards*.

carry a torch (for someone) AND **carry the torch**   estar enamorado de alguien que no corresponde el amor; dar vueltas a una relación amorosa que es imposible. □ *John is carrying a torch for Jane.* □ *Is John still carrying a torch?* □ *Yes, he'll carry the torch for months.*

carry coals to Newcastle   hacer algo innecesario; hacer algo que es redundante. (La frase es refrán viejo de Inglaterra. Mandaron carbón a otras partes del país desde Newcastle hace un siglo. Sería estúpida llevar carbón a esta ciudad.) → **ir a vendimiar y llevar uvas de postre; llevar leña al monte.** □ *Taking food to a farmer is like carrying coals to Newcastle.* □ *Mr. Smith is so rich he doesn't need any more money. To give him money is like carrying coals to Newcastle.*

carry one's cross   Véase *bear one's cross.*

carry the ball   1. ser el jugador que agarra de la pelota, especialmente en el fútbol americano cuando el equipo del jugador hace un gol. □ *It was the fullback carrying the ball.* □ *Yes, Tom always carries the ball.* 2. ser el encargado; asegurarse de que una tarea está terminada. □ *We need someone who knows how to get the job done. Hey, Sally! Why don't you carry the ball for us?* □ *John can't carry the ball. He isn't organized enough.*

carry the torch   defender unas ideas; dirigir o participar en una cruzada (figurada). □ *The battle was over, but John continued to carry the torch.* □ *If Jane hadn't carried the torch, no one would have followed, and the whole thing would have failed.*

carry the weight of the world on one's shoulders   parecer preocupado de todos los problemas del mundo. □ *Look at Tom. He appears to be carrying the weight of the world on his shoulders.* □ *Cheer up, Tom! You don't need to carry the weight of the world on your shoulders.*

carry weight (with someone)   tener influencia sobre alguien (referente a la persona que tiene la influencia); tener importancia para alguien (referente a la cosa que tiene la influencia). (Muchas veces se usa en el sentido negativo.) → **ser de peso; ser de influencia.** □ *Everything Mary says carries weight with me.* □ *Don't pay any attention to John. What he says carries no weight around here.* □ *Your proposal is quite good, but since you're not a member of the club, it carries no weight.*

case in point   un ejemplo de la idea que una persona está expresando. → **ejemplo claro; caso pertinente.** □ *Now, as a case in point, let's* *look at nineteenth-century England.* □ *Fireworks can be danger-ous. For a case in point, look what happened to Bob Smith last week.*

cash-and-carry   algo que tiene que ver con un modo de vender productos en que el comprador paga al mismo tiempo que la venta y se lleva el producto inmediatamente. → **al chas chas.** □ *I'm sorry. We don't deliver. It's strictly cash-and-carry.* □ *You cannot get credit at that drugstore. They only sell cash-and-carry.*

cash in (on something)   ganar mucho dinero por algo; sacar un beneficio de algo. → **sacar partido de algo.** □ *This is a good year for farming, and you can cash in on it if you're smart.* □ *It's too late to cash in on that particular clothing fad.*

cast (one's) pearls before swine   gastar algo de buena calidad para alguien que no lo aprecia. (De un refrán bíblico. Como si uno estuviera tirando algo de mucho valor debajo de los pies de cerdos. Es insultante referirse a las personas como cerdos.) □ *To sing for them is to cast pearls before swine.* □ *To serve them French cuisine is like casting one's pearls before swine.*

cast the first stone   hacer la primera crítica de alguien o algo; ser la primera persona que ataca a alguien o algo. (De un refrán bíblico.) □ *Well, I don't want to be the one to cast the first stone, but she sang horribly.* □ *John always casts the first stone. Does he think he's perfect?*

catch cold AND **take cold**   contraer un resfriado o catarro. → **coger catarro; coger un resfriado.** □ *Please close the window, or we'll all catch cold.* □ *I take cold every year at this time.*

catch one's death (of cold) AND **take one's death of cold**   contraer un resfriado o catarro; contraer un resfriado o catarro muy grave. □ *If I go out in this weather, I'll catch my death of cold.* □ *Dress up warm or you'll take your death of cold.* □ *Put on your raincoat or you'll catch your death.*

catch someone off-balance   coger a alguien desprevenido; sorprender a alguien. (También se usa literalmente.) □ *Sorry I acted so flustered. You caught me off-balance.* □ *The robbers caught Ann off-balance and stole her purse.*

catch someone's eye AND **get someone's eye** establecer contacto visual con alguien; atraer la atención de alguien. (También se usa con *have,* como en los ejemplos.) → **llamar la atención de alguien.** □ *The shiny red car caught Mary's eye.* □ *Tom got Mary's eye and waved to her.* □ *When Tom had her eye, he smiled at her.*

caught in the cross fire colocado entre dos personas o grupos que se están peleando o luchando. (Como si uno estuviera colocado entre dos ejércitos opuestos que se están disparando, uno a otro.) □ *In western movies, innocent people are always getting caught in the cross fire.* □ *In the war, Corporal Smith was killed when he got caught in the cross fire.*

caught short no tener algo que uno necesita, especialmente dinero. → **andar escaso de algo; no andar sobrado de algo.** □ *I needed eggs for my cake, but I was caught short.* □ *Bob had to borrow money from John to pay for the meal. Bob is caught short quite often.*

cause (some) eyebrows to raise escandalizar a otros; sorprender y consternar a otros. □ *John caused eyebrows to raise when he married a poor girl from Toledo.* □ *If you want to cause some eyebrows to raise, just start singing as you walk down the street.*

cause (some) tongues to wag causar cotilleo; dar motivo de cotilleo. → **seguro que la gente murmurará.** □ *The way John was looking at Mary will surely cause some tongues to wag.* □ *The way Mary was dressed will also cause tongues to wag.*

champ at the bit estar listo para y ansioso por hacer algo. (Originalmente referente a los caballos.) □ *The kids were champing at the bit to get into the swimming pool.* □ *The dogs were champing at the bit to begin the hunt.*

change horses in midstream hacer cambios importantes en una actividad que ya se ha empezado; elegir a alguien o algo para una actividad demasiado tarde. (Normalmente el cambio está considerado como una mala idea.) □ *I'm already baking a cherry pie. I can't bake an apple pie. It's too late to change horses in midstream.* □ *The house is half-built. It's too late to hire a different architect. You can't change horses in midstream.*

channels, go through   Véase *go through channels.*

Charity begins at home.   un refrán significando que uno debe ayudar a su familia, amigos, o compañeros de patria antes de ayudar a otros. → **La caridad bien entendida empieza por casa.** □ *"Mother, may I please have some pie?" asked Mary. "Remember, charity begins at home." □ At church, the minister reminded us that charity begins at home, but we must remember others also.*

chip off the old block, a   Véase *a chip off the old block.*

chip on one's shoulder, have a   Véase *have a chip on one's shoulder.*

circulation, back in   Véase *back in circulation.*

circulation, out of   Véase *out of circulation.*

clean hands, have   Véase *have clean hands.*

clear as mud, (as)   Véase *(as) clear as mud.*

clear blue sky, out of a   Véase *out of a clear blue sky.*

clear the table   quitar los platos y otros utensilios de la mesa después de una comida. → **levantar la mesa; quitar la mesa.** □ *Will you please help clear the table? □ After you clear the table, we'll play cards.*

climb on the bandwagon   unirse con otros para apoyar a alguien o algo. → **apuntarse al carro; subirse al carro; arrimarse al que lleva la batuta.** □ *Come join us! Climb on the bandwagon and support Senator Smith! □ Look at all those people climbing on the bandwagon! They don't know what they are getting into!*

clip someone's wings   contener a alguien; reducir o poner fin a los privilegios de un adolescente. (A veces los pájaros o las aves tienen las alas recortadas para que no se escapen.) □ *You had better learn to get home on time, or I will clip your wings. □ My mother clipped my wings. I can't go out tonight.*

clock, against the Véase *against the clock.*

clockwork, go like Véase *go like clockwork.*

close at hand al alcance de uno; cerca. → **a mano.** □ *I'm sorry, but your letter isn't close at hand. Please remind me what you said in it.* □ *When you're cooking, you should keep all the ingredients close at hand.*

close call, have a Véase *have a close call.*

close ranks - **1.** mover más cerca de los otros soldados en una formación militar. → **cerrar las filas.** □ *The soldiers closed ranks and marched on the enemy.* □ *All right! Stop that talking and close ranks.* **2.** unirse (con alguien). □ *We can fight this menace only if we close ranks.* □ *Let's all close ranks behind Ann and get her elected.*

close shave, have a Véase *have a close shave.*

cloud nine, on Véase *on cloud nine.*

cloud (of suspicion), under a Véase *under a cloud (of suspicion).*

coast is clear, The. Véase *The coast is clear.*

coast-to-coast del océano Atlántico al océano Pacífico (en los Estados Unidos); toda la tierra entre el océano Atlántico y el océano Pacífico. □ *My voice was once heard on a coast-to-coast radio broadcast.* □ *Our car made the coast-to-coast trip in eighty hours.*

cock-and-bull story un cuento estúpido e inventado; un cuento que es mentira. → **cuento chino.** □ *Don't give me that cock-and-bull story.* □ *I asked for an explanation, and all I got was your ridiculous cock-and-bull story!*

cold, out Véase *out cold.*

color, off Véase *off-color.*

come a cropper   tener mala suerte; fracasar. (Literalmente, caerse de un caballo.) → **darse un batacazo; pegar un patinazo; irse a la porra (cuando el fracaso o la mala suerte tiene que ver con los negocios.)** ☐ *Bob invested all his money in the stock market just before it fell. Boy, did he come a cropper.* ☐ *Jane was out all night before she took her tests. She really came a cropper.*

come apart at the seams   perder el mando de las emociones de repente. (Del sentido original de la frase, que se refiere a la ropa que se deshace.) ☐ *Bill was so upset that he almost came apart at the seams.* ☐ *I couldn't take anymore. I just came apart at the seams.*

come away empty-handed   volver sin algo. ☐ *All right, go gambling. Don't come away empty-handed, though.* ☐ *Go to the bank and ask for the loan again. This time don't come away empty-handed.*

come by something   1. viajar por un modo específico de transporte, como un avión, un barco, o un coche. (El sentido literal.) ☐ *We came by train. It's more relaxing.* ☐ *Next time, we'll come by plane. It's faster.* 2. conseguir o recibir algo. ☐ *How did you come by that haircut?* ☐ *Where did you come by that new shirt?*

come down in the world   bajar de nivel social o económico. → **venir a menos.** ☐ *Mr. Jones has really come down in the world since he lost his job.* ☐ *If I were unemployed, I'm sure I'd come down in the world, too.*

come home (to roost)   volver a causar molestias (para alguien). (Como las gallinas o las otras aves que vuelven al gallinero para posarse para dormir.) ☐ *As I feared, all my problems came home to roost.* ☐ *Yes, problems all come home eventually.*

come in out of the rain   ponerse atento y sensato. (También se usa literalmente.) ☐ *Pay attention, Sally! Come in out of the rain!* ☐ *Bill will fail if he doesn't come in out of the rain and study.*

come into one's or its own   1. lograr el reconocimiento que una persona merece. ☐ *Sally finally came into her own.* ☐ *After years of trying, she finally came into her own.* 2. lograr el reconocimiento que una cosa merece. ☐ *The idea of an electric car* *finally came into its own.* □ *Film as an art medium finally came into its own.*

come of age   llegar a una edad en que uno puede poseer tierrra, casarse, y firmar contratos legales. → **llegar a la mayoría de edad; hacerse mayor de cdad.** □ *When Jane comes of age, she will buy her own car.* □ *Sally, who came of age last month, entered into an agreement to purchase a house.*

come off second-best   ganar el segundo lugar o un lugar menor en una competencia; salir perdiendo en una competencia. □ *John came off second-best in the race.* □ *Why do I always come off second-best in an argument with you?*

come out ahead   acabar con beneficios en una empresa; mejorar la situación de uno. → **salir ganando.** □ *I hope you come out ahead with your investments.* □ *It took a lot of money to buy the house, but I think I'll come out ahead.*

come out in the wash   salir bien. (La frase significa que los problemas o las dificultades van a desaparecer, como la suciedad desaparece de la ropa en el lavado.) → **al final todo se arreglará.** □ *Don't worry about that problem. It'll all come out in the wash.* □ *This trouble will go away. It'll come out in the wash.*

come out of the closet   **1.** revelar los intereses secretos de sí mismo. → **salir a la luz.** □ *Tom Brown came out of the closet and admitted that he likes to knit.* □ *It's time that all of you lovers of chamber music came out of the closet and attended our concerts.* **2.** revelar a otros que uno es homosexual. □ *Tom surprised his parents when he came out of the closet.* □ *It was difficult for him to come out of the closet.*

come to a bad end   experimentar un desastre, posiblemente un desastre merecido o esperado; morir de una manera inoportuna o desdicha. □ *My old car came to a bad end. Its engine burned up.* □ *The evil merchant came to a bad end.*

come to a dead end   llegar a un punto absoluto de parar o dejar de hacer algo. → **llegar a un callejón sin salida.** □ *The building project came to a dead end.* □ *The street came to a dead end.* □ *We were driving along and came to a dead end.*

come to a head llegar a un punto o momento crítico; llegar a un momento en que se necesita resolver un problema. □ *Remember my problem with my neighbors? Well, last night the whole thing came to a head.* □ *The battle between the two factions of the city council came to a head yesterday.*

come to an end terminar; acabar. □ *The party came to an end at midnight.* □ *Her life came to an end late yesterday.*

come to an untimely end morir premaduramente. □ *Poor Mr. Jones came to an untimely end in a car accident.* □ *Cancer caused Mrs. Smith to come to an untimely end.*

come to a standstill terminar, temporal o permanentemente. → **pararse; estancarse; llegar a un punto muerto.** □ *The building project came to a standstill. because the workers went on strike.* □ *The party came to a standstill until the lights were turned on again.*

come to grief fracasar; tener preocupaciones o problemas. → **sufrir un percance; irse al traste.** □ *The artist wept when her canvas came to grief.* □ *The wedding party came to grief when the bride passed out.*

come to grips with something enfrentarse a algo; comprender algo. → **habérselas con algo.** □ *He found it difficult to come to grips with his grandmother's death.* □ *Many students have a hard time coming to grips with algebra.*

come to light ser revelado. → **salir a la luz.** □ *Some interesting facts about your past have just come to light.* □ *If too many bad things come to light, you may lose your job.*

come to one's senses despertarse; volver en sí; empezar a pensar con claridad. → **recobrar el juicio; entrar en razón.** □ *John, come to your senses. You're being quite stupid.* □ *In the morning I don't come to my senses until I have had two cups of coffee.*

come to pass ocurrir (Se usa la frase en la literatura.) → **llegar a suceder.** □ *When did all of this come to pass?* □ *When will this event come to pass?*

come to the point AND **get to the point**   llegar a la parte importante (de algo). → **dejarse de cuentos; ir al grano.** □ *He has been talking a long time. I wish he would come to the point.* □ *Quit wasting time! Get to the point!* □ *We are talking about money, Bob! Come on, get to the point.*

come to think of it   lo recordé hace un momento . . .; ahora que lo pienso . . . □ *Come to think of it, I know someone who can help.* □ *I have a screwdriver in the trunk of my car, come to think of it.*

come true   hacerse realidad; suceder de veras (como un sueño o deseo). □ *When I got married, all my dreams came true.* □ *Coming to the big city was like having my wish come true.*

come up in the world   mejorar el estado o la situación de uno en la vida. □ *Since Mary got her new job, she has really come up in the world.* □ *A good education helped my brother come up in the world.*

come what may   suceda lo que suceda. → **contra viento y marea.** □ *I'll be home for the holidays, come what may.* □ *Come what may, the mail will get delivered.*

comfortable as an old shoe, (as)   Véase *(as) comfortable as an old shoe.*

commission, out of   Véase *out of commission.*

conspicuous by one's absence   tener la ausencia notada por otros. → **brillar uno por su ausencia.** □ *We missed you last night. You were conspicuous by your absence.* □ *How could the bride's father miss the wedding party? He was certainly conspicuous by his absence.*

construction, under   Véase *under construction.*

contrary, on the   Véase *on the contrary.*

control the purse strings   tener cargo del dinero en una empresa o casa. □ *I control the purse strings at our house.* □ *Mr. Williams is the treasurer. He controls the purse strings.*

cook someone's goose   dañar o arruinar a alguien. (Hacer algo que no se puede deshacer.) → **malograrle los planes a uno.** □ *I cooked my own goose by not showing up on time.* □ *Sally cooked Bob's goose for treating her the way he did.*

cook the accounts   estafar en la contabilidad; cambiar las cuentas en la contabilidad para que aparezcan cuadrar cuando, en realidad, no cuadran. □ *Jane was sent to jail for cooking the accounts of her mother's store.* □ *It's hard to tell whether she really cooked the accounts or just didn't know how to add.*

cool as a cucumber, (as)   Véase *(as) cool as a cucumber.*

cool one's heels   esperar (para alguien). → **hacer antesala larga.** □ *I spent all afternoon cooling my heels in the waiting room while the doctor talked on the telephone.* □ *All right. If you can't behave properly, just sit down here and cool your heels until I call you.*

copycat, be a   Véase *be a copycat.*

corner of one's eye, out of the   Véase *out of the corner of one's eye.*

cost an arm and a leg   Véase en *pay an arm and a leg (for something).*

cost a pretty penny   costar mucho dinero. → **costar un ojo de la cara.** □ *I'll bet that diamond cost a pretty penny.* □ *You can be sure that house cost a pretty penny. It has seven bathrooms.*

counter, under the   Véase *under the counter.*

count noses AND **count heads**   contar el número de personas. (Porque sólo hay una cabeza por persona.) □ *I'll tell you how many people are here after I count noses.* □ *Everyone is here. Let's count heads so we can order hamburgers.*

count one's chickens before they hatch   planear la manera de utilizar algo antes de que uno lo tenga. (Muchas veces se usa esta frase en el sentido negativo.) □ *You're way ahead of yourself. Don't* *count your chickens before they hatch.* □ *You may be disappointed if you count your chickens before they hatch.*

cover a lot of ground 1. viajar una distancia muy larga; investigar mucha tierra. □ *The prospectors covered a lot of ground, looking for gold.* □ *My car can cover a lot of ground in one day.* 2. tratar de mucha información y de muchos hechos. □ *The history lecture covered a lot of ground today.* □ *Mr. and Mrs. Franklin always cover a lot of ground when they argue.*

cover for someone 1. dar excusas para alguien; ocultar los errores de alguien. □ *If I miss class, please cover for me.* □ *If you're late, I'll cover for you.* 2. encargarse del trabajo de otra persona. □ *Dr. Johnson's partner agreed to cover for him during his vacation.* □ *I'm on duty this afternoon. Will you please cover for me? I have a doctor's appointment.*

crack a joke contar un chiste. □ *She's never serious. She's always cracking jokes.* □ *As long as she's cracking jokes, she's okay.*

crack a smile sonreír un poco, posiblemente de mala gana. □ *She cracked a smile, so I knew she was kidding.* □ *The soldier cracked a smile at the wrong time and had to march for an hour as punishment.*

cramp someone's style limitar a alguien de algún modo. □ *I hope this doesn't cramp your style, but could you please not hum while you work?* □ *To ask him to keep regular hours would really be cramping his style.*

crazy as a loon, (as) Véase *(as) crazy as a loon.*

cream of the crop el mejor de todo. (Es cliché.) □ *This particular car is the cream of the crop.* □ *The kids are very bright. They are the cream of the crop.*

creation, in Véase *in creation.*

Crime doesn't pay. un refrán significando que la delincuencia no va a ayudar a una persona. □ *At the end of the radio program,* *a voice said, "Remember, crime doesn't pay."* □ *No matter how tempting it may appear, crime doesn't pay.*

cross a bridge before one comes to it   preocuparse demasiado por algo antes de que ocurra. (Observe las variaciones en los ejemplos.) □ *There is no sense in crossing that bridge before you come to it.* □ *She's always crossing bridges before coming to them. She needs to learn to relax.*

cross a bridge when one comes to it   enfrentarse a algún problema sólo cuando tenga que hacerlo. (Observe las variaciones en los ejemplos.) □ *Please wait and cross that bridge when you come to it.* □ *He shouldn't worry about it now. He can cross that bridge when he comes to it.*

cross-examine someone   preguntar detalles; interrogar al sospechoso o testigo con detenimiento. □ *The police cross-examined the suspect for three hours.* □ *The lawyer plans to cross-examine the witness tomorrow morning.*

cross one's heart (and hope to die)   prometer o jurar que uno dice la verdad. □ *It's true, cross my heart and hope to die.* □ *It's really true—cross my heart.*

cross swords (with someone)   entrar en una discusión con alguien. (No es literal.) □ *I don't want to cross swords with Tom.* □ *The last time we crossed swords, we had a terrible time.*

crow flies, as the   Véase *as the crow flies.*

crux of the matter   la cuestión más importante de algún asunto. (*Crux* es palabra vieja en inglés significando "cross.") □ *All right, this is the crux of the matter.* □ *It's about time that we looked at the crux of the matter.*

cry before one is hurt   llorar o quejarse antes de que uno esté herido. □ *Bill always cries before he's hurt.* □ *There is no point in crying before one is hurt.*

cry bloody murder AND **scream bloody murder**   gritar como si algo muy grave hubiera occurido. (Gritar como si uno

hubiera encontrado el cadáver sangriento después de un asesinato.)
□ *Now that Bill is really hurt, he's screaming bloody murder.* □
*There is no point in crying bloody murder about the bill if you aren't
going to pay it.*

cry one's eyes out   llorar muy fuerte. (No es literal.) □ *When we
heard the news, we cried our eyes out with joy.* □ *She cried her eyes
out after his death.*

cry over spilled milk   estar triste por hacer algo que no se puede
deshacer. (Normalmente se ve como acción inmadura. Se puede
deletrear *spilled* como *spilt* también.) □ *I'm sorry that you broke
your bicycle, Tom. But there is nothing that can be done now. Don't
cry over spilled milk.* □ *Ann is always crying over spilt milk.*

cry wolf   llorar o quejarse de algo cuando, en realidad, nada anda
mal. □ *Pay no attention. She's just crying wolf again.* □ *Don't cry
wolf too often. No one will come.*

cup of tea, not someone's   Véase *not someone's cup of tea.*

Curiosity killed the cat.   un refrán significando que es peligroso
estar curioso. □ *Don't ask so many questions, Billy. Curiosity killed
the cat.* □ *Curiosity killed the cat. Mind your own business.*

curl someone's hair   espantar o atemorizar a alguien gravemente;
dar susto a alguien con la vista, el sonido, o el sabor de algo.
(También se usa literalmente.) □ *Don't ever sneak up on me like
that again. You really curled my hair.* □ *The horror film curled my
hair.*

curl up and die   retirarse para morir. □ *When I heard you say that,
I could have curled up and died.* □ *No, it wasn't an illness. She just
curled up and died.*

cut class   no ir a clase. (Referente a las clases de la escuela secundaria
o de la universidad.) □ *If Mary keeps cutting classes, she'll fail the
course.* □ *I can't cut that class. I've missed too many already.*

cut off one's nose to spite one's face   una frase significando
que uno causa daño a sí mismo cuando intenta castigar a otros.

(Observe las variaciones en la forma en los ejemplos.) □ *Billy loves the zoo, but he refused to go with his mother because he was mad at her. He cut off his nose to spite his face.* □ *Find a better way to be angry. It is silly to cut your nose off to spite your face.*

cut one's (own) throat   experimentar fracaso seguro; causar daño a alguien. (También se usa literalmente.) □ *If I were to run for office, I'd just be cutting my throat.* □ *Judges who take bribes are cutting their own throats.*

cut someone or something (off) short   terminar con algo antes de que sea terminado; interrumpir a alguien antes de que acabe. □ *We cut the picnic short because of the storm.* □ *I'm sorry to cut you off short, but I must go now.*

cut someone or something to the bone   **1.** cortar muy hondo, hasta el hueso. (El sentido literal.) □ *The knife cut John to the bone. He had to be sewed up.* □ *Cut each slice of ham to the bone. Then each slice will be as big as possible.* **2.** [con *something*] reducir (algo) mucho. (No es literal.) □ *We cut our expenses to the bone and are still losing money.* □ *Congress had to cut the budget to the bone in order to balance it.*

cut someone's losses   reducir la pérdida de dinero, artículos, u otras cosas de valor de alguien. □ *I sold the stock as it went down, thus cutting my losses.* □ *He cut his losses by putting better locks on the doors. There were fewer robberies.* □ *The mayor's reputation suffered because of the scandal. He finally resigned to cut his losses.*

cut someone to the quick   ofender a alguien muy gravemente. (Se puede usar literalmente cuando *quick* es referente a la carne tierna a la base de las uñas de la mano o del pie.) □ *Your criticism cut me to the quick.* □ *Tom's sharp words to Mary cut her to the quick.*

cut the ground out from under someone AND **cut out the ground from under someone**   deshacer la base de los planes o del argumento de una persona. □ *The politician cut the ground out from under his opponent.* □ *Congress cut out the ground from under the president.*

D

dance to another tune   cambiar rápidamente a otra conducta; cambiar de conducta o actitud. □ *After being yelled at, Ann danced to another tune.* □ *A stern talking-to will make her dance to another tune.*

dash cold water on something   Véase en *pour cold water on something.*

date back (to sometime)   ser parte de otra época; haber vivido durante una época específica del pasado. □ *My late grandmother dated back to the Civil War.* □ *This record dates back to the sixties.* □ *How far do you date back?*

Davy Jones's locker, go to   Véase *go to Davy Jones's locker.*

dead and buried   pasado (o muerto) para siempre. (La frase se refiere literalmente a personas y figuradamente a ideas y otras cosas.) □ *Now that Uncle Bill is dead and buried, we can read his will.* □ *That kind of thinking is dead and buried.*

dead as a dodo, (as)   Véase *(as) dead as a dodo.*

dead as a doornail, (as)   Véase *(as) dead as a doornail.*

dead heat, in a   Véase *in a dead heat.*

dead to rights, have someone   Véase *have someone dead to rights.*

dead to the world   cansado; agotado; durmiendo profundamente. (Dormido e inconsciente del mundo.) → **dormir como un tronco.** □ *I've had such a hard day. I'm really dead to the world.* □ *Look at her sleep. She's dead to the world.*

death on someone or something   1. muy eficaz contra alguien o algo. □ *This road is terribly bumpy. It's death on tires.* □ *The sergeant is death on lazy soldiers.* 2. [con *something*] preciso o absoluto en hacer algo que require mucha habilidad o mucho esfuerzo. □ *John is death on curve balls. He's our best pitcher.* □ *The boxing champ is really death on those fast punches.*

death's door, at   Véase *at death's door.*

deep end, go off the   Véase *go off the deep end.*

deep water, in   Véase *in deep water.*

depth, beyond one's   Véase *beyond one's depth.*

desert a sinking ship AND **leave a sinking ship**   salir de un lugar, dejar una situación, o dejar a una persona cuando las cosas se ponen difíciles o desagradables. (Se dice que las ratas salen primero de un buque que está hundiéndose.) □ *I hate to be the one to desert a sinking ship, but I can't stand it around here anymore.* □ *There goes Tom. Wouldn't you know he'd leave a sinking ship rather than stay around and try to help?*

devil and the deep blue sea, between the   Véase *between the devil and the deep blue sea.*

devil of it, for the   Véase *for the devil of it.*

diamond in the rough   una persona o cosa de mucho valor o excelencia potencial ocultado por un exterior tosco o sin encerar. □ *Ann looks like a stupid woman, but she's a fine person—a real diamond in the rough.* □ *That piece of property is a diamond in the rough. Someday it will be valuable.*

dibs on something, have   Véase *have dibs on something.*

die of a broken heart   1. morir de pena emocional. □ *I was not surprised to hear of her death. They say she died of a broken heart.* □ *In the movie, the heroine appeared to die of a broken heart, but the audience knew she was poisoned.* 2. sufrir de pena emocional, especialmente a causa de un amorío roto. □ *Tom and Mary broke* *off their romance and both died of broken hearts.* □ *Please don't leave me. I know I'll die of a broken heart.*

die of boredom   sufrir aburrimiento; estar muy aburrido. □ *No one has ever really died of boredom.* □ *We sat there and listened politely, even though we almost died of boredom.*

die on the vine   Véase en *wither on the vine.*

different as night and day, (as)   Véase *(as) different as night and day.*

dig some dirt up on someone AND **dig up some dirt on someone**   averiguar una cosa mala acerca de una persona. (*Dirt* significa "cotilleo" en este caso.) □ *If you don't stop trying to dig some dirt up on me, I'll get a lawyer and sue you.* □ *The citizens' group dug up some dirt on the mayor and used it against her at election time.*

dirty one's hands   Véase en *get one's hands dirty.*

dishes, do the   Véase *do the dishes.*

distance, go the   Véase *go the distance.*

do a land-office business   hacer muchos negocios durante un período corto. (Como si uno estuviera vendiendo tierra durante una época en que muchas personas compraran tierrra.) □ *The ice-cream shop always does a land-office business on a hot day.* □ *The tax collector's office did a land-office business on the day that taxes were due.*

doghouse, in the   Véase *in the doghouse.*

dogs, go to the   Véase *go to the dogs.*

doldrums, in the   Véase *in the doldrums.*

dollar-for-dollar   considerando la cantidad de dinero; considerando el precio. (Muchas veces se ve esta frase en la publicidad.) □ *Dollar-for-dollar, you cannot buy a better car.* □ *Dollar-for-dollar,* *this laundry detergent washes cleaner and brighter than any other product on the market.*

Don't hold your breath.   una frase significando que una persona no debe pensar que una cosa esperada necesariamente vaya a ocurrir. (Literalmente, la frase manda que la persona no deje de respirar.) □ *You think he'll get a job? Ha! Don't hold your breath.* □ *I'll finish building the fence as soon as I have time, but don't hold your breath.*

Don't let someone or something get you down.   una frase significando que una persona no debe permitir que esté abrumado por alguien o algo. □ *Don't let their constant teasing get you down.* □ *Don't let Tom get you down. He's not always unpleasant.*

Don't look a gift horse in the mouth.   un refrán signficando que uno no debe esperar regalos perfectos. (Normalmente se usa en el sentido negativo. Observe las variaciones en los ejemplos. Se puede averiguar la edad de un caballo, y por eso su utilidad, si examina sus dientes. Sería codicioso examinar los dientes de un caballo recibido como regalo.) □ *Don't complain. You shouldn't look a gift horse in the mouth.* □ *John complained that the television set he got for his birthday was black and white rather than color. He was told, "Don't look a gift horse in the mouth."*

doorstep, at someone's   Véase *at someone's doorstep.*

doorstep, on someone's   Véase *on someone's doorstep.*

dose of one's own medicine   la misma manera en que una persona trata a otras personas. (Muchas veces se usa con *get* o *have.*) □ *Sally never is very friendly. Someone is going to give her a dose of her own medicine someday.* □ *He didn't like getting a dose of his own medicine.*

do someone's heart good   hacer que otra persona se sienta feliz. (También se usa literalmente.) □ *It does my heart good to hear you talk that way.* □ *When she sent me a get-well card, it really did my heart good.*

do something by hand   hacer algo con las manos en vez de una máquina. □ *The computer was broken so I had to do the calculations by hand.* □ *All this tiny stitching was done by hand. Machines cannot do this kind of work.*

do something hands down   hacer algo fácilmente y sin oposición. (Sin que una persona levante la mano en oposición.) □ *The mayor won the election hands down.* □ *She was the choice of the people hands down.*

do the dishes   fregar los platos; fregar y secar los platos. □ *Bill, you cannot go out and play until you've done the dishes.* □ *Why am I always the one who has to do the dishes?*

do the honors   como anfitrón, servir las bebidas, trinchar la carne, o hacer el brindis. □ *All the guests were seated, and a huge juicy turkey sat on the table. Jane Thomas turned to her husband and said, "Bob, will you do the honors?" Mr. Jones smiled and began slicing thick slices of meat from the turkey.* □ *The mayor stood up and addressed the people who were still eating their salads. "I'm delighted to do the honors this evening and propose a toast to your friend and mine, Bill Jones. Bill, good luck and best wishes in your new job in Washington." And everyone sipped a bit of wine.*

dot, on the   Véase *on the dot.*

down in the dumps   triste o deprimido. □ *I've been down in the dumps for the past few days.* □ *Try to cheer Jane up. She's down in the dumps for some reason.*

down in the mouth   con expresión triste; deprimido. (Referente al ceño.) □ *Since her dog died, Barbara has been down in the mouth.* □ *Bob has been down in the mouth since the car wreck.*

down the drain   perdido para siempre; gastado. (También se usa literalmente.) □ *I just hate to see all that money go down the drain.* □ *Well, there goes the whole project, right down the drain.*

down to the wire   al último momento posible; hasta el último momento posible. (Referente al alambre que marca el fin de una carrera de caballos. □ *I have to turn this in tomorrow, and I'll be* *working down to the wire.* □ *When we get down to the wire, we'll know better what to do.*

drain, down the   Véase *down the drain.*

draw a blank   1. no recibir una respuesta; no encontrar nada. □ *I asked him about Tom's financial problems, and I just drew a blank.* □ *We looked in the files for an hour, but we drew a blank.* 2. no recordar (algo). □ *I tried to remember her telephone number, but I could only draw a blank.* □ *It was a very hard test with just one question to answer, and I drew a blank.*

draw a line between something and something else   separar dos cosas; distinguir entre dos cosas. (Se puede usar *the* en vez de *a.* También se puede usar literalmente.) □ *It's necessary to draw a line between bumping into people and striking them.* □ *It's very hard to draw the line between slamming a door and just closing it loudly.*

draw blood   1. golpear o morder (un animal o a una persona) hasta causar un herido que sangra. □ *The dog chased me and bit me hard, but it didn't draw blood.* □ *The boxer landed just one punch and drew blood immediately.* 2. enfadar o insultar a una persona. □ *Sally screamed out a terrible insult at Tom. Judging by the look on his face, she really drew blood.* □ *Tom started yelling and cursing, trying to insult Sally. He wouldn't be satisfied until he had drawn blood, too.*

dream come true   un deseo o sueño que se realiza. □ *Going to Hawaii is like having a dream come true.* □ *Having you for a friend is a dream come true.*

drink to excess   beber demasiado alcohol; beber alcohol continuamente. □ *Mr. Franklin drinks to excess.* □ *Some people drink to excess only at parties.*

drive a hard bargain   trabajar mucho para negociar precios o acuerdos a favor de sí mismo. □ *I saved $200 by driving a hard bargain when I bought my new car.* □ *All right, sir, you drive a hard bargain. I'll sell you this car for $12,450.* □ *You drive a hard bargain, Jane, but I'll sign the contract.*

drive someone to the wall Véase en *force someone to the wall*.

drop in one's tracks parar o derrumbarse de agotamiento; morir de repente. □ *If I keep working this way, I'll drop in my tracks.* □ *Uncle Bob was working in the garden and dropped in his tracks. We are all sorry that he's dead.*

drop of a hat, at the Véase *at the drop of a hat*.

drop someone a few lines Véase la entrada siguiente.

drop someone a line AND **drop someone a few lines** escribirle una carta o una nota a alguien. (*Line* se refiere a las líneas de la escritura.) → **mandarle unas letras a alguien.** □ *I dropped Aunt Jane a line last Thanksgiving.* □ *She usually drops me a few lines around the first of the year.*

drop the ball meter la pata; fracasar de algún modo. (También se usa literalmente cuando la frase trata de los deportes.) □ *Everything was going fine in the election until my campaign manager dropped the ball.* □ *You can't trust John to do the job right. He's always dropping the ball.*

drop the other shoe hacer la acción que termina con algo; hacer la parte que queda por hacer. (Referente a la acción de quitarse los zapatos al acostarse. La persona se quita un zapato y lo deja caer, se quita el otro, y termina con el proceso cuando deja caer el segundo zapato.) □ *Mr. Franklin has left his wife. Soon he'll drop the other shoe and divorce her.* □ *Tommy has just failed three classes in school. We expect him to drop the other shoe and quit altogether any day now.*

drown one's sorrows Véase la entrada siguiente.

drown one's troubles AND **drown one's sorrows** intentar olvidarse de los problemas de uno bebiendo mucho alcohol. □ *Bill is in the bar, drowning his troubles.* □ *Jane is at home, drowning her sorrows.*

drug on the market a la venta en abundancia; un exceso a la venta. □ *Right now, small computers are a drug on the market.* □ *Ten years ago, small transistor radios were a drug on the market.*

drum some business up AND **drum up some business**
animar a las personas a comprar lo que uno vende. (Como si alguien
estuviera golpeando el tambor para llamar la atención de los
compradores.) □ *I need to do something to drum some business up.*
□ *A little bit of advertising would drum up some business.*

dry behind the ears   muy joven e inmaduro. (Normalmente se
usa en el sentido negativo.) □ *Tom is going into business by
himself? Why, he's hardly dry behind the ears.* □ *That kid isn't dry
behind the ears. He'll go broke in a month.*

duck takes to water, as a   Véase *as a duck takes to water.*

dumps, down in the   Véase *down in the dumps.*

Dutch, go   Véase *go Dutch.*

duty, off   Véase *off duty.*

duty, on   Véase *on duty.*

E

early bird gets the worm, The. Véase *The early bird gets the worm.*

Early to bed, early to rise (, makes a man healthy, wealthy, and wise). un refrán significando que es beneficioso acostarse temprano y levantarse temprano. (A veces se dice cuando una persona está levantándose temprano. Se puede omitir la parte entre paréntesis.) → **A quien madruga, Dios le ayuda.** □ *Tom left the party at ten o'clock, saying "Early to bed, early to rise, makes a man healthy, wealthy, and wise."* □ *I always get up at six o'clock. After all, early to bed, early to rise.*

earn one's keep echar una mano a las tareas en recompensa de comida y alojamiento; ganar la paga cumpliendo los deberes del puesto. □ *I earn my keep at college by shoveling snow in the winter.* □ *Tom hardly earns his keep around here. He should be fired.*

ears (in something), up to one's Véase *up to one's ears (in something).*

earth, on Véase *on earth.*

ear to the ground, have one's Véase *have one's ear to the ground.*

easy as (apple) pie, (as) Véase *(as) easy as (apple) pie.*

easy as duck soup, (as) Véase *(as) easy as duck soup.*

easy come, easy go una frase dicha para explicar la pérdida de algo que no requirió mucho esfuerzo para obtener. □ *Ann found twenty dollars in the morning and spent it foolishly at noon. "Easy* come, easy go," she said. □ John spends his money as fast as he can earn it. With John it's easy come, easy go.

Easy does it.   Tenga cuidado; Tenga calma. □ Be careful with that glass vase. Easy does it! □ Now, now, Tom. Don't get angry. Easy does it.

eat humble pie   1. estar muy humilde cuando uno está equivocado en algo. □ I think I'm right, but if I'm wrong, I'll eat humble pie. □ You think you're so smart. I hope you have to eat humble pie. **2.** aceptar insultos e humillación. □ John, stand up for your rights. You don't have to eat humble pie all the time. □ Beth seems quite happy to eat humble pie. She should stand up for her rights.

eat like a bird   comer poco; picotear la comida. □ Jane is very slim because she eats like a bird. □ Bill is trying to lose weight by eating like a bird.

eat like a horse   comer mucho. □ No wonder he's so fat. He eats like a horse. □ John works like a horse and eats like a horse, so he never gets fat.

eat one's cake and have it too   Véase en have one's cake and eat it too.

eat one's hat   una frase contando las cosas que haría uno si un suceso improbable pasara en realidad. (Siempre se usa con if. Nunca se usa literalmente.) □ If we get there on time, I'll eat my hat. □ I'll eat my hat if you get a raise. □ He said he'd eat his hat if she got elected.

eat one's heart out   1. estar muy triste (sobre alguien o algo.) □ Bill spent a lot of time eating his heart out after his divorce. □ Sally ate her heart out when she had to sell her house. **2.** estar envidioso (de alguien o algo.) □ Do you like my new watch? Well, eat your heart out. It was the last one in the store. □ Don't eat your heart out about my new car. Go get one of your own.

eat one's words   tener que retirar una declaración; confesar que las predicciones de uno eran equivocadas. □ You shouldn't say that to me. I'll make you eat your words. □ John was wrong about the election and had to eat his words.

eat out of someone's hands   hacer lo que quiere otra persona; obedecer a alguien con entusiasmo. (Muchas veces se usa con *have;* observe los ejemplos.) □ *Just wait! I'll have everyone eating out of my hands. They'll do whatever I ask.* □ *The president has Congress eating out of his hands.* □ *A lot of people are eating out of his hands.*

eat someone out of house and home   comer mucho (en la casa de otra persona); comer toda la comida en la casa. □ *Billy has a huge appetite. He almost eats us out of house and home.* □ *When the kids come home from college, they always eat us out of house and home.*

egg on one's face, have   Véase *have egg on one's face.*

element, out of one's   Véase *out of one's element.*

eleventh hour, at the   Véase *at the eleventh hour.*

empty-handed, come away   Véase *come away empty-handed.*

empty-handed, go away   Véase *go away empty-handed.*

end in itself   por sí mismo; hacia sus propios fines. → **un fin en sí mismo.** □ *For Bob, art is an end in itself. He doesn't hope to make any money from it.* □ *Learning is an end in itself. Knowledge does not have to have a practical application.*

end of one's rope, at the   Véase *at the end of one's rope.*

end of one's tether, at the   Véase *at the end of one's rope.*

end of the line   Véase la entrada siguiente.

end of the road AND **end of the line**   el fin; el fin del proceso entero; la muerte. (*Line* se refirió originalmente a las vías del ferrocarril. □ *Our house is at the end of the road.* □ *We rode the train to the end of the line.* □ *When we reach the end of the road on this project, we'll get paid.* □ *You've come to the end of the line. I'll not lend you another penny.* □ *When I reach the end of the road, I wish to be buried in a quiet place, near some trees.*

ends of the earth, to the   Véase *to the ends of the earth.*

end up with the short end of the stick   Véase en *get the short end of the stick.*

Enough is enough.   Ya basta, no queremos más. □ *Stop asking for money! Enough is enough!* □ *I've heard all the complaining from you that I can take. Stop! Enough is enough!*

enter one's mind   pensar en algo; entrar en la conciencia [una idea o una memoria]. □ *Leave you behind? The thought never even entered my mind.* □ *A very interesting idea just entered my mind. What if I ran for Congress?*

Every cloud has a silver lining.   un refrán significando que se puede encontrar algo bueno en cada cosa mala. □ *Jane was upset when she saw that all her flowers had died from the frost. But when she saw that the weeds had died too, she said, "Every cloud has a silver lining." □ Sally had a sore throat and had to stay home from school. When she learned she missed a math test, she said, "Every cloud has a silver lining."*

Every dog has its day. AND **Every dog has his day.**   un refrán significando que todos tendrán oportunidades, aún los más desgraciados. □ *Don't worry, you'll get chosen for the team. Every dog has its day.* □ *You may become famous someday. Every dog has his day.*

every living soul   cada persona. □ *I expect every living soul to be there and be there on time.* □ *This is the kind of problem that affects every living soul.*

every minute counts AND **every moment counts**   el tiempo es muy importante. □ *Doctor, please try to get here quickly. Every minute counts.* □ *When you take a test, you must work rapidly because every minute counts.* □ *When you're trying to meet a deadline, every moment counts.*

every moment counts   Véase la entrada previa.

every (other) breath, with   Véase *with every (other) breath.*

everything but the kitchen sink   casi todo en que puede pensar uno. □ *When Sally went off to college, she took everything but the kitchen sink.* □ *John orders everything but the kitchen sink when he goes out to dinner, especially if someone else is paying for it.*

everything from A to Z   Véase la entrada siguiente.

everything from soup to nuts AND **everything from A to Z**   casi todo en que puede pensar uno. (Se usa la primera entrada especialmente en la descripción de los platos de una comida.) □ *For dinner we had everything from soup to nuts.* □ *In college I studied everything from soup to nuts.* □ *She mentioned everything from A to Z.*

expecting (a child)   embarazada. (Es eufemismo.) □ *Tommy's mother is expecting a child.* □ *Oh, I didn't know she was expecting.*

eye for an eye, a tooth for a tooth, An.   Véase *An eye for an eye, a tooth for a tooth.*

eye out (for someone or something), have an   Véase *have an eye out (for someone or something).*

eyes bigger than one's stomach, have   Véase *have eyes bigger than one's stomach.*

eyes in the back of one's head, have   Véase *have eyes in the back of one's head.*

F

face the music   recibir castigo; aceptar los resultados desagradables de las acciones de sí mismo. □ *Mary broke a dining-room window and had to face the music when her father got home.* □ *After failing a math test, Tom had to go home and face the music.*

fair-weather friend   una persona que sólo es amigo cuando la vida va bien para uno. (La persona no será amigo cuando las cosas van mal.) □ *Bill wouldn't help me with my homework. He's just a fair-weather friend.* □ *A fair-weather friend isn't much help in an emergency.*

fall down on the job   no hacer algo bien; no cumplir con los deberes de un puesto. (También se usa literalmente.) □ *The team kept losing because the coach was falling down on the job.* □ *Tom was fired because he fell down on the job.*

fall flat (on one's face) AND **fall flat (on its face)**   no tener éxito. □ *I fell flat on my face when I tried to give my speech.* □ *The play fell flat on its face.* □ *My jokes fall flat most of the time.*

fall in(to) place   caber; ponerse organizado. □ *After we heard the whole story, things began to fall in place.* □ *When you get older, the different parts of your life begin to fall into place.*

fall short (of something)   **1.** carecer de algo; carecer bastante de algo. □ *We fell short of money at the end of the month.* □ *When baking a cake, the cook fell short of eggs and had to go to the store for more.* **2.** no llegar a una meta. □ *We fell short of our goal of collecting a thousand dollars.* □ *Ann ran a fast race, but fell short of the record.*

Familiarity breeds contempt. un refrán significando que conocer a otra persona muy bien durante mucho tiempo lleva al resentimiento. □ *Bill and his brothers are always fighting. As they say: "Familiarity breeds contempt."* □ *Mary and John were good friends for many years. Finally they got into a big argument and became enemies. That just shows that familiarity breeds contempt.*

familiar ring, have a Véase *have a familiar ring.*

fan of someone, be a Véase *be a fan of someone.*

far as it goes, as Véase *as far as it goes.*

farm someone or something out AND **farm out someone or something** 1. [con *someone*] mandar a alguien a algún lugar para el cuidado o la educación. □ *When my mother died, they farmed me out to my aunt and uncle.* □ *The team manager farmed out the baseball player to the minor leagues until he improved.* 2. [con *something*] mandar algo a algún lugar para resolverse. □ *I farmed out various parts of the work to different people.* □ *Bill farmed his chores out to his brothers and sisters and went to a movie.*

fat is in the fire, The. Véase *The fat is in the fire.*

fear of something, for Véase *for fear of something.*

feast one's eyes (on someone or something) mirar a alguien o algo con gusto, envidia, o admiración. (Como si la vista diera un banquete de placer a los ojos.) □ *Just feast your eyes on that beautiful juicy steak!* □ *Yes, feast your eyes. You won't see one like that again for a long time.*

feather in one's cap un honor; una recompensa de algo. □ *Getting a new client was really a feather in my cap.* □ *John earned a feather in his cap by getting an A in physics.*

feather one's (own) nest 1. decorar y amueblar la casa de uno con estilo y también con comodidad. (Los pájaros forran el nido con plumas para hacerlo caliento y cómodo. □ *Mr. and Mrs. Simpson have feathered their nest quite comfortably.* □ *It costs a great deal of money to feather one's nest these days.* **2.** utilizar el poder y el prestigio con egoísmo para propocionar mucho a sí mismo. (Se dice mucho de políticos que abusan de sus puesto para ganar dinero.) □ *The mayor seemed to be helping people, but she was really feathering her own nest.* □ *The building contractor used a lot of public money to feather his nest.*

feed the kitty   dar dinero. (*Kitty* es el nombre del recipiente en que se pone el dinero.) □ *Please feed the kitty. Make a contribution to help sick children.* □ *Come on, Bill. Feed the kitty. You can afford a dollar for a good cause.*

feel like a million (dollars)   sentirse bien y sano, física y emocionalmente. (Casi es imposible sentirse tan bien.) □ *A quick swim in the morning makes me feel like a million dollars.* □ *What a beautiful day! It makes you feel like a million.*

feel like a new person   sentirse vigorizado y reavivado, especialmente después de ponerse buena ropa o de estar enfermo. □ *I bought a new suit, and now I feel like a new person.* □ *Bob felt like a new person when he got out of the hospital.*

feel out of place   sentir que uno no se encaja en algún lugar. □ *I feel out of place at formal dances.* □ *Bob and Ann felt out of place at the picnic, so they went home.*

feel something in one's bones AND **know something in one's bones**   percibir algo; intuir algo. □ *The train will be late. I feel it in my bones.* □ *I failed the test. I know it in my bones.*

feet of clay, have   Véase *have feet of clay.*

feet, on one's   Véase *on one's feet.*

fell swoop, at one   Véase *at one fell swoop.*

fell swoop, in one   Véase *in one fell swoop.*

fight someone or something hammer and tongs AND **fight someone or something tooth and nail; go at it hammer and tongs; go at it tooth and nail**   luchar contra alguien o algo con energía y mucha determinación. (Son frases antiguas que se refieren a la lucha con o sin armas.) □ *They fought against the robber tooth and nail.* □ *The dogs were fighting each other hammer and tongs.* □ *The mayor fought the new law hammer and tongs.* □ *We'll fight this zoning ordinance tooth and nail.*

fight someone or something tooth and nail   Véase la entrada previa.

fill someone's shoes   tomar el puesto de otra persona y trabajar satisfactoriamente. (Como si uno estuviera llevando los zapatos de la persona, o sea, llenando [*filling*] los zapatos con los pies.) □ *I don't know how we'll be able to do without you. No one can fill your shoes.* □ *It'll be difficult to fill Jane's shoes. She did her job very well.*

fill the bill   ser exactamente lo que se necesita. □ *Ah, this steak is great. It really fills the bill.* □ *This new pair of shoes fills the bill nicely.*

Finders keepers(, losers weepers).   una frase dicha cuando se encuentra algo. (Un refrán significando que la persona que encuentra algo puede quedarse con ello. La persona que lo pierde sólo puede llorar.) □ *John lost a quarter in the dining room yesterday. Ann found the quarter there today. Ann claimed that since she found it, it was hers. She said, "Finders keepers, losers weepers."* □ *John said, "I'll say finders keepers when I find something of yours!"*

find it in one's heart (to do something)   tener la valentiá o la compasión para hacer algo. □ *She couldn't find it in her heart to refuse to come home to him.* □ *I can't do it! I can't find it in my heart.*

find one's or something's way somewhere   1. [con *one's*] encontrar el camino a algún lugar. □ *Mr. Smith found his way to* *the museum.* □ *Can you find your way home?* **2.** [con *something's*] estar en algún lugar. (Esta frase evita la acusación a alguien de mover la cosa a este lugar. □ *The money found its way into the mayor's pocket.* □ *The secret plans found their way into the enemy's hands.*

fine feather, in   Véase *in fine feather.*

fine kettle of fish   un lío; una situación insatisfactoria. (No se usa literalmente.) □ *The dog has eaten the steak we were going to have for dinner. This is a fine kettle of fish!* □ *This is a fine kettle of fish. It's below freezing outside, and the furnace won't work.*

fine-tooth comb, go over something with a   Véase *go over something with a fine-tooth comb.*

finger in the pie, have one's   Véase *have one's finger in the pie.*

fingertips, have something at one's   Véase *have something at one's fingertips.*

fire, under   Véase *under fire.*

first and foremost   primero y el más importante. (Es cliché.) □ *First and foremost, I think you should work harder on your biology.* □ *Have this in mind first and foremost: Keep smiling!*

First come, first served.   Las primeras personas que llegan van a ser servidos primero. (Es cliché.) □ *They ran out of tickets before we got there. It was first come, first served, but we didn't know that.* □ *Please line up and take your turn. It's first come, first served.*

first of all   la primera cosa; antes de todo. (Frases similares, "second of all" o "third of all," no tienen mucho sentido.) □ *First of all, put your name on this piece of paper.* □ *First of all, we'll try to find a place to live.*

first thing (in the morning)   antes de todo por la mañana. □ *Please call me first thing in the morning. I can't help you now.* □ *I'll do that first thing.*

first things first se debe hacer las cosas más importantes primero.
□ *It's more important to get a job than to buy new clothes. First
things first!* □ *Do your homework now. Go out and play later. First
things first.*

first water, of the Véase *of the first water.*

fish for a compliment intenta hacer que alguien lo elogie. □
*When she showed me her new dress, I could tell that she was fishing
for a compliment.* □ *Tom was certainly fishing for a compliment
when he modeled his fancy haircut for his friends.*

fishing expedition, go on a Véase *go on a fishing expedition.*

fish or cut bait hacer el trabajo o dejarlo para que otra persona
lo haga. (Por ejemplo, pescar o dejarlo y cebar para los pescadores.)
□ *Mary is doing much better on the job since her manager told her
to fish or cut bait.* □ *The boss told Tom, "Quit wasting time! Fish
or cut bait!"*

fish out of water, like a Véase *like a fish out of water.*

fish to fry, have other Véase *have other fish to fry.*

fit as a fiddle, (as) Véase *(as) fit as a fiddle.*

fit for a king totalmente adecuado; adecuado para la realeza. (Es
cliché.) □ *What a delicious meal. It was fit for a king.* □ *Our room
at the hotel was fit for a king.*

fit like a glove estar bien de talla; ir justo. □ *My new shoes fit
like a glove.* □ *My new coat is a little tight. It fits like a glove.*

fit someone to a T Véase en *suit someone to a T.*

fix someone's wagon castigar a alguien; ajustarle las cuentas a
alguien; conspirar contra alguien. □ *If you ever do that again, I'll
fix your wagon!* □ *Tommy! You clean up your room this instant, or
I'll fix your wagon!* □ *He reported me to the boss, but I fixed his
wagon. I knocked his lunch on the floor.*

flames, go up in   Véase *go up in flames.*

flash, in a   Véase *in a flash.*

flash in the pan   alguien o algo que llama mucha atención durante un período muy breve. □ *I'm afraid that my success as a painter was just a flash in the pan.* □ *Tom had hoped to be a singer, but his career was only a flash in the pan.*

flat as a pancake, (as)   Véase *(as) flat as a pancake.*

flat broke   sin un duro; sin ningún dinero. □ *I spent my last dollar, and I'm flat broke.* □ *The bank closed its doors to the public. It was flat broke!*

flesh and blood   1. un cuerpo humano vivo, especialmente referente a sus límites naturales; un ser humano. □ *This cold weather is more than flesh and blood can stand.* □ *Carrying 300 pounds is beyond mere flesh and blood.* 2. la calidad de tener vida. □ *The paintings of this artist are lifeless. They lack flesh and blood.* □ *These ideas have no flesh and blood.* 3. los parientes de uno. □ *That's no way to treat one's own flesh and blood.* □ *I want to leave my money to my own flesh and blood.* □ *Grandmother was happier living with her flesh and blood.*

flesh, in the   Véase *in the flesh.*

float a loan   recibir un préstamo; hacer lo necesario para conseguir un préstamo. □ *I couldn't afford to pay cash for the car, so I floated a loan.* □ *They needed money, so they had to float a loan.*

flying colors, with   Véase *with flying colors.*

fly in the face of someone or something AND **fly in the teeth of someone or something**   no hacer caso de, desafiar a, o faltar al respeto a alguien o algo. □ *John loves to fly in the face of tradition.* □ *Ann made it a practice to fly in the face of standard procedures.* □ *John finds great pleasure in flying in the teeth of his father.*

fly in the ointment un asunto sin mucha importancia pero desagradable que estropea algo; una desventaja. □ *We enjoyed the play, but the fly in the ointment was not being able to find our car afterward.* □ *It sounds like a good idea, but there must be a fly in the ointment somewhere.*

fly in the teeth of someone or something Véase en *fly in the face of someone or something.*

fly off the handle perder la paciencia. □ *Every time anyone mentions taxes, Mrs. Brown flies off the handle.* □ *If she keeps flying off the handle like that, she'll have a heart attack.*

foam at the mouth estar muy enfadado. (Referente a un perro rabioso que echa espuma por la boca.) □ *Bob was raving—foaming at the mouth. I've never seen anyone so angry.* □ *Bill foamed at the mouth in anger.*

follow one's heart comportarse según los sentimientos; obedecer las inclinaciones comprensivas o compasivas. □ *I couldn't decide what to do, so I just followed my heart.* □ *I trust that you will follow your heart in this matter.*

food for thought algo en que pensar. □ *I don't like your idea very much, but it's food for thought.* □ *Your lecture was very good. It contained much food for thought.*

fool and his money are soon parted, A. Véase *A fool and his money are soon parted.*

foot-in-mouth disease, have Véase *have foot-in-mouth disease.*

foot the bill pagar la cuenta; pagar (por algo). □ *Let's go out and eat. I'll foot the bill.* □ *If the bank goes broke, don't worry. The government will foot the bill.*

force someone's hand forzar a alguien a revelar sus planes, estrategias, o secretos. (Referente a la mano en los naipes.) □ *We didn't know what she was doing until Tom forced her hand.* □ *We couldn't plan our game until we forced the other team's hand in the last play.*

force someone to the wall AND **drive someone to the wall** empujar a alguien hasta una posición extrema; poner a alguien en una situación incómoda. □ *He wouldn't tell the truth until we forced him to the wall.* □ *They don't pay their bills until you drive them to the wall.*

for fear of something por miedo de algo; a causa del miedo de algo. □ *He doesn't drive for fear of an accident.* □ *They lock their doors for fear of being robbed.*

forgive and forget perdonarle algo a alguien y olvidarse de que ocurrió. (Es cliché.) □ *I'm sorry, John. Let's forgive and forget. What do you say?* □ *It was nothing. We'll just have to forgive and forget.*

fork money out (for something) AND **fork out money (for something)** pagar (posiblemente sin ganas) por algo. (Muchas veces se dice la cantidad de dinero. Véase en los ejemplos.) □ *I like that stereo, but I don't want to fork out a lot of money.* □ *Do you think I'm going to fork twenty dollars out for that book?* □ *I hate having to fork out money day after day.* □ *Forking money out to everyone is part of life in a busy economy.*

form an opinion formarse una opinión. (Observe las variaciones en los ejemplos.) □ *I don't know enough about the issue to form an opinion.* □ *Don't tell me how to think! I can form my own opinion.* □ *I don't form opinions without careful consideration.*

for the devil of it AND **for the heck of it; for the hell of it** sólo por diversión; porque es un poco malo; sin motivo bueno. (Algunas personas pueden tener objeción al uso de *hell*.) □ *We filled their garage with leaves just for the devil of it.* □ *Tom tripped Bill for the heck of it.* □ *John picked a fight with Tom just for the hell of it.*

for the heck of it Véase la entrada previa.

for the odds to be against one sin mucha suerte en general; sin mucha probalidad de tener éxito. □ *You can give it a try, but the odds are against you.* □ *I know the odds are against me, but I wish to run in the race anyway.*

for the record para que se sepa la opinión o observación de uno; para que haya declaración pública de un hecho en particular. (Muchas veces dicha a los periodistas.) □ *I'd like to say—for the record— that at no time have I ever accepted a bribe from anyone.* □ *For the record, I've never been able to get anything done around city hall without bribing someone.*

foul play actividad ilegal; costumbres malas. □ *The police investigating the death suspect foul play.* □ *Each student got an A on the test, and the teacher imagined it was the result of foul play.*

free and easy casual. □ *John is so free and easy. How can anyone be so relaxed?* □ *Now, take it easy. Just act free and easy. No one will know you're nervous.*

free as a bird, (as) Véase *(as) free as a bird.*

free-for-all una lucha o una competencia desorganizada y con todo el mundo metido en ella; una gresca. □ *The picnic turned into a free-for-all after midnight.* □ *The race started out in an organized manner, but ended up being a free-for-all.*

friend in need is a friend indeed, A. Véase *A friend in need is a friend indeed.*

from hand to hand de una persona a una serie de otras personas; pasado de persona en persona. □ *The book traveled from hand to hand until it got back to its owner.* □ *By the time the baby had been passed from hand to hand, it was crying.*

from pillar to post de un lugar a una serie de otros lugares; (figuradamente) de persona en persona, como en el caso del cotilleo. (Es cliché.) □ *My father was in the army, and we moved from pillar to post year after year.* □ *After I told one person my secret, it went quickly from pillar to post.*

from rags to riches de la pobreza a la riqueza; de la modestia a la elegancia. □ *The princess used to be quite poor. She certainly moved from rags to riches.* □ *After I inherited the money, I went from rags to riches.*

from start to finish   del principio al fin; todo el tiempo. □ *I disliked the whole business from start to finish.* □ *Mary caused problems from start to finish.*

from stem to stern   de un lado al otro. (Referente a la proa delantera y la popa atrás de un buque. También se usa literalmente referente a los buques.) □ *Now, I have to clean the house from stem to stern.* □ *I polished my car carefully from stem to stern.*

from the bottom of one's heart   sinceramente. □ *When I returned the lost kitten to Mrs. Brown, she thanked me from the bottom of her heart.* □ *Oh, thank you! I'm grateful from the bottom of my heart.*

from the ground up   del principio; del principio al fin. (Se usa literalmente referente a la construcción de una casa u otro edificio.) □ *We must plan our sales campaign carefully from the ground up.* □ *Sorry, but you'll have to start all over again from the ground up.*

from the word go   del principio. (Del momento en que se dice "go" al principio de una carrera.) □ *I knew about the problem from the word go.* □ *She was failing the class from the word go.*

from top to bottom   del nivel más alto al nivel más bajo; por todo. □ *I have to clean the house from top to bottom today.* □ *We need to replace our elected officials from top to bottom.*

frying pan into the fire, out of the   Véase *out of the frying pan into the fire.*

full as a tick, (as)   Véase *(as) full as a tick.*

full swing, in   Véase *in full swing.*

fun and games   divirtiéndose; haciendo cosas de poca importancia o actividades que son una pérdida de tiempo. □ *All right, Bill, the fun and games are over. It's time to get down to work.* □ *This isn't a serious course. It's nothing but fun and games.*

funny as a crutch, (as)   Véase *(as) funny as a crutch.*

further ado, without   Véase *without further ado.*

G

gas, out of Véasc *out of gas.*

get a black eye (También con *have.* Observe las variaciones en los ejemplos. *Get* normalmente significa ponerse, adquirir, o causar. *Have* normalmente significa tener, ser, o tener algo como resultado.) **1.** tener una magulladura cerca del ojo a causa de un golpe. □ *I got a black eye from walking into a door.* □ *I have a black eye where John hit me.* **2.** tener el carácter o la reputación dañado. □ *Mary got a black eye because of her complaining.* □ *The whole group now has a black eye.* ALSO: **give someone a black eye 1.** golpear a alguien cerca del ojo, resultando en una magulladura. □ *John became angry and gave me a black eye.* **2.** dañar el carácter o la reputación de alguien. □ *The constant complaining gave the whole group a black eye.*

get a clean bill of health ser declarado sano por un médico. (También se usa con *have.* Veáse en *get a black eye.*) □ *Sally got a clean bill of health from the doctor.* □ *Now that Sally has a clean bill of health, she can go back to work.* ALSO: **give someone a clean bill of health** declarar [un médico] que una persona es sana. □ *The doctor gave Sally a clean bill of health.*

get (all) dolled up ponerse ropa buena. (Normalmente, pero no siempre, se usa referente a las mujeres.) □ *I have to get all dolled up for the dance tonight.* □ *I just love to get dolled up in my best clothes.*

get a load off one's feet AND **take a load off one's feet** sentarse; disfrutar de estar sentado. □ *Come in, John. Sit down and take a load off your feet.* □ *Yes, I need to get a load off my feet. I'm really tired.*

get a load off one's mind   decir lo que piensa uno. □ *He sure talked a long time. I guess he had to get a load off his mind.* □ *You aren't going to like what I'm going to say, but I have to get a load off my mind.*

get along (on a shoestring)   vivir con poco dinero. □ *For the last two years, we have had to get along on a shoestring.* □ *With so little money, it's hard to get along.*

get a lump in one's throat   sentir que algo está en la garganta, como si uno fuera a llorar. (También se usa con *have*. Véase en *get a black eye*.) □ *Whenever they play the national anthem, I get a lump in my throat.* □ *I have a lump in my throat because I'm frightened.*

get a word in edgewise AND **get a word in edgeways**   lograr hablar cuando otros están hablando mucho y no están haciendo caso de uno. (Muchas veces se usa en el sentido negativo. Como si uno tratara de aportar algo a la conversación.) □ *It was such an exciting conversation that I could hardly get a word in edgewise.* □ *Mary talks so fast that nobody can get a word in edgeways.*

get cold feet   ponerse asustado. (Los pies hielan de miedo. También se usa con *have*. Véase *get a black eye*.) □ *I usually get cold feet when I have to speak in public.* □ *John got cold feet and wouldn't run in the race.* □ *I can't give my speech now. I have cold feet.*

get down to brass tacks   empezar a hablar de temas importantes. □ *Let's get down to brass tacks. We've wasted too much time chatting.* □ *Don't you think that it's about time to get down to brass tacks?*

get down to business AND **get down to work**   empezar a hablar en serio; empezar a negociar. □ *All right, everyone. Let's get down to business. There has been enough playing around.* □ *When the president and vice president arrive, we can get down to business.* □ *They're here. Let's get down to work.*

get down to work   Véase la entrada previa.

get fresh (with someone)   actuar con demasiada audacidad o impertinencia. □ *When I tried to kiss Mary, she slapped me and shouted, "Don't get fresh with me!"* □ *I can't stand people who get fresh.*

get goose bumps AND **get goose pimples**   sentir abollada o áspera la piel a causa del miedo o la emoción. (También se usa con *have*. Véase en *get a black eye*. La frase se hace referencia a la piel de una gallina desplumada, aunque muchos norteamericanos no han visto una gallina desplumada.) □ *When he sings, I get goose bumps.* □ *I never get goose pimples.* □ *That really scared her. Now she's got goose pimples.*

get goose pimples   Véase la entrada previa.

get in someone's hair   molestar a alguien. (Normalmente no se usa literalmente.) □ *Billy is always getting in his mother's hair.* □ *I wish you'd stop getting in my hair.*

get into the swing of things   unirse a las actividades. (Referente al ritmo de una actividad rutinaria.) □ *Come on, Bill. Try to get into the swing of things.* □ *John just couldn't seem to get into the swing of things.*

get off scot-free   Véase en *go scot-free.*

get one's ducks in a row   poner los asuntos en orden; arreglar las cosas. (Es informal o argot. Como si uno estuviera poniendo patos de madera en una fila para disparar hacia ellos, como en el juego de un parque de atracciones.) □ *You can't hope to go into a company and sell something until you get your ducks in a row.* □ *As soon as you people get your ducks in a row, we'll leave.*

get one's feet on the ground   establecerse o establecerse de nuevo. (También se usa con *have*. Véase en *get a black eye.*) □ *He's new at the job, but soon he'll get his feet on the ground.* □ *Her productivity will improve after she gets her feet on the ground again.* □ *Don't worry about Sally. She has her feet on the ground.* ALSO: **keep one's feet on the ground**   permanecer establecido. □ *Sally will have no trouble keeping her feet on the ground.*

get one's feet wet   empezar algo; hacer algo por primera vez. (Como si uno estuviera caminando por el agua por primera vez.) □ *Of course he can't do the job right. He's hardly got his feet wet yet.* □ *I'm looking forward to learning to drive. I can't wait to get behind the steering wheel and get my feet wet.*

get one's fill of someone or something   recibir bastante de algo o pasar bastante tiempo con alguien. (También se usa con *have.* Véase en *get a black eye.*) □ *You'll soon get your fill of Tom. He can be quite a pest.* □ *I can never get my fill of shrimp. I love it.* □ *Three weeks of visiting grandchildren is enough. I've had my fill of them.*

get one's fingers burned   tener una experiencia mala. (También se usa literalmente.) □ *I tried that once before and got my fingers burned. I won't try it again.* □ *If you go swimming and get your fingers burned, you won't want to swim again.*

get one's foot in the door   llegar a un puesto o posición favorable (hacia el futuro); dar el primer paso en algún proceso. (En el pasado, los vendedores a domicilio ponían el pie en la puerta de una casa para que el comprador posible no la cerrara. También se usa con *have.* Véase en *get a black eye.*) □ *I think I could get the job if I could only get my foot in the door.* □ *It pays to get your foot in the door. Try to get an appointment with the boss.* □ *I have a better chance now that I have my foot in the door.*

get one's hands dirty AND **dirty one's hands; soil one's hands**   estar metido en asuntos ilegales; hacer algo vergonzoso; hacer algo indigno de su posición. □ *The mayor would never get his hands dirty by giving away political favors.* □ *I will not dirty my hands by breaking the law.* □ *Sally felt that to talk to the hobo was to soil her hands.*

get one's head above water   abrirse camino después de los problemas; ponerse al día con el trabajo o las responsabilidades de uno. (También se usa literalmente. También se usa con *have.* Véase en *get a black eye.*) □ *I can't seem to get my head above water. Work just keeps piling up.* □ *I'll be glad when I have my head above water.* ALSO: **keep one's head above water**   permanencer por delante de las responsabilidades. □ *Now that I have more space to work in, I can easily keep my head above water.*

get one's just desserts   recibir lo que merece alguien. □ *I feel better now that Jane got her just desserts. She really insulted me.* □ *Bill got back exactly the treatment that he gave out. He got his just desserts.*

get one's second wind   (También se usa con *have*. Véase en *get a black eye*.) **1.** repirar normalmente después de un esfuerzo físico breve.) □ *John was having a hard time running until he got his second wind.* □ *Bill had to quit the race because he never got his second wind.* □ *"At last," thought Ann, "I have my second wind. Now I can really swim fast."* **2.** llegar a ser más activo o productivo (después de un principio despacio.) □ *I usually get my second wind early in the afternoon.* □ *Mary is a better worker now that she has her second wind.*

get one's teeth into something   empezar a hacer algo en serio, especialmente una tarea difícil. (También se usa literalmente referente a la comida.) □ *Come on, Bill. You have to get your teeth into your biology.* □ *I can't wait to get my teeth into this problem.*

get on someone's nerves   molestar a alguien. □ *Please stop whistling. It's getting on my nerves.* □ *All this arguing is getting on their nerves.*

get on the bandwagon AND **jump on the bandwagon**   afiliarse al lado popular (de una cuestión); tener una opinión común. □ *You really should get on the bandwagon. Everyone else is.* □ *Jane has always had her own ideas about things. She's not the kind of person to jump on the bandwagon.*

get out of the wrong side of the bed   Véase en *get up on the wrong side of the bed*.

get second thoughts about someone or something   estar dudando acerca de alguien o algo. (También se usa con *have*. Véase en *get a black eye*.) □ *I'm beginning to get second thoughts about Tom.* □ *Tom is getting second thoughts about it, too.* □ *We now have second thoughts about going to Canada.*

get (someone) off the hook   librar a alguien de una obligación; ayudar a alguien en una situación incómoda.) □ *Thanks for getting me off the hook. I didn't want to attend that meeting.* □ *I couldn't get off the hook by myself.*

get someone over a barrel AND **get someone under one's thumb**   poner a alguien a merced de uno; tomar control de alguien. (También se usa con *have*. Véase en *get a black eye*.) □ *He got me over a barrel, and I had to do what he said.* □ *Ann will do exactly what I say. I've got her over a barrel.* □ *All right, John. You've got me under your thumb. What do you want me to do?*

get someone's back up   Véase la entrada siguiente.

get someone's dander up AND **get someone's back up; get someone's hackles up; get someone's Irish up**   enfadar a alguien. (También se usa con *have*. Véase en *get a black eye*.) □ *Now, don't get your dander up. Calm down.* □ *Bob had his Irish up all day yesterday. I don't know what was wrong.* □ *She really got her back up when I asked her for money.* □ *Now, now, don't get your hackles up. I didn't mean any harm.*

get someone's ear   conseguir que alguien escucha a uno; atraer la atención de alguien. (También se usa con *have*. Véase en *get a black eye*. No es literal.) □ *He got my ear and talked for an hour.* □ *While I have your ear, I'd like to tell you about something I'm selling.*

get someone's eye   Véase en *catch someone's eye.*

get someone's hackles up   Véase en *get someone's dander up.*

get someone's Irish up   Véase en *get someone's dander up.*

get someone under one's thumb   Véase en *get someone over a barrel.*

get something into someone's thick head   Véase en *get something through someone's thick skull.*

get something off one's chest   contar algo que ha preocupado a uno. (También se usa con *have*. Véase en *get a black eye*.) □ *I have to get this off my chest. I broke your window with a stone.* □ *I knew I'd feel better when I had that off my chest.*

get something off (the ground)   empezar algo. □ *I can relax after I get this project off the ground.* □ *You'll have a lot of free time when you get the project off.*

get something sewed up   (También se usa con *have*. Véase en *get a black eye*.) **1.** tener algo cosido (por alguien). (Es literal.) □ *I want to get this tear sewed up now.* □ *I'll have this hole sewed up tomorrow.* **2.** AND **get something wrapped up**   terminar o resolver algo. (También se usa con *have*.) □ *I'll take the contract to the mayor tomorrow morning. I'll get the whole deal sewed up by noon.* □ *Don't worry about the car loan. I'll have it sewed up in time to make the purchase.* □ *I'll get the loan wrapped up, and you'll have the car this week.*

get something straight   comprender algo perfectamente. (También se usa con *have*. Véase en *get a black eye*.) □ *Now get this straight. You're going to fail history.* □ *Let me get this straight. I'm supposed to go there in the morning?* □ *Let me make sure I have this straight.*

get something through someone's thick skull AND **get something into someone's thick head**   hacer que alguien comprenda algo; aprender algo. □ *He can't seem to get it through his thick skull.* □ *If I could get this into my thick head once, I'd remember it.*

get something under one's belt   (También se usa con *have*. Véase en *get a black eye*.) **1.** comer o beber algo. (Significa que la comida o bebida entra en el estómago, debajo del cinturón de uno.) □ *I'd feel a lot better if I had a cool drink under my belt.* □ *Come in out of the cold and get a nice warm meal under your belt.* **2.** aprender algo muy bien; comprender alguna información. (No es literal.) □ *I have to study tonight. I have to get a lot of algebra under my belt.* □ *Now that I have my lessons under my belt, I can rest easy.*

get something under way   empezar algo. (También se usa con *have*. Véase en *get a black eye*. La frase es de origen marítimo.) ☐ *The time has come to get this meeting under way.* ☐ *Now that the president has the meeting under way, I can relax.*

get something wrapped up   Véase en *get something sewed up*.

get stars in one's eyes   estar obsesionado con el mundo del espectáculo; estar apasionado por el teatro. (También con *have*. Véase en *get a black eye*. Referente a las estrellas del cine o del teatro.) ☐ *Many young people get stars in their eyes at this age.* ☐ *Ann has stars in her eyes. She wants to go to Hollywood.*

get the benefit of the doubt   recibir un juicio a favor de uno cuando las pruebas lo desmienten. (También se usa con *have*. Véase en *get a black eye*.) ☐ *I was right between a B and an A. I got the benefit of the doubt—an A.* ☐ *I thought I should have had the benefit of the doubt, but the judge made me pay a fine.* ALSO: **give someone the benefit of the doubt** ☐ *I'm glad the teacher gave me the benefit of the doubt.* ☐ *Please, judge. Give me the benefit of the doubt.*

get the blues   ponerse triste o deprimido; ponerse melancólico. (También se usa con *have*. Véase en *get a black eye*.) ☐ *You'll have to excuse Bill. He has the blues tonight.* ☐ *I get the blues every time I hear that song.*

get the final word   Véase en *get the last word*.

get the hang of something   aprender a hacer algo; aprender como funciona algo. (También se usa con *have*. Véase en *get a black eye*.) ☐ *As soon as I get the hang of this computer, I'll be able to work faster.* ☐ *Now that I have the hang of starting the car in cold weather, I won't have to get up so early.*

get the inside track   tener ventaja (sobre alguien) a causa de los contactos, el conocimiento especial, o el favoritismo. (También se usa con *have*. Véase en *get a black eye*.) ☐ *If I could get the inside track, I could win the contract.* ☐ *The boss likes me. Since I have the inside track, I'll probably be the new office manager.*

get the jump on someone   hacer algo antes de alguien; llegar por delante de o frente a alguien. (También se usa con *have*. Véase en *get a black eye*.) □ *I got the jump on Tom and got a place in line ahead of him.* □ *We'll have to work hard to get the contract, because they have the jump on us.*

get the last laugh   reírse o burlarse de alguien que se ha reído o burlado de uno; poner a alguien en la misma situación mala en que estaba uno una vez. (También se usa con *have*. Véase en *get a black eye*.) □ *John laughed when I got a D on the final exam. I got the last laugh, though. He failed the course.* □ *Mr. Smith said I was foolish when I bought an old building. I had the last laugh when I sold it a month later for twice what I paid for it.*

get the last word AND **get the final word**   tener la última palabra (en una discusión o debate); tomar la última decisión (en algún asunto. También se usa con *have*. Véase en *get a black eye*.) □ *The boss gets the last word in hiring.* □ *Why do you always have to have the final word in an argument?*

get the message   Véase en *get the word*.

get the nod   ser elegido. (También se usa con *have*. Véase en *get a black eye*.) □ *The boss is going to pick the new sales manager. I think Ann will get the nod.* □ *I had the nod for captain of the team, but I decided not to do it.*

get the red-carpet treatment   recibir trato especial; recibir trato real. (Referente—a veces literalmente—a la costumbre de extender una alfombra roja para los invitados o las personas importantes.) □ *I love to go to fancy stores where I get the red-carpet treatment.* □ *The queen expects to get the red-carpet treatment wherever she goes.* ALSO: **give someone the red-carpet treatment**   darle trato muy especial a alguien; darle trato real a alguien. □ *We always give the queen the red-carpet treatment when she comes to visit.* ALSO: **roll out the red carpet for someone**   proporcionarle trato especial a alguien. □ *There's no need to roll out the red carpet for me.* □ *We rolled out the red carpet for the king and queen.*

get the runaround   recibir una serie de disculpas y retrasos. □ *You'll get the runaround if you ask to see the manager.* □ *I hate it when I get the runaround.* ALSO: **give someone the runaround** dar una serie de disculpas y retrasos. □ *If you ask to see the manager, they'll give you the runaround.*

get the shock of one's life   experimentar un susto (emocional). (También se usa con *have*. Véase en *get a black eye*.) □ *I opened the telegram and got the shock of my life.* □ *I had the shock of my life when I won $5,000.*

get the short end of the stick AND **end up with the short end of the stick**   acabar con menos (que otra persona); ser estafado o engañado. (También se usa con *have*. Véase en *get a black eye*.) □ *Why do I always get the short end of the stick? I want my fair share!* □ *She's unhappy because she has the short end of the stick again.* □ *I hate to end up with the short end of the stick.*

get the upper hand (on someone)   alcanzar una posición más alta que la de otra persona; tener la ventaja sobre alguien. (También se usa con *have*. Véase en *get a black eye*.) □ *John is always trying to get the upper hand on someone.* □ *He never ends up having the upper hand, though.*

get the word AND **get the message**   recibir una explicación; recibir la explicación final y autorizada. (También se usa con *have*. Véase en *get a black eye*.) □ *I'm sorry, I didn't get the word. I didn't know the matter had been settled.* □ *Now that I have the message, I can be more effective in answering questions.*

get time to catch one's breath   encontrar tiempo para relajarse. (También se usa con *have*. Véase en *get a black eye*.) □ *When things slow down around here, I'll get time to catch my breath.* □ *Sally was so busy she didn't even have time to catch her breath.*

get to first base (with someone or something) AND **reach first base (with someone or something)**   hacer un avance importante con alguien o en algo. □ *I wish I could get to first base with this business deal.* □ *John adores Sally, but he can't even reach first base with her. She won't even speak to him.* □ *He smiles and acts friendly, but he can't get to first base.*

get to one's feet ponerse de pie. □ *On a signal from the director, the singers got to their feet.* □ *I was so weak, I could hardly get to my feet.*

get to the bottom of something llegar a comprender las causas de algo. □ *We must get to the bottom of this problem immediately.* □ *There is clearly something wrong here, and I want to get to the bottom of it.*

get to the heart of the matter llegar a los elementos esenciales de un asunto. □ *We have to stop wasting time and get to the heart of the matter.* □ *You've been very helpful. You really seem to be able to get to the heart of the matter.*

get to the point Véase en *come to the point.*

get two strikes against one tener muchas cosas que van mal para uno; estar en una posición sin mucha posibilidad de éxito. (Referente al béisbol. También se usa con *have.* Véase en *get a black eye.*) □ *Poor Bob got two strikes against him when he tried to explain where he was last night.* □ *I can't win. I've got two strikes against me before I start.*

get under someone's skin molestar a alguien. (Referente a una cosa, como un insecto o una sustancia química, que penetra la piel.) □ *John is so annoying. He really gets under my skin.* □ *I know he's bothersome, but don't let him get under your skin.* □ *This kind of problem gets under my skin.*

get up enough nerve (to do something) adquirir la valentía para hacer algo. □ *I could never get up enough nerve to sing in public.* □ *I'd do it if I could get up enough nerve, but I'm shy.*

get up on the wrong side of the bed AND **get out of the wrong side of the bed** levantarse por la mañana de mal humor. (Como si el lado de la cama tuviera que ver con el humor de uno.) □ *What's wrong with you? Did you get up on the wrong side of the bed today?* □ *Excuse me for being grouchy. I got out of the wrong side of the bed.*

get wind of something   haber oído hablar de algo; recibir información sobre algo. (*Wind* se refiere posiblemente al aliento o a las palabras de uno, pero probablemente se refiere a que el viento lleva el olor de cosas.) □ *I just got wind of your marriage. Congratulations.* □ *Wait until the boss gets wind of this. Somebody is going to get in trouble.*

get worked up about something   Véase la entrada siguiente.

get worked up (over something) AND **get worked up about something**   ponerse emocionado o preocupado por algo. □ *Please don't get worked up over this matter.* □ *They get worked up about these things very easily.* □ *I try not to get worked up.*

gild the lily   añadir adornos a algo que ya es agradable o bonito; intentar mejorar algo que no necesita mejoras. (Muchas veces se refiere a halagos o exageración. Se consider el lirio bonito en su estado natural; es demasiado dorarlo.) □ *Your house has lovely brickwork. Don't paint it. That would be gilding the lily.* □ *Oh, Sally. You're beautiful the way you are. You don't need makeup. You would be gilding the lily.*

gird (up) one's loins   prepararse (para algo). (Es cliché. Significa, esencialmente, ponerse ropa para hacer algo. Una referencia bíblica.) □ *Well, I guess I had better gird up my loins and go to work.* □ *Somebody has to do something about the problem. Why don't you gird your loins and do something?*

give a good account of oneself   hacer algo bien o a fondo. □ *John gave a good account of himself when he gave his speech last night.* □ *Mary was not hungry, and she didn't give a good account of herself at dinner.*

give as good as one gets   hacer tanto como recibe alguien; pagar en especie. (Normalmente se usa en el presente.) □ *John can take care of himself in a fight. He can give as good as he gets.* □ *Sally usually wins a formal debate. She gives as good as she gets.*

give credit where credit is due   reconocer a alguien que lo merece el mérito de hacer algo; darle gracias a alguien que las merece. (Es cliché.) □ *We must give credit where credit is due.*

Thank you very much, Sally. □ *Let's give credit where credit is due. Mary is the one who wrote the report, not Jane.*

Give one an inch, and one will take a mile. AND **If you give one an inch, one will take a mile.** un refrán significando que una persona que obtiene un poco de algo (como una tregua) querrá más. □ *I told John he could turn in his paper one day late, but he turned it in three days late. Give him an inch, and he'll take a mile.* □ *First we let John borrow our car for a day. Now he wants to go on a two-week vacation. If you give him an inch, he'll take a mile.*

give one an inch, one will take a mile, If you. Véase la entrada previa.

give one one's freedom liberar a alguien; divorciar a alguien. (Normalmente se usa como eufemismo para el divorcio.) □ *Mrs. Brown wanted to give her husband his freedom.* □ *Well, Tom, I hate to break it to you this way, but I have decided to give you your freedom.*

give oneself airs comportarse con arrogancia y altanería. □ *Sally is always giving herself airs. You'd think she had royal blood.* □ *Come on, John. Don't act so haughty. Stop giving yourself airs.*

give one's right arm (for someone or something) estar dispuesto a dar algo de mucho valor por alguien o algo. (Nunca se usa literalmente.) □ *I'd give my right arm for a nice cool drink.* □ *I'd give my right arm to be there.* □ *Tom really admired John. Tom would give his right arm for John.*

give someone a black eye Véase en *get a black eye.*

give someone a buzz Véase en *give someone a ring.*

give someone a clean bill of health Véase en *get a clean bill of health.*

give someone a piece of one's mind vociferar a alguien; reprender a alguien. □ *I've had enough from John. I'm going to give him a piece of my mind.* □ *Sally, stop it, or I'll give you a piece of my mind.*

give someone a ring AND **give someone a buzz**   llamar a alguien por teléfono. (*Ring* y *buzz* se refieren al sonido del timbre del teléfono.) □ *Nice talking to you. Give me a ring sometime.* □ *Give me a buzz when you're in town.*

give someone or something a wide berth   estar a bastante distancia de alguien o algo; evitar a alguien o algo. (Originalmente se refirió a los buques.) □ *The dog we are approaching is very mean. Better give it a wide berth.* □ *Give Mary a wide berth. She's in a very bad mood.*

give someone the benefit of the doubt   Véase en *get the benefit of the doubt.*

give someone the eye   mirar a alguien de un modo que expresa interés romántico. (No es literal.) □ *Ann gave John the eye. It really surprised him.* □ *Tom kept giving Sally the eye. She finally left.*

give someone the red-carpet treatment   Véase en *get the red-carpet treatment.*

give someone the runaround   Véase en *get the runaround.*

give someone the shirt off one's back   estar muy generoso o solícito a alguien. □ *Tom really likes Bill. He'd give Bill the shirt off his back.* □ *John is so friendly that he'd give anyone the shirt off his back.*

give someone tit for tat   dar tanto como recibe uno; intercambiar una serie de cosas, uno por uno, con alguien. □ *They gave me the same kind of difficulty that I gave them. They gave me tit for tat.* □ *He punched me, so I punched him. Every time he hit me, I hit him. I just gave him tit for tat.*

give something a lick and a promise   hacer algo mal— rápida y descuidadamente. □ *John! You didn't clean your room! You just gave it a lick and a promise.* □ *This time, Tom, comb your hair. It looks as if you just gave it a lick and a promise.*

give the bride away   acompañar [el padre de la novia] a la novia en elcamino hacia el novio durante la boda. □ *Mr. Brown is ill.*

Who'll give the bride away? □ *In the traditional wedding ceremony, the bride's father gives the bride away.*

give the devil his due AND **give the devil her due** dar mérito al enemigo de uno (para algo). (Es cliché. La frase normalmente se refiere a una persona que se ha comportado como el diablo.) □ *She's generally impossible, but I have to give the devil her due. She cooks a terrific cherry pie.* □ *John may cheat on his taxes and yell at his wife, but he keeps his car polished. I'll give the devil his due.*

give up the ghost morir. (Es cliché. Se considera literaria o humorística.) □ *The old man sighed, rolled over, and gave up the ghost.* □ *I'm too young to give up the ghost.*

go about one's business no hablar de o preocuparse por los asuntos de otros. → **no meterse donde no te llaman.** □ *Leave me alone! Just go about your business!* □ *I have no more to say. I would be pleased if you would go about your business.*

go against the grain ir en contra de la dirección o inclinación natural. (Referente a la madera.) → **ir a contrapelo.** □ *Don't expect me to help you cheat. That goes against the grain.* □ *Would it go against the grain for you to call in sick for me?*

go along for the ride acompañar (a alguien) por el placer de ir; acompañar a alguien sin razón específica. □ *Join us. You can go along for the ride.* □ *I don't really need to go to the grocery store, but I'll go along for the ride.* □ *We're having a little party next weekend. Nothing fancy. Why don't you go along for the ride?*

go and never darken my door again marchar y nunca volver. (Es cliché.) □ *The heroine of the drama told the villain to go and never darken her door again.* □ *She touched the back of her hand to her forehead and said, "Go and never darken my door again!"*

go (a)round the bend **1.** viajar por una curva del camino; doblar (la esquina). □ *You'll see the house you're looking for as you go round the bend.* □ *John waved to his father until the car went round the bend.* **2.** volverse loco; perder la cordura. □ *If I don't get some* *rest, I'll go round the bend.* □ *Poor Bob. He has been having trouble for a long time. He finally went around the bend.*

go away empty-handed   salir sin nada. □ *I hate for you to go away empty-handed, but I cannot afford to contribute any money.* □ *They came hoping for some food, but they had to go away empty-handed.*

go back on one's word   faltar a una promesa. □ *I hate to go back on my word, but I won't pay you $100 after all.* □ *Going back on your word makes you a liar.*

go down in history   ser recordado como alguien o algo importante en la historia (Es cliché.) → **pasar a la historia.** □ *Bill is so great. I'm sure that he'll go down in history.* □ *This is the greatest party of the century. I bet it'll go down in history.*

go Dutch   compartir el precio de una comida u otra cosa. □ JANE: *Let's go out and eat.* MARY: *Okay, but let's go Dutch.* □ *It's getting expensive to have Sally for a friend. She never wants to go Dutch.*

go in one ear and out the other   escuchar [algo] y luego olvidarlo. (No es literal.) □ *Everything I say to you seems to go in one ear and out the other. Why don't you pay attention?* □ *I can't concentrate. Things people say to me just go in one ear and out the other.*

go into a nosedive AND **take a nosedive**   **1.** caer en picado [un avión] de repente hacia la tierra, con el morro en frente. □ *It was a bad day for flying, and I was afraid we'd go into a nosedive.* □ *The small plane took a nosedive. The pilot was able to bring it out at the last minute, so the plane didn't crash.* **2.** entrar en un declive rápido de las emociones, las finanzas, o la salud. □ *Our profits took a nosedive last year.* □ *After he broke his hip, Mr. Brown's health went into a nosedive, and he never recovered.*

go into a tailspin   **1.** perder control [un avión] y dar vueltas hacia la tierra, con el morro en frente. □ *The plane shook and then suddenly went into a tailspin.* □ *The pilot was not able to stop the*

plane from going into a tailspin, and it crashed into the sea.
2. ponerse desorientado o preso; ir mal las cosas [para uno]. □
*Although John was a great success, his life went into a tailspin. It
took him a year to get straightened out.* □ *After her father died,
Mary's world fell apart, and she went into a tailspin.*

go into one's song and dance about something   empezar
a dar las explicaciones o disculpas que siempre da uno. (Es cliché.
No es literal. Se puede usar *the same old* en vez de *one's*.) □ *Please
don't go into your song and dance about how you always tried to
do what was right.* □ *John went into his song and dance about how
he won the war all by himself.* □ *He always goes into the same old
song and dance every time he makes a mistake.*

go like clockwork   avanzar o progresar normalmente. (Referente
más al funcionamiento mecánico que el funcionamiento de los
relojes.) □ *The building project is progressing nicely. Everything
is going like clockwork.* □ *The elaborate pageant was a great
success. It went like clockwork from start to finish.*

good as done, (as)   Véase *(as) good as done.*

good as gold, (as)   Véase *(as) good as gold.*

good condition, in   Véase *in good condition.*

good head on one's shoulders, have a   Véase *have a good
head on one's shoulders.*

good shape, in   Véase *in good shape.*

go off the deep end AND **jump off the deep end**   meterse
en algo o hacerse aliado con alguien antes de que uno esté preparado;
seguir las emociones en vez del razonamiento. (Referente al entrar
en una piscina en el lado profundo en vez del lado poco profundo.
La frase atañe especialmente a los enamorados.) □ *Look at the way
Bill is looking at Sally. I think he's about to go off the deep end.* □
*Now, John, I know you really want to go to Australia, but don't go
jumping off the deep end. It isn't all perfect there.*

go on a fishing expedition   intentar averiguar información. (Tambíen se usa literalmente.) □ *We are going to have to go on a fishing expedition to try to find the facts.* □ *One lawyer went on a fishing expedition in court, and the other lawyer objected.*

go, on the   Véase *on the go.*

go (out) on strike   tener huelga; dejar de trabajar [un grupo de personas] hasta recibir alguna reivindicación. □ *If we don't have a contract by noon tomorrow, we'll go out on strike.* □ *The entire work force went on strike at noon today.*

go overboard   1. caerse de un barco o buque. □ *My fishing pole just went overboard. I'm afraid it's lost.* □ *That man just went overboard. I think he jumped.* **2.** hacer demasiado; estar derrochado. □ *Look, Sally, let's have a nice party, but don't go overboard. It doesn't need to be fancy.* □ *Okay, you can buy a big comfortable car, but don't go overboard.*

go over someone's head   ser demasiado difícil para comprender. (Como si la cosa no comprendida volara en vez de entrar en el cerebro.) □ *All that talk about computers went over my head.* □ *I hope my lecture didn't go over the students' heads.*

go over something with a fine-tooth comb AND **search something with a fine-tooth comb**   examinar algo muy detenidamente. (Como si uno estuviera buscando algo muy pequeño en alguna fibra.) □ *I can't find my calculus book. I went over the whole place with a fine-tooth comb.* □ *I searched this place with a fine-tooth comb and didn't find my ring.*

go over with a bang   ser [algo] divertido o humorístico. (Referente principalmente a los chistes u obras de teatro.) □ *The play was a success. It really went over with a bang.* □ *That's a great joke. It went over with a bang.*

go scot-free AND **get off scot-free**   escaparse sin castigo; ser absuelto de un crimen. (*Scot* es palabra inglesa antigua que significa "impuesto".) □ *The thief went scot-free.* □ *Jane cheated on the test and got caught, but she got off scot-free.*

go stag   ir solo a alguna fiesta u otro suceso para las parejas (Originalmente se refirió sólo a los hombres.) □ *Is Tom going to take you, or are you going stag?* □ *Bob didn't want to go stag, so he took his sister to the party.*

go the distance   hacerlo todo; jugar durante todo el juego; correr una carrera entera. (Originalmente se refirió sólo a los deportes.) □ *That horse runs fast. I hope it can go the distance.* □ *This is going to be a long, hard project. I hope I can go the distance.*

go the limit   hacer todo lo posible. □ *What do I want on my hamburger? Go the limit!* □ *Don't hold anything back. Go the limit.*

go through channels   consultar a las personas o las oficinas importantes para averiguar algo. (*Channels* se refiere a la ruta de algún asunto de negocios por la jerarquía o burocracia de una empresa.) □ *If you want an answer to your questions, you'll have to go through channels.* □ *If you know the answers, why do I have to go through channels?*

go through the motions   hacer un esfuerzo débil para hacer algo; hacer algo sin sinceridad. □ *Jane isn't doing her best. She's just going through the motions.* □ *Bill was supposed to be raking the yard, but he was just going through the motions.*

go through the roof   ir muy alto; llegar a un nivel muy alto (de algo). (No es literal.) □ *It's so hot! The temperature is going through the roof.* □ *Mr. Brown got so angry he almost went through the roof.*

go to bat for someone   apoyar o ayudar a alguien. (Referente al uso del substituto para el bateador en el béisbol.) □ *I tried to go to bat for Bill, but he said he didn't want any help.* □ *I heard them gossiping about Sally, so I went to bat for her.*

go to Davy Jones's locker   ir al fondo del mar. (Posiblemente un dicho náutico.) □ *My camera fell overboard and went to Davy Jones's locker.* □ *My uncle was a sailor. He went to Davy Jones's locker during a terrible storm.*

go to pot AND **go to the dogs**   caer en ruinas; deteriorarse. □ *My whole life seems to be going to pot.* □ *My lawn is going to pot. I had better weed it.* □ *The government is going to the dogs.*

go to rack and ruin AND **go to wrack and ruin**   arruinarse; estropearse. (*Rack* and *wrack* significan restos y sólo se encuentran en esta frase.) □ *That lovely old house on the corner is going to go to rack and ruin.* □ *My lawn is going to wrack and ruin.*

go to seed   Véase en *run to seed*.

go to someone's head   causar que alguien se ponga vanidoso; causar que alguien se ponga soberbio. → **subir a la cabeza de uno.** □ *You did a fine job, but don't let it go to your head.* □ *He let his success go to his head, and soon he became a complete failure.*

go to the dogs   Véase en *go to pot*.

go to the wall   fracasar o ser vencido después de un esfuerzo muy fuerte. □ *We really went to the wall on that deal.* □ *The company went to the wall because of that contract. Now it's broke.*

go to town   trabajar duro o rápido. (También se usa literalmente.) □ *Look at all those ants working. They are really going to town.* □ *Come on, you guys! Let's go to town. We have to finish this job before noon.*

go to wrack and ruin   Véase en *go to rack and ruin*.

go up in flames AND **go up in smoke**   quemar; ser consumido por llamas. → **estallar en llamas.** □ *The whole museum went up in flames.* □ *My paintings—my whole life's work—went up in flames.* □ *What a shame for all that to go up in smoke.*

go up in smoke   Véase la entrada previa.

grain, go against the   Véase *go against the grain*.

green thumb, have a   Véase *have a green thumb*.

green with envy envidioso; celoso. (Es cliché. No es literal.) □ *When Sally saw me with Tom, she turned green with envy. She likes him a lot.* □ *I feel green with envy whenever I see you in your new car.*

grin and bear it aguantar algo desagradable con buen humor. □ *There is nothing you can do but grin and bear it.* □ *I hate having to work for rude people. I guess I have to grin and bear it.*

grind to a halt aminorar hasta pararse. □ *By the end of the day, the factory had ground to a halt.* □ *The car ground to a halt, and we got out to stretch our legs.*

grit one's teeth moler los dientes a causa de la ira o la determinación. □ *I was so mad, all I could do was stand there and grit my teeth.* □ *All through the race, Sally was gritting her teeth. She was really determined.*

ground up, from the Véase *from the ground up.*

gun for someone buscar a alguien, posiblemente para dañarlo con una pistola. (Originalmente usado en las películas del oeste o de los gángsters). □ *The coach is gunning for you. I think he's going to bawl you out.* □ *I've heard that the sheriff is gunning for me, so I'm getting out of town.*

gutter, in the Véase *in the gutter.*

H

hail-fellow-well-met simpático con todos; símpatico, pero no sinceramente, con todos. (Normalmente se dice de los hombres.) □ *Yes, he's friendly, sort of hail-fellow-well-met.* □ *He's not a very sincere person. Hail-fellow-well-met—you know the type.* □ *What a pain he is! Good old Mr. Hail-fellow-well-met. What a phony!*

hair of the dog that bit one una bebida alcohólica que alguien toma cuando tiene resaca. (No tiene que ver con los perros ni con el cabello). □ *Oh, I'm miserable. I need some of the hair of the dog that bit me.* □ *That's some hangover you've got there, Bob. Here, drink this. It's some of the hair of the dog that bit you.*

hair's breadth, by a Véase *by a hair's breadth.*

hale and hearty sano. □ *Doesn't Ann look hale and hearty?* □ *I don't feel hale and hearty. I'm really tired.*

Half a loaf is better than none. un refrán significando que tener una parte de algo es mejor que no tener nada. □ *When my raise was smaller than I wanted, Sally said, "Half a loaf is better than none."* □ *People who keep saying "Half a loaf is better than none" usually have as much as they need.*

halfhearted (about someone or something), be Véase *be halfhearted (about someone or something).*

half-mast, at Véase *at half-mast.*

hand, do something by Véase *do something by hand.*

hand, have something at Véase *have something at hand.*

hand in glove (with someone) muy unido a alguien. □ *John is really hand in glove with Sally.* □ *The teacher and the principal work hand in glove.*

hand in the till, have one's Véase *have one's hand in the till.*

handle someone with kid gloves tener cuidado con una persona susceptible; enfrentarse a una persona difícil. □ *Bill has become so sensitive. You really have to handle him with kid gloves.* □ *You don't have to handle me with kid gloves. I can take it.*

hand, out of Véase *out of hand.*

hand over fist muy rápido [en el intercambio de dinero y mercancías]. □ *What a busy day. We took in money hand over fist.* □ *They were buying things hand over fist.*

hand over hand [poner] una mano después de la otra [continuamente]. □ *Sally pulled in the rope hand over hand.* □ *The man climbed the rope hand over hand.*

hands down, do something Véase *do something hands down.*

hands full (with someone or something), have one's Véase *have one's hands full (with someone or something).*

hands, have someone or something in one's Véase *have someone or something in one's hands.*

hands tied, have one's Véase *have one's hands tied.*

hand tied behind one's back, with one Véase *with one hand tied behind one's back.*

hand to hand, from Véase *from hand to hand.*

hang by a hair AND **hang by a thread** estar en una posición incierta; depender de algo poco sustancioso como apoyo. (También se usa con *on,* como en el segundo ejemplo.) □ *Your whole argument is hanging by a thread.* □ *John isn't failing geometry, but he's just hanging on by a hair.*

hang by a thread   Véase la entrada previa.

hanging over one's head, have something   Véase *have something hanging over one's head.*

hang in the balance   no estar decidido; estar indeciso entre dos posibilidades iguales. ☐ *The prisoner stood before the judge with his life hanging in the balance.* ☐ *This whole issue will have to hang in the balance until Jane gets back from her vacation.*

Hang on!   estar preparado para el movimiento rápido o desigual. ☐ *Hang on! Here we go!* ☐ *The airplane passengers suddenly seemed weightless. Someone shouted, "Hang on!"*

hang on someone's every word   escuchar atentamente a todo lo que dice alguien. ☐ *He gave a great lecture. We hung on his every word.* ☐ *Look at the way John hangs on Mary's every word. He must be in love with her.*

Hang on to your hat! AND **Hold on to your hat!**   "Agarren el sombrero"; "Preparen para una sorpresa o choque repentino." ☐ *What a windy day. Hang on to your hat!* ☐ *Here we go! Hold on to your hat!* ☐ *Are you ready to hear the final score? Hang on to your hat! We won ten to nothing!*

hang someone in effigy   ahorcar una efigie de un enemigo. ☐ *They hanged the dictator in effigy.* ☐ *The angry mob hanged the president in effigy.*

happy as a clam, (as)   Véase *(as) happy as a clam.*

happy as a lark, (as)   Véase *(as) happy as a lark.*

hard-and-fast rule   una regla estricta. ☐ *It's a hard-and-fast rule that you must be home by midnight.* ☐ *You should have your project completed by the end of the month, but it's not a hard-and-fast rule.*

hard as nails, (as)   Véase *(as) hard as nails.*

hardly have time to breathe   estar muy ocupado. ☐ *This was such a busy day. I hardly had time to breathe.* ☐ *They made him work so hard that he hardly had time to breathe.*

hard on someone's heels   seguir a alguien con mucha proximidad; seguir a una persona muy cerca de los talones. □ *I ran as fast as I could, but the dog was still hard on my heels.* □ *Here comes Sally, and John is hard on her heels.*

Haste makes waste.   un refrán significando que el tiempo que uno gana en hacer algo rápidamente pero sin cuidado será perdido cuando uno tiene que hacer la cosa de nuevo correctamente. □ *Now, take your time. Haste makes waste.* □ *Haste makes waste, so be careful as you work.*

hat, be old   Véase *be old hat.*

hate someone's guts   odiar a alguien mucho (La frase es familiar y grosera.) □ *Oh, Bob is terrible. I hate his guts!* □ *You may hate my guts for saying so, but I think you're getting gray hair.*

haul someone over the coals   Véase en *rake someone over the coals.*

have a bee in one's bonnet   tener una idea o un pensamiento que permanece en la mente; obsesionarse. (La abeja es la idea en la mente, o cabeza, lo cual tiene una toca que cubre ella. → **tener una fijación con algo.** □ *I have a bee in my bonnet that you'd be a good manager.* □ *I had a bee in my bonnet about swimming. I couldn't stop wanting to go swimming.* ALSO: **put a bee in someone's bonnet**   darle una idea a alguien. □ *Somebody put a bee in my bonnet that we should go to a movie.* □ *Who put a bee in your bonnet?*

have a big mouth   ser una persona que cotillea mucho; ser una persona que cuenta los secretos de otros. □ *Mary has a big mouth. She told Bob what I was getting him for his birthday.* □ *You shouldn't say things like that about people all the time. Everyone will say you have a big mouth.*

have a bone to pick (with someone)   tener que hablar de un asunto con alguien; tener que discutir algo con alguien. □ *Hey, Bill. I've got a bone to pick with you. Where is the money you owe me?* □ *I had a bone to pick with her, but she was so sweet that I forgot about it.* □ *You always have a bone to pick.*

have a brush with something   tener contacto muy breve con algo; experimentar algo. (Se usa especialmente referente al derecho. A veces se dice *close brush* en vez de *brush*.) □ *Ann had a close brush with the law. She was nearly arrested for speeding.* □ *When I was younger, I had a brush with scarlet fever, but I got over it.*

have a chip on one's shoulder   provocar a alguien a reñir o a luchar. (Se puede expresar la invitación a luchar como una invitación a dar un golpe al hombro de alguien, así echando un pedacito de él y empezando la lucha. Una persona que tiene *chip* siempre está provocando a otros). → **estar resentido; tener uno un poco de complejo.** □ *Who are you mad at? You always seem to have a chip on your shoulder.* □ *John's had a chip on his shoulder ever since he got his speeding ticket.*

have a close call   Véase la entrada siguiente.

have a close shave AND **have a close call**   escapar sin daño de algo peligroso. □ *What a close shave I had! I nearly fell off the roof when I was working there.* □ *I almost got struck by a speeding car. It was a close shave.*

have a familiar ring   sonar [un cuento o una explicación]. □ *Your excuse has a familiar ring. Have you done this before?* □ *This term paper has a familiar ring. I think it has been copied.*

have a good head on one's shoulders   tener sentido común; ser sensato e inteligente. □ *Mary doesn't do well in school, but she's got a good head on her shoulders.* □ *John has a good head on his shoulders and can be depended on to give good advice.*

have a green thumb   cultivar las plantas muy bien. (No es literal.) □ *Just look at Mr. Simpson's garden. He has a green thumb.* □ *My mother has a green thumb when it comes to house plants.*

have a heart   ser compasivo; ser generoso e indulgente; tener un corazón especialmente compasivo. □ *Oh, have a heart! Give me some help!* □ *If Ann had a heart, she'd have made us feel more welcome.*

have a heart of gold ser generoso, sincero, y simpático. (No es literal.) □ *Mary is such a lovely person. She has a heart of gold.* □ *You think Tom stole your watch? Impossible! He has a heart of gold.*

have a heart of stone ser insensible y antipático. (No es literal.) □ *Sally has a heart of stone. She never even smiles.* □ *The villain in the play had a heart of stone. He was an ideal villain.*

have a lot going (for one) tener muchas cosas que van bien para uno. □ *Jane is so lucky. She has a lot going for her.* □ *She has a good job and a nice family. She has a lot going.*

have a low boiling point enojarse fácilmente. □ *Be nice to John. He's upset and has a low boiling point.* □ *Mr. Jones sure has a low boiling point. I hardly said anything, and he got angry.*

have an ax to grind tener algo de que quejarse. □ *Tom, I need to talk to you. I have an ax to grind.* □ *Bill and Bob went into the other room to argue. They had an ax to grind.*

have an eye out (for someone or something) AND **keep an eye out (for someone or something)** estar atento a la llegada o la aparición de alguien o algo. (Se puede usar *one's* en vez de *an.*) □ *Please try to have an eye out for the bus.* □ *Keep an eye out for rain.* □ *Have your eye out for a raincoat on sale.* □ *Okay. I'll keep my eye out.*

have an in (with someone) poder pedir un favor de alguien; tener influencia con alguien. (*In* sustantivo en este caso.) □ *Do you have an in with the mayor? I have to ask him a favor.* □ *Sorry, I don't have an in, but I know someone who does.*

have an itchy palm AND **have an itching palm** necesitar dinero; tener la tendencia a pedir propinas; ansiar el dinero. (Como si poner el dinero en la palma pusiera fin al picor.) □ *All the waiters at that restaurant have itchy palms.* □ *The cab driver had an itching palm. Since he refused to carry my bags, I gave him nothing.*

have a price on one's head   ser buscado por la policía, que ha ofrecido una recompensa por la captura. (No se usa literalmente. Normalmente usado sólo en las películas del oeste o de los gángsters. Como si la cabeza misma produjera una recompensa o un premio.) □ *We captured a thief who had a price on his head, and the sheriff gave us the reward.* □ *The crook was so mean, he turned in his own brother, who had a price on his head.*

have a scrape (with someone or something)   chocarse con alguien o algo; luchar o reñir con alguien o contra algo. □ *I had a scrape with the county sheriff.* □ *John and Bill had a scrape, but they are friends again now.*

have a soft spot in one's heart for someone or something   tener cariño por alguien o algo. □ *John has a soft spot in his heart for Mary.* □ *I have soft spot in my heart for chocolate cake.*

have a sweet tooth   querer comer mucha comida azucarada— especialmente los dulces y los pasteles. (Como si un diente en particular tuviera antojo de la comida azucarada.) □ *I have a sweet tooth, and if I don't watch it, I'll really get fat.* □ *John eats candy all the time. He must have a sweet tooth.*

have a weakness for someone or something   no poder resistir a alguien o algo; tener cariño por alguien o algo; no tener ningún poder (figuradamente) contra alguien o algo. □ *I have a weakness for chocolate.* □ *John has a weakness for Mary. I think he's in love.*

have bats in one's belfry   ser un poco loco. (*Belfry,* que significa "campanario," representa la mente o el cerebro de uno. Los murciélagos representan una plaga de confusión allí.) □ *Poor old Tom has bats in his belfry.* □ *Don't act so silly, John. People will think you have bats in your belfry.*

have clean hands   no tener ninguna culpa. (Como si la persona culpable tuviera manos ensangrentadas.) □ *Don't look at me. I have clean hands.* □ *The police took him in, but let him go again because he had clean hands.*

have dibs on something AND **put one's dibs on something**   reservar algo para sí misso; reclamar algo para sí mismo. □ *I have dibs on the last piece of cake.* □ *John put his dibs on the last piece again. It isn't fair.*

have egg on one's face   tener vergüenza a causa de un error de que todo el mundo sabe. (Casi nunca se usa literalmente.) □ *Bob has egg on his face because he wore jeans to the party and everyone else wore formal clothing.* □ *John was completely wrong about the weather for the picnic. It snowed! Now he has egg on his face.*

have eyes bigger than one's stomach   Véase en *one's eyes are bigger than one's stomach*.

have eyes in the back of one's head   parecer como si uno pudiera ver cosas fuera de su visión. (No es literal.) □ *My teacher seems to have eyes in the back of her head.* □ *My teacher doesn't need to have eyes in the back of his head. He watches us very carefully.*

have feet of clay   tener [una persona fuerte] un defecto del carácter. □ *All human beings have feet of clay. No one is perfect.* □ *Sally was popular and successful. She was nearly fifty before she learned that she, too, had feet of clay.*

have foot-in-mouth disease   ponerse avergonzado a causa de meterse la pata. (La frase es parodia de *foot-and-mouth disease* or *hoof-and-mouth disease,* una enfermedad de los vacos y de los ciervos.) □ *I'm sorry I keep saying stupid things. I guess I have foot-in-mouth disease.* □ *Yes, you really have foot-in-mouth disease tonight.*

have mixed feelings (about someone or something)   no haber decidido algo [de alguien o algo]. □ *I have mixed feelings about Bob. Sometimes I think he likes me; other times I don't.* □ *I have mixed feelings about my trip to England. I love the people, but the climate upsets me.* □ *Yes, I also have mixed feelings.*

have money to burn   tener mucho dinero; tener más dinero que necesita uno; tener dinero que uno puede gastar. □ *Look at the way*

Tom buys things. You'd think he had money to burn. □ *If I had money to burn, I'd just put it in the bank.*

have one's back to the wall   estar a la defensiva. □ *He'll have to give in. He has his back to the wall.* □ *How can I bargain when I've got my back to the wall?*

have one's cake and eat it too AND **eat one's cake and have it too**   disfrutar de los dos lados de algo. (Normalmente se usa en el sentido negativo.) → **no se puede estar en la misa y picando.** □ *Tom wants to have his cake and eat it too. It can't be done.* □ *Don't buy a car if you want to walk and stay healthy. You can't eat your cake and have it too.*

have one's ear to the ground AND **keep one's ear to the ground**   escuchar atentamente, esperando que uno tiene aviso de algo. (No es literal. Como si uno estuviera escuchando para oír el sonido de los cascos del caballo.) □ *John had his ear to the ground, hoping to find out about new ideas in computers.* □ *His boss told him to keep his ear to the ground so that he'd be the first to know of a new idea.*

have one's finger in the pie,   estar metido en algo. (No es literal.) □ *I like to have my finger in the pie so I can make sure things go my way.* □ *As long as John has his finger in the pie, things will happen slowly.*

have one's hand in the till   malversar de una empresa o una organización. (*Till* es la caja para el dinero de la empresa o organización.) □ *Mr. Jones had his hand in the till for years before he was caught.* □ *I think that the new clerk has her hand in the till. There is cash missing every morning.*

have one's hands full (with someone or something)   estar muy ocupado con alguien o algo. □ *I have my hands full with my three children.* □ *You have your hands full with the store.* □ *We both have our hands full.*

have one's hands tied   estar impedido de hacer algo. □ *I can't help you. I was told not to, so I have my hands tied.* □ *John can help. He doesn't have his hands tied.*

have one's head in the clouds   no estar consciente de lo que pasa. ☐ *"Bob, do you have your head in the clouds?" said the teacher.* ☐ *She walks around all day with her head in the clouds. She must be in love.*

have one's heart in one's mouth   sentirse muy emocional en cuanto a alguien o algo. ☐ *"Gosh, Mary," said John, "I have my heart in my mouth whenever I see you."* ☐ *My heart is in my mouth whenever I hear the national anthem.* ALSO: **one's heart is in one's mouth**   sentirse muy emocional. ☐ *It was a touching scene. My heart was in my mouth the whole time.*

have one's heart set on something   querer y esperar algo. ☐ *Jane has her heart set on going to London.* ☐ *Bob will be disappointed. He had his heart set on going to college this year.* ☐ *His heart is set on it.* ALSO: **set one's heart on something**   ponerse decidido para hacer algo. ☐ *Jane set her heart on going to London.* ALSO: **one's heart is set on something**   querer y esperar algo. ☐ *Jane's heart is set on going to London.*

have one's nose in a book   estar leyendo un libro; leer los libros siempre. ☐ *Bob has his nose in a book every time I see him.* ☐ *His nose is always in a book. He never gets any exercise.*

have one's tail between one's legs   tener miedo o estar amedrentado. (Referente al perro asustado. También se usa literalmente referente a los perros.) ☐ *John seems to lack courage. Whenever there is an argument, he has his tail between his legs.* ☐ *You can tell that the dog is frightened because it has its tail between its legs.* ALSO: **one's tail is between one's legs**   tener miedo o estar amedrentado. ☐ *He should have stood up and argued, but—as usual—his tail was between his legs.*

have one's words stick in one's throat   ponerse tan abrumado por la emoción que casi no se puede hablar. ☐ *I sometimes have my words stick in my throat.* ☐ *John said that he never had his words stick in his throat.* ALSO: **one's words stick in one's throat**   tener dificultad de hablar a causa de la emoción. ☐ *My words stick in my throat whenever I try to say something kind or tender.*

have other fish to fry tener otras cosas que hacer; tener cosas más importantes que hacer. (Se puede usar *bigger, better, more important,* etc. en vez de *other.* No se usa literalmente.) □ *I can't take time for your problem. I have other fish to fry.* □ *I won't waste time on your question. I have bigger fish to fry.*

have someone dead to rights demostrar que alguien es culpable, fuera de duda. □ *The police burst in on the robbers while they were at work. They had the robbers dead to rights.* □ *All right, Tom! I've got you dead to rights! Get your hands out of the cookie jar.*

have someone in one's pocket controlar a alguien. □ *Don't worry about the mayor. She'll cooperate. I've got her in my pocket.* □ *John will do just what I tell him. I've got him and his brother in my pocket.*

have someone or something in one's hands tener control de o reponsabilidad por alguien o algo. (Se puede usar *leave* o *put* en vez de *have.*) □ *You have the whole project in your hands.* □ *The boss put the whole project in your hands.* □ *I have to leave the baby in your hands while I go to the doctor.*

have something at hand Véase la entrada siguiente.

have something at one's fingertips AND **have something at hand** tener algo cerca. (Se puede usar *keep* en vez de *have.*) → **tener algo al alcance de la mano.** □ *I have a dictionary at my fingertips.* □ *I try to have everything I need at hand.* □ *I keep my medicine at my fingertips.*

have something hanging over one's head tener algo que se preocupa o molesta a uno; tener una fecha tope que molesta a uno. (También se usa literalmente.) □ *I keep worrying about getting drafted. I hate to have something like that hanging over my head.* □ *I have a history paper that is hanging over my head.*

have something in stock tener mercancías en el almacén, disponible para la venta. □ *Do you have extra large sizes in stock?* □ *Of course, we have all sizes and colors in stock.*

have something to spare   tener más que uno necesita de algo. □ *Ask John for some firewood. He has firewood to spare.* □ *Do you have any candy to spare?*

have the right-of-way   tener el derecho de ocupar una parte específica de una calzada pública. □ *I had a traffic accident yesterday, but it wasn't my fault. I had the right-of-way.* □ *Don't pull out onto a highway if you don't have the right-of-way.*

have the shoe on the other foot   experimentar la situación opuesta (a una situación previa). (También se usa con *be* en vez de *have*. Véanse en los ejemplos.) □ *I used to be a student, and now I'm the teacher. Now I have the shoe on the other foot.* □ *You were mean to me when you thought I was cheating. Now that I have caught you cheating, the shoe is on the other foot.*

have the time of one's life   pasarlo muy bien; pasarlo mejor que en toda la vida. □ *What a great party! I had the time of my life.* □ *We went to Florida last winter and had the time of our lives.*

have too many irons in the fire   haciendo demasiadas cosas a la vez. (Es cliché. Como si el herrero tuviera demasiadas cosas calientes en el fuego a la vez.) □ *Tom had too many irons in the fire and missed some important deadlines.* □ *It's better if you don't have too many irons in the fire.*

head and shoulders above someone or something   ser obviamente superior a alguien. (Muchas veces se usa con *stand*, como en los ejemplos.) □ *This wine is head and shoulders above that one.* □ *John stands head and shoulders above Bob.*

head, go over someone's   Véase *go over someone's head.*

head, go to someone's   Véase *go to someone's head.*

head, in over one's   Véase *in over one's head.*

head in the clouds, have one's   Véase *have one's head in the clouds.*

head, on someone's   Véase *on someone's head.*

head, out of one's   Véase *out of one's head.*

heart and soul, with all one's   Véase *with all one's heart and soul.*

heart good, do someone's   Véase *do someone's heart good.*

heart, have a   Véase *have a heart.*

heart in one's mouth, have one's   Véase *have one's heart in one's mouth.*

heart of gold, have a   Véase *have a heart of gold.*

heart of stone, have a   Véase *have a heart of stone.*

heart set on something, have one's   Véase *have one's heart set on something.*

heat, in   Véase *in heat.*

heck of it, for the   Véase *for the heck of it.*

heels of something, on the   Véase *on the heels of something.*

He laughs best who laughs last.   Véase la entrada siguiente.

He who laughs last, laughs longest. AND **He laughs best who laughs last.**   un refrán signficando que la persona que hace el último movimiento o gasta la última broma goza más que todos. □ *Bill had pulled many silly tricks on Tom. Finally Tom pulled a very funny trick on Bill and said, "He who laughs last, laughs longest."* □ *Bill pulled another, even bigger trick on Tom, and said, laughing, "He laughs best who laughs last."*

hide one's head in the sand   Véase en *bury one's head in the sand.*

hide one's light under a bushel   ocultar las ideas inteligentes o las habilidades de uno. (Es tema bíblico.) □ *Jane has some good ideas, but she doesn't speak very often. She hides her light under* *a bushel.* □ *Don't hide your light under a bushel. Share your gifts with other people.*

high as a kite, (as)   Véase *(as) high as a kite.*

high as the sky, (as)   Véase *(as) high as the sky.*

high man on the totem pole   la persona que tiene control de la jerarquía; la persona encargada de una organización. (Véase también *low man on the totem pole.*) □ *I don't want to talk to a secretary. I demand to talk to the high man on the totem pole.* □ *Who's in charge around here? Who's high man on the totem pole?*

hill, over the   Véase *over the hill.*

history, go down in   Véase *go down in history.*

hit a happy medium   Véase en *strike a happy medium.*

hit a snag   encontrar un problema. □ *We've hit a snag with the building project.* □ *I stopped working on the roof when I hit a snag.*

hit a sour note   Véase en *strike a sour note.*

hit bottom   llegar al momento peor o más difícil. □ *Our profits have hit bottom. This is our worst year ever.* □ *When my life hit bottom, I began to feel much better. I knew that if there was going to be any change, it would be for the better.*

hitch a ride   Véase en *thumb a ride.*

hit someone between the eyes   llegar a ser evidente; sorprender o impresionar a alguien. (También se usa con *right,* como en los ejemplos. También se usa literalmente.) □ *Suddenly, it hit me right between the eyes. John and Mary were in love.* □ *Then—as he was talking—the exact nature of the evil plan hit me between the eyes.*

hit (someone) like a ton of bricks   sorprender, asustar, o conmover a alguien. □ *Suddenly, the truth hit me like a ton of bricks.* □ *The sudden tax increase hit like a ton of bricks. Everyone became angry.*

hit the bull's-eye   1. dar en el centro de un blanco circular. (Se usa literalmente.) → **dar en el blanco.** □ *The archer hit the bull's-eye three times in a row.* □ *I didn't hit the bull's-eye even once.* **2.** alcanzar un objetivo precisamente. □ *Your idea really hit the bull's-eye. Thank you!* □ *Jill has a lot of insight. She knows how to hit the bull's-eye.*

hit the nail (right) on the head   hacer la cosa más adecuada; hacer algo de la manera más eficaz y eficiente. (Es cliché.) □ *You've spotted the flaw, Sally. You hit the nail on the head.* □ *Bob doesn't say much, but every now and then he hits the nail right on the head.*

hit the spot   estar correcto; ser refrescante. □ *This cool drink really hits the spot.* □ *That was a delicious meal, dear. It hit the spot.*

hold one's end (of the bargain) up AND **hold up one's end (of the bargain)**   hacer lo que ha accedido a hacer; cumplir con las responsabilidades como ha accedido uno. □ *Tom has to learn to cooperate. He must hold up his end of the bargain.* □ *If you don't hold your end up, the whole project will fail.*

hold one's ground   Véase en *stand one's ground.*

hold one's head up AND **hold up one's head**   tener dignidad; mantener o demostrar la dignidad. □ *I've done nothing wrong. I can hold my head up in public.* □ *I'm so embarrassed and ashamed. I'll never be able to hold up my head again.*

hold one's own   hacer algo tanto como otras personas. □ *I can hold my own in a footrace any day.* □ *She was unable to hold her own, and she had to quit.*

hold one's peace   permanecer callado. □ *Bill was unable to hold his peace any longer. "Don't do it!" he cried.* □ *Quiet, John. Hold your peace for a little while longer.*

hold one's temper   Véase en *keep one's temper.*

hold one's tongue   abstenerse de hablar; abstenerse de decir algo desagradable. (No se usa literalmente.) □ *I felt like scolding her, but I held my tongue.* □ *Hold your tongue, John. You can't talk to me that way.*

Hold on to your hat! Véase en *Hang on to your hat!*

hold out the olive branch ofrecer acabar con un desacuerdo y hacerse amigo de alguien; ofrecerle la reconciliación de algo a alguien. (El ramo del olivo es símbolo de la paz y la reconciliación. Es una referencia bíblica.) □ *Jill was the first to hold out the olive branch after our argument.* □ *I always try to hold out the olive branch to someone I have hurt. Life is too short for a person to bear grudges for very long.*

hold the fort cuidar algún lugar, como la tienda o la casa. (La frase origina en las películas del oeste.) □ *I'm going next door to visit Mrs. Jones. You stay here and hold the fort.* □ *You should open the store at eight o'clock and hold the fort until I get there at ten o'clock.*

hold true ser la verdad [algo]; seguir siendo la verdad [algo]. □ *Does this rule hold true all the time?* □ *Yes, it holds true no matter what.*

hold water, not Véase *not hold water.*

hole in one 1. hacer que la bola [en el golf] entre en el hoyo después de un intento. → **hoyo en uno.** □ *John made a hole in one yesterday.* □ *I've never gotten a hole in one.* 2. tener éxito después del primer intento de hacer algo. □ *It worked the first time I tried it—a hole in one.* □ *Bob got a hole in one on that sale. A lady walked in the door, and he sold her a car in five minutes.*

hole, in the Véase *in the hole.*

hole, out of the Véase *out of the hole.*

honeymoon is over, The. Véase *The honeymoon is over.*

honor, on one's Véase *on one's honor.*

honors, do the Véase *do the honors.*

honor someone's check aceptar el cheque personal de una persona. □ *The clerk at the store wouldn't honor my check. I had to pay cash.* □ *The bank didn't honor your check when I tried to deposit it. Please give me cash.*

hope against all hope tener esperanzas aún en una situación que no parece esperanzadora. □ *We hope against all hope that she'll see the right thing to do and do it.* □ *There is little point in hoping against all hope, except that it makes you feel better.*

horizon, on the Véase *on the horizon.*

horn in (on someone) intentar cambiar los planes de alguien. □ *I'm going to ask Sally to the party. Don't you dare try to horn in on me!* □ *I wouldn't think of horning in.*

horns of a dilemma, on the Véase *on the horns of a dilemma.*

horse of a different color Véase la entrada siguiente.

horse of another color AND **horse of a different color** totalmente de otro asunto. □ *I was talking about the tree, not the bush. That's a horse of another color.* □ *Gambling is not the same as investing in the stock market. It's a horse of a different color.*

hot under the collar muy enfadado. (Es cliché.) □ *The boss was really hot under the collar when you told him you lost the contract.* □ *I get hot under the collar every time I think about it.*

hour, on the Véase *on the hour.*

house, on the Véase *on the house.*

huff, in a Véase *in a huff.*

hump, over the Véase over the hump.

hungry as a bear, (as) Véase *(as) hungry as a bear.*

I

(ifs, ands, or) buts about it, no Véase *no (ifs, ands, or) buts about it.*

If the shoe fits, wear it. un refrán significando que uno debe prestar atención a algo que lo concierne. □ *Some people here need to be quiet. If the shoe fits, wear it.* □ *This doesn't apply to everyone. If the shoe fits, wear it.*

if worst comes to worst en el peor caso posible; si las cosas se ponen peores. (Es cliché.) □ *If worst comes to worst, we'll hire someone to help you.* □ *If worst comes to worst, I'll have to borrow some money.*

If you give one an inch, one will take a mile. Véase en *Give one an inch, and one will take a mile.*

in a dead heat terminando una carrera al mismo momento que otra persona o cosa; empatado. (En este caso, "dead" significa "exact" o "total.") □ *The two horses finished the race in a dead heat.* □ *They ended the contest in a dead heat.*

in a flash rápidamente; inmediatamente. □ *I'll be there in a flash.* □ *It happened in a flash. Suddenly my wallet was gone.*

in a huff de una manera enfadada u ofendido. (Se puede usar *into* en vez de *in.* Véanse los ejemplos.) □ *He heard what we had to say, then left in a huff.* □ *She came in a huff and ordered us to bring her something to eat.* □ *She gets into a huff very easily.*

in a mad rush de prisa. □ *I ran around all day today in a mad rush, looking for a present for Bill.* □ *Why are you always in a mad rush?*

in a (tight) spot   envuelto en un problema; en una situación difícil. (Se puede usar *into* en vez de *in*. Véanse los ejemplos.) □ *Look, John, I'm in a tight spot. Can you lend me twenty dollars?* □ *I'm in a spot too. I need $300.* □ *I have never gotten into a tight spot.*

in a vicious circle   en una situación en que la solución de un problem lleva a otro problema, y la solución de éste lleva otra vez al primer problema, etc. (Se puede usar *into* en vez de *in*. Véanse los ejemplos.) → **callejón sin salida; la pescadilla que se muerde la cola.** □ *Life is so strange. I seem to be in a vicious circle most of the time.* □ *I put lemon in my tea to make it sour, then sugar to make it sweet. I'm in a vicious circle.* □ *Don't let your life get into a vicious circle.*

in a world of one's own   frío; distante; egocéntrico. (Se puede usar *into* en vez de *in*. Véanse los ejemplos.) □ *John lives in a world of his own. He has very few friends.* □ *Mary walks around in a world of her own, but she's very intelligent.* □ *When she's thinking, she drifts into a world of her own.*

in bad faith   sin sinceridad; con intención mala o deshonesta. □ *It appears that you acted in bad faith and didn't live up to the terms of our agreement.* □ *If you do things in bad faith, you'll get a bad reputation.*

in bad sorts   de mal humor. □ *Bill is in bad sorts today. He's very grouchy.* □ *I try to be extra nice to people when I'm in bad sorts.*

in bad taste AND **in poor taste**   grosero; vulgar; indecente. □ *Mrs. Franklin felt that your joke was in bad taste.* □ *We found the play to be in poor taste, so we walked out in the middle of the second act.*

in black and white   autorizado, por escrito o en letra impresa. (Dicha de algo, como de un acuerdo o una declaración, que ha sido recordado por su forma escrita o en letra impresa. Se puede usar *into* en vez de *in*. Véanse los ejemplos.) □ *I have it in black and white that I'm entitled to three weeks of vacation each year.* □ *It says right here in black and white that oak trees make acorns.* □ *Please put the agreement into black and white.*

in broad daylight visible por todos de día. □ *The thief stole the car in broad daylight.* □ *There they were, selling drugs in broad daylight.*

inch by inch de una pulgada a otra; poco a poco. □ *Traffic moved along inch by inch.* □ *Inch by inch, the snail moved across the stone.*

inch of one's life, within an Véase *within an inch of one's life.*

in creation Véase en *on earth.*

in deep water en una situación peligrosa o vulnerable; en una situación seria; con problemas. (Como si uno estuviera nadando, o se hubiera caído, en aguas demasiado profundas para él. Se puede usar *into* en vez de *in*. Véanse los ejemplos.) □ *John is having trouble with his taxes. He's in deep water.* □ *Bill is in deep water in algebra class. He's almost failing.* □ *He really got himself into deep water.*

in fine feather de buen humor; de buena salud. (Es cliché. Se puede usar *into* en vez de *in*. Véanse los ejemplos. Referente a un pájaro sano, y por lo tanto guapo.) □ *Hello, John. You appear to be in fine feather.* □ *Of course I'm in fine feather. I get lots of sleep.* □ *Good food and lots of sleep put me into fine feather.*

in full swing en curso; funcionando, operando, o teniendo lugar sin restricción. (*In* can be replaced with *into*. Se puede usar *into* en vez de *in*. Véanse los ejemplos.) □ *We can't leave now! The party is in full swing.* □ *Our program to help the starving people is in full swing. You should see results soon.* □ *Just wait until our project gets into full swing.*

in good condition Véase la entrada siguiente.

in good shape AND **in good condition** sólido y sano, físicamente y en su funcionamiento. (Referente a las personas y las cosas. Se puede usar *into* en vez de *in*. Véanse los ejemplos.) □ *This car isn't in good shape.* □ *I'd like to have one that's in good condition.* □ *Mary is in good condition. She works hard to keep healthy.* □ *You have to make an effort to get into good shape.*

in heat   en un período de emoción sexual; en estro. (Estro es el período en que las hembras están más dispuestos a procrear. Véase también *in season*. Normalmente referente a los animales, pero a veces se usa como chiste para referirse a los seres humanos. Se puede usar *into* en vez de *in*. Véanse los ejemplos.) □ *Our dog is in heat.* □ *She goes into heat every year at this time.* □ *When my dog is in heat, I have to keep her locked in the house.*

in less than no time   muy rápidamente. □ *I'll be there in less than no time.* □ *Don't worry. This won't take long. It'll be over with in less than no time.*

in mint condition   en perfecto estado. (Referente al perfecto estado de una moneda justamente acuñada. Se puede usar *into* en vez de *in*. Véanse los ejemplos.) □ *This is a fine car. It runs well and is in mint condition.* □ *We went through a house in mint condition and decided to buy it.* □ *We put our house into mint condition before we sold it.*

in name only   nominalmente; no de hecho, sólo por la forma. □ *The president is head of the country in name only. Congress makes the laws.* □ *Mr. Smith is the boss of the Smith Company in name only. Mrs. Smith handles all the business affairs.*

innocent as a lamb, (as)   Véase *(as) innocent as a lamb.*

in no mood to do something   no tener ganas de hacer nada; no querer hacer nada. □ *I'm in no mood to cook dinner tonight.* □ *Mother is in no mood to put up with our arguing.*

in nothing flat   sin pasar tiempo. (No es literal.) □ *Of course I can get there in a hurry. I'll be there in nothing flat.* □ *We covered the distance between New York and Philadelphia in nothing flat.*

in one ear and out the other   hacer casa omiso de algo; no ser [algo] oído o tenido en cuenta. (Es cliché. Se puede usar *into* en vez de *in*. Véanse los ejemplos.) □ *Everything I say to you goes into one ear and out the other!* □ *Bill just doesn't pay attention. Everything is in one ear and out the other.*

in one fell swoop   Véase en *at one fell swoop.*

in one's birthday suit   desnudo. (En la "ropa" en que uno nació. Se puede usar *into* en vez de *in.* Véanse los ejemplos.) ☐ *I've heard that John sleeps in his birthday suit.* ☐ *We used to go down to the river and swim in our birthday suits.* ☐ *You have to get into your birthday suit to bathe.*

in one's mind's eye   en la mente. (Referente a ver algo en la mente.) ☐ *In my mind's eye, I can see trouble ahead.* ☐ *In her mind's eye, she could see a beautiful building beside the river. She decided to design such a building.*

in one's or its prime   al apogeo o la mejor época de alguien o algo. → **en la flor de la vida [referente a personas].** ☐ *Our dog— that is in its prime—is very active.* ☐ *The program ended in its prime when we ran out of money.* ☐ *I could work long hours when I was in my prime.*

in one's right mind   cuerdo; racional y sensato. (Muchas veces se usa en el sentido negativo.) ☐ *That was a stupid thing to do. You're not in your right mind.* ☐ *You can't be in your right mind! That sounds crazy!*

in one's second childhood   interesado en las cosas que normalmente a los niños les interesan. ☐ *My father bought himself a toy train, and my mother said he was in his second childhood.* ☐ *Whenever I go to the river and throw stones, I feel as though I'm in my second childhood*

in one's spare time   en el tiempo de sobra que tiene uno; en el tiempo no reservado para hacer otra cosa. ☐ *I write novels in my spare time.* ☐ *I'll try to paint the house in my spare time.*

in over one's head   con más dificultades que uno puede aguantar. ☐ *Calculus is very hard for me. I'm in over my head.* ☐ *Ann is too busy. She's really in over her head.*

in poor taste   Véase en *in bad taste.*

in print   disponible [un libro] para la venta. (Compare a *out of print*.)
□ *I think I can get that book for you. It's still in print.* □ *This is the only book in print on this subject.*

in rags   en harapas ya para tirar. □ *Oh, look at my clothing. I can't go to the party in rags!* □ *I think the new casual fashions make you look as if you're in rags.*

in round figures   Véase la entrada siguiente.

in round numbers AND **in round figures**   un número calculado; una cifra redondeada al número entero más cercano. Se puede usar *into* en vez de *in*. Véanse los ejemplos.) □ *Please tell me in round numbers what it'll cost.* □ *I don't need the exact amount. Just give it to me in round figures.*

ins and outs of something   el modo correcto de hacer algo; las cosas que necesita saber uno para hacer algo. □ *I don't understand the ins and outs of politics.* □ *Jane knows the ins and outs of working with computers.*

in season   **1.** actualmente disponible para la venta. (Algunas comidas y otras cosas sólo están disponibles para la venta durante estaciones específicas. Se puede usar *into* en vez de *in*, especialmente cuando se usa con *come*. Véanse los ejemplos.) □ *Oysters are available in season.* □ *Strawberries aren't in season in January.* □ *When do strawberries come into season?* **2.** cazado o pescado legalmente. □ *Catfish are in season all year round.* □ *When are salmon in season?* **3.** [un perro] en estro. □ *My dog is in season every year at this time.* □ *When my dog is in season, I have to keep her locked in the house.*

in seventh heaven   en un estado muy contento. (Es cliché. El cielo séptimo es donde existe Dios.) □ *Ann was really in seventh heaven when she got a car of her own.* □ *I'd be in seventh heaven if I had a million dollars.*

in short order   muy rápidamente. □ *I can straighten out this mess in short order.* □ *The people came in and cleaned the place up in short order.*

in short supply escaso. (Se puede usar *into* en vez de *in*. Véanse los ejemplos.) ☐ *Fresh vegetables are in short supply in the winter.* ☐ *Yellow cars are in short supply because everyone likes them and buys them.* ☐ *At this time of the year, fresh vegetables go into short supply.*

in stock inmediatamente disponible, como los productos de una tienda. ☐ *I'm sorry, I don't have that in stock. I'll have to order it for you.* ☐ *We have all our Christmas merchandise in stock now.*

in the air por todas partes. (También se usa literalmente.) ☐ *There is such a feeling of joy in the air.* ☐ *We felt a sense of tension in the air.*

in the bargain en adición a lo accedido. (Se puede usar *into* en vez de *in*. Véanse los ejemplos.) ☐ *I bought a car, and they threw an air conditioner into the bargain.* ☐ *When I bought a house, I asked the seller to include the furniture in the bargain.*

in the black sin deudas; en una situación financiera en que uno puede sacar beneficios. (Referente a escribir las cifras en negro en vez de rojo, lo cual indicaría una deuda. Véase también *in the red*. Se puede usar *into* en vez de *in*. Véanse los ejemplos.) ☐ *I wish my accounts were in the black.* ☐ *Sally moved the company into the black.*

in the blood AND **in one's blood** parte de la personalidad o del carácter de uno. (De hecho en los genes, no en la sangre.) ☐ *John's a great runner. It's in his blood.* ☐ *The whole family is very athletic. It's in the blood.*

in the bullpen en un sitio específico cerca del campo de béisbol [el lanzador], calentando los músculos para el lanzamiento. (Se puede usar *into* en vez de *in*. Véanse los ejemplos.) ☐ *You can tell who is pitching next by seeing who is in the bullpen.* ☐ *Our best pitcher just went into the bullpen. He'll be pitching soon.*

in the cards en el futuro. ☐ *Well, what do you think is in the cards for tomorrow?* ☐ *I asked the boss if there was a raise in the cards for me.*

in the doghouse   el estado de tener muchos problemas; en desgracia con alguien. (Se puede usar *into* en vez de *in*. Véanse los ejemplos. Como si alguien mandara que alguien saliera de la casa a causa del mal comportamiento—como alguien mandaría el perro de la casa al patio.) □ *I'm really in the doghouse. I was late for an appointment.* □ *I hate being in the doghouse all the time. I don't know why I can't stay out of trouble.*

in the doldrums   aturdido; inactivo; de mal humor. (Se puede usar *into* en vez de *in*. Véanse los ejemplos.) □ *He's usually in the doldrums in the winter.* □ *I had some bad news yesterday, which put me into the doldrums.*

in the flesh   presente de verdad; en persona. □ *I've heard that the queen is coming here in the flesh.* □ *Is she really here? In the flesh?* □ *I've wanted a color television for years, and now I've got one right here in the flesh.*

in the gutter   en un estado bajo de la vida; depravado. (Se puede usar *into* en vez de *in*. Véanse los ejemplos.) □ *You had better straighten out your life, or you'll end up in the gutter.* □ *His bad habits put him into the gutter.*

in the hole   en deuda. (Se puede usar *into* en vez de *in*. Véanse los ejemplos. También se usa literalmente.) □ *I'm $200 in the hole.* □ *Our finances end up in the hole every month.*

in the know   entendido. (Se puede usar *into* en vez de *in*. Véanse los ejemplos.) □ *Let's ask Bob. He's in the know.* □ *I have no knowledge of how to work this machine. I think I can get into the know very quickly though.*

in the lap of luxury   en un ambiente lujoso. (Es cliché. Se puede usar *into* en vez de *in*. Véase en los ejemplos.) □ *John lives in the lap of luxury because his family is very wealthy.* □ *When I retire, I'd like to live in the lap of luxury.*

in the limelight AND **in the spotlight**   al centro de atención de muchas personas. (Se puede usar *into* en vez de *in*. Véanse los ejemplos. También se usa literalmente. *Limelight* es una clase de foco del teatro que ya no existe, y la palabra sólo aparece en inglés en esta frase.) □ *John will do almost anything to get himself into the limelight.* □ *I love being in the spotlight.* □ *All elected officials spend a lot of time in the limelight.*

in the line of duty   como parte de los deberes esperados (militares o policíacos). □ *When soldiers fight people in a war, it's in the line of duty.* □ *Police officers have to do things they may not like in the line of duty.*

in the long run   durante un período muy largo; al fin. (Es cliché.) □ *We'd be better off in the long run buying one instead of renting one.* □ *In the long run, we'd be happier in the South.*

in the money   1. rico. □ *John is really in the money. He's worth millions.* □ *If I am ever in the money, I'll be generous.* 2. en el primer lugar de una carrera o un concurso. (Como si uno hubiera ganado dinero como premio.) □ *I knew when Jane came around the final turn that she was in the money.* □ *The horses coming in first, second, and third are said to be in the money.*

in the nick of time   justo a tiempo; al último momento posible; antes de que sea demasiado tarde. (Es cliché.) → **justo a tiempo.** □ *The doctor arrived in the nick of time. The patient's life was saved.* □ *I reached the airport in the nick of time.*

in the pink (of condition)   de muy buena salud; en estado muy bueno, física y emocionalmente. (Se puede usar *into* en vez de *in*. Véanse los ejemplos.) □ *The garden is lovely. All the flowers are in the pink of condition.* □ *Jane has to exercise hard to get into the pink of condition.* □ *I'd like to be in the pink, but I don't have the time.*

in the prime of life   en la época mejor o más productiva de la vida de uno. (Se puede usar *into* en vez de *in*. Véanse los ejemplos.) → **en la flor de la vida [referente a personas].** □ *The good health of one's youth can carry over into the prime of life.* □ *He was struck down by a heart attack in the prime of life.*

in the public eye   públicamente; visible por todos. (Se puede usar *into* en vez de *in*. Véanse los ejemplos.) □ *Elected officials find themselves constantly in the public eye.* □ *The mayor made it a practice to get into the public eye as much as possible.*

in the red en deuda. (Referente a escribir cifras de débitos en rojo en vez de negro. (Véase también *in the black.* Se puede usar *into* en vez de *in.* Véanse los ejemplos.) □ *My accounts are in the red at the end of every month.* □ *It's easy to get into the red if you don't pay close attention to the amount of money you spend.*

in the right al lado moral o legal de una cuestión; al lado correcto de una cuestión. □ *I felt I was in the right, but the judge ruled against me.* □ *It's hard to argue with Jane. She always believes that she's in the right.*

in the same boat en la misma situación; con el mismo problema. (Es cliché. Se puede usar *into* en vez de *in.* Véanse los ejemplos.) □ TOM: *I'm broke. Can you lend me twenty dollars?* BILL: *Sorry. I'm in the same boat.* □ *Jane and Mary are in the same boat. They both have been called for jury duty.*

in the same breath [dicho] casi al mismo momento; como parte del mismo pensamiento o de la misma conversación. □ *He told me I was lazy, but then in the same breath he said I was doing a good job.* □ *The teacher said that the students were working hard and, in the same breath, that they were not working hard enough.*

in the spotlight Véase en *in the limelight.*

in the twinkling of an eye muy rápidamente. (Es referencia bíblica.) □ *In the twinkling of an eye, the deer had disappeared into the forest.* □ *I gave Bill ten dollars and, in the twinkling of an eye, he spent it.*

in the wind a punto de pasar. (También se usa literalmente.) □ *There are some major changes in the wind. Expect these changes to happen soon.* □ *There is something in the wind. We'll find out what it is soon.*

in the world Véase en *on earth.*

in the wrong al lado malo o ilegal de una cuestión; culpable o equivocado. □ *I felt she was in the wrong, but the judge ruled in her favor.* □ *It's hard to argue with Jane. She always believes that everyone else is in the wrong.*

in two shakes of a lamb's tail   muy rápidamente. (Es cliché.) □ *I'll be there in two shakes of a lamb's tail.* □ *In two shakes of a lamb's tail, the bird flew away.*

itchy palm, have an   Véase *have an itchy palm.*

It never rains but it pours.   un refrán significando que muchas cosas malas suelen pasar a la vez. → **las desgracias nunca vienen solas.** □ *The car won't start, the stairs broke, and the dog died. It never rains but it pours.*

J

Johnny-come-lately   una persona que se une a algo después de que ha empezado. □ *Don't pay any attention to Sally. She's just a Johnny-come-lately and doesn't know what she's talking about.* □ *We've been here for thirty years. Why should some Johnny-come-lately tell us what to do?*

Johnny-on-the-spot   una persona que está en el sitio oportuno en el momento oportuno. □ *Here I am, Johnny-on-the-spot. I told you I would be here at 12:20.* □ *Bill is late again. You can hardly call him Johnny-on-the-spot.*

jump off the deep end   Véase en *go off the deep end.*

jump on the bandwagon   Véase en *get on the bandwagon.*

jump out of one's skin   reaccionar con susto o sorpresa fuerte. (Normalmente se usa con *nearly, almost,* etc. Nunca se usa literalmente.) □ *Oh! You really scared me. I nearly jumped out of my skin.* □ *Bill was so startled he almost jumped out of his skin.*

jump the gun   empezar antes de la señal de empezar. (La frase origina en las competencias deportivas, que a veces empiezan con el disparo de una pistola.) □ *We all had to start the race again because Jane jumped the gun.* □ *When we took the test, Tom jumped the gun and started early.*

jump the track   1. descarrilar (Normalmente dicho de los trenes.) □ *The train jumped the track, causing many injuries to the passengers.* □ *The engine jumped the track, but the other cars stayed on.* 2. cambiar de repente de una cosa, un pensamiento, un plan, o una actividad a otro. □ *The entire project jumped the track, and we finally had to give up.* □ *John's mind jumped the track while he was in the play, and he forgot his lines.*

just what the doctor ordered   exactamente lo que se necesita, especialmente para la salud o la comodidad. (Es cliché.) □ *That meal was delicious, Bob. Just what the doctor ordered.* □ BOB: *Would you like something to drink?* MARY: *Yes, a cold glass of water would be just what the doctor ordered.*

K

keep a civil tongue (in one's head) hablar decentemente y con cortesía. (También se usa con *have*.) ☐ *Please, John. Don't talk like that. Keep a civil tongue in your head.* ☐ *John seems unable to keep a civil tongue.* ☐ *He'd be welcome here if he had a civil tongue in his head.*

keep an eye out (for someone or something) Véase en *have an eye out (for someone or something).*

keep a stiff upper lip estar tranquilo y permanecer impasible ante acontecimientos inquietantes. (También se usa con *have*. Véase en *keep a straight face.*) ☐ *John always keeps a stiff upper lip.* ☐ *Now, Billy, don't cry. Keep a stiff upper lip.* ☐ *Bill can take it. He has a stiff upper lip.*

keep a straight face no reírse. (Se puede usar *have* en vez de *keep*. Nota: *Keep* implica un esfuerzo, y *have* significa que uno ya tiene calma.) ☐ *It's hard to keep a straight face when someone tells a funny joke.* ☐ *I knew it was John who played the trick. He couldn't keep a straight face.* ☐ *John didn't have a straight face.*

keep body and soul together alimentarse, vestirse, y alojarse. (Es cliché.) ☐ *I hardly have enough money to keep body and soul together.* ☐ *How the old man was able to keep body and soul together is beyond me.*

keep late hours quedarse levantado o afuera de la casa hasta muy tarde por la noche; trabajar hasta muy tarde por la noche. ☐ *I'm always tired because I keep late hours.* ☐ *If I didn't keep late hours, I wouldn't sleep so late in the morning.*

keep one's ear to the ground Véase en *have one's ear to the ground.*

keep one's eye on the ball **1.** mirar o seguir la pelota [la bola, el balón] atentamente, especialmente al jugar en algún partido; seguir atentamente los detalles de algún partido, como un partido de béisbol o baloncesto. □ *John, if you can't keep your eye on the ball, I'll have to take you out of the game.* □ *"Keep your eye on the ball," the coach roared at the players.* **2.** estar atento a los sucesos. □ *If you want to get along in this office, you're going to have to keep your eye on the ball.* □ *Bill would do better in his classes if he would just keep his eye on the ball.*

keep one's feet on the ground Véase en *get one's feet on the ground.*

keep one's head above water Véase en *get one's head above water.*

keep one's nose to the grindstone Véase en *put one's nose to the grindstone.*

keep one's temper AND **hold one's temper** no ponerse enojado; reprimir una cara de ira. □ *She should have learned to keep her temper when she was a child.* □ *Sally got thrown off the team because she couldn't hold her temper.*

keep one's weather eye open estar atento a algo [que va a ocurrir]; estar en alerta; estar al acecho. □ *Some trouble is brewing. Keep your weather eye open.* □ *Try to be more alert. Learn to keep your weather eye open.*

keep one's word cumplir con una promesa. □ *I told her I'd be there to pick her up, and I intend to keep my word.* □ *Keeping one's word is necessary in the legal profession.*

keep someone in stitches causar a alguien que se ría alto y fuerte durante mucho tiempo. (También se usa con *have.* Véase la nota en *keep a straight face.*) □ *The comedian kept us in stitches for nearly an hour.* □ *The teacher kept the class in stitches, but the students didn't learn anything.*

keep someone on tenterhooks mantener a alguien en un estado de ansiedad o incertidumbre. (También se usa con *have.* Véase la nota en *keep a straight face.*) □ *Please tell me now. Don't* *keep me on tenterhooks any longer!* □ *Now that we have her on tenterhooks, shall we let her worry, or shall we tell her?*

keep someone or something hanging in midair   Véase en *leave someone or something hanging in midair.*

keep someone or something in mind AND **bear someone or something in mind**   recordar y pensar en alguien o algo. □ *When you're driving a car, you must bear this in mind at all times: Keep your eyes on the road.* □ *As you leave home, keep your family in mind.*

keep someone posted   informar a alguien de lo que pasa; mantener a alguien al día. → **mantener a alguien al tanto.** □ *If the price of corn goes up, I need to know. Please keep me posted.* □ *Keep her posted about the patient's status.*

keep something to oneself   guardar algo como secreto. (Observe el uso de *but* en los ejemplos.) □ *I'm quitting my job, but please keep that to yourself.* □ *Keep it to yourself, but I'm quitting my job.* □ *John is always gossiping. He can't keep anything to himself.*

keep something under one's hat   guardar algo como secreto; guardar un pensamiento sin decírselo a nadie. (Si el secreto queda debajo del sombrero, queda en la mente también. Observe el uso de *but* en los ejemplos.) → **de esto ni palabra a nadie.** □ *Keep this under your hat, but I'm getting married.* □ *I'm getting married, but keep it under your hat.*

keep something under wraps   ocultar o guardar algo (hasta otra época). □ *We kept the plan under wraps until after the election.* □ *The automobile company kept the new model under wraps until most of the old models had been sold.*

keep the home fires burning   mantener los asuntos de casa o algún otro sitio central en marcha. (Es cliché.) □ *My uncle kept the home fires burning when my sister and I went to school.* □ *The manager stays at the office and keeps the home fires burning while I'm out selling our products.*

keep the wolf from the door   subsistir al nivel mínimo; evitar que alguien muera de hambre o se congele. (Es cliché.) □ *I don't make a lot of money, just enough to keep the wolf from the door.* □ *We have a small amount of money saved, hardly enough to keep the wolf from the door.*

keep up (with the Joneses)   trabajar muy duro para tener el mismo nivel económico que tienen los amigos y vecinos de uno. □ *Mr. and Mrs. Brown bought a new car simply to keep up with the Joneses.* □ *Keeping up with the Joneses can take all your money.*

keep up (with the times)   seguir la moda [la ropa que lleva uno]; seguir las noticias; estar contemporáneo o moderno. □ *I try to keep up with the times. I want to know what's going on.* □ *I bought a whole new wardrobe because I want to keep up with the times.* □ *Sally learns all the new dances. She likes to keep up.*

kick up a fuss AND **kick up a row; kick up a storm**   hacerse pesado; portarse mal y molestar alguien. (*Row* rima con *cow*. Observe las variaciones en los ejemplos.) □ *The customer kicked up such a fuss about the food that the manager came to apologize.* □ *I kicked up such a row that they kicked me out.*

kick up a row   Véase la entrada previa.

kick up a storm   Véase en *kick up a fuss.*

kick up one's heels   estar retozón; estar animado y divertido. □ *I like to go to an old-fashioned square dance and really kick up my heels.* □ *For an old man, your uncle is really kicking up his heels.*

kill the fatted calf   preparar un banquete lujoso (en honor de alguien). (Referente al cuento bíblico en que el hijo pródigo vuelve a la familia.) □ *When Bob got back from college, his parents killed the fatted calf and threw a great party.* □ *Sorry this meal isn't much, John. We didn't have time to kill the fatted calf.*

kill the goose that laid the golden egg   un refrán que tiene que ver con la destrucción de la fuente de la buena suerte de alguien. (Basado en una fábula antigua.) □ *If you fire your best office* *worker, you'll be killing the goose that laid the golden egg.* □ *He sold his computer, which was like killing the goose that laid the golden egg.*

kill time   gastar tiempo. □ *Stop killing time. Get to work!* □ *We went over to the record shop just to kill time.*

kill two birds with one stone   resolver dos problemas con una solución.) (Es cliché.) → **matar dos pájaros de un tiro.** □ *John learned the words to his part in the play while peeling potatoes. He was killing two birds with one stone.* □ *I have to cash a check and make a payment on my bank loan. I'll kill two birds with one stone by doing them both in one trip to the bank.*

kiss and make up   perdonar (a alguien) y hacerse amigos otra vez. (También se usa literalmente.) □ *They were very angry, but in the end they kissed and made up.* □ *I'm sorry. Let's kiss and make up.*

kiss of death   una cosa que pasa que pone fin a alguien o algo. □ *The mayor's veto was the kiss of death for the new law.* □ *Fainting on stage was the kiss of death for my acting career.*

kiss something good-bye   prever o experimentar la pérdida de algo. (No se usa literalmente.) □ *If you leave your camera on a park bench, you can kiss it good-bye.* □ *You kissed your wallet good-bye when you left it in the store.*

knit one's brow   fruncir la frente; fruncir el ceño. □ *The woman knit her brow and asked us what we wanted from her.* □ *While he read his book, John knit his brow occasionally. He must not have agreed with what he was reading.*

knock on wood   una frase que borra la mala suerte, se dice. (Es igual a la frase británica "touch wood.") □ *My stereo has never given me any trouble—knock on wood.* □ *We plan to be in Florida by tomorrow evening—knock on wood.*

knock someone for a loop   Véase en *throw someone for a loop.*

know all the tricks of the trade tener las habilidades y los conocimientos necesarios para hacer algo. (También se usa sin *all*.) □ *Tom can repair car engines. He knows the tricks of the trade.* □ *If I knew all the tricks of the trade, I could be a better plumber.*

know enough to come in out of the rain, not Véase *not know enough to come in out of the rain*.

know, in the Véase *in the know*.

know one's ABCs saber el alfabeto; saber lo básico de algo. □ *Bill can't do it. He doesn't even know his ABCs.* □ *You can't expect to write novels when you don't even know your ABCs.*

know someone by sight saber el nombre y reconocer la cara de alguien. □ *I've never met the man, but I know him by sight.* □ BOB: *Have you ever met Mary?* JANE: *No, but I know her by sight.*

know someone from Adam, not Véase *not know someone from Adam*.

know someone or something like a book Véase en *know someone or something like the palm of one's hand*.

know someone or something like the back of one's hand Véase la entrada siguiente.

know someone or something like the palm of one's hand AND **know someone or something like the back of one's hand; know someone or something like a book** conocer a alguien o algo muy bien. □ *Of course I know John. I know him like the back of my hand.* □ *I know him like a book.*

know something from memory saber algo de memoria, así que uno no tiene que consultar una copia escrita; saber algo bien de memoria a causa de verlo mucho. □ *Mary didn't need the script because she knew the play from memory.* □ *The conductor went through the entire concert without music. He knew it from memory.*

know something in one's bones Véase en *feel something in one's bones*.

know something inside out   saber algo en detalle. □ *I know my geometry inside out.* □ *I studied and studied for my driver's test until I knew the rules inside out.*

know the ropes   saber hacer algo. □ *I can't do the job because I don't know the ropes.* □ *Ask Sally to do it. She knows the ropes.* ALSO: **show someone the ropes**   explicar o mostrar como se hace algo. □ *Since this was my first day on the job, the manager spent a lot of time showing me the ropes.*

know the score AND **know what's what**   saber los hechos; conocer la vida y sus dificultades. (También se usa literalmente.) □ *Bob is so naive. He sure doesn't know the score.* □ *I know what you're trying to do. Oh, yes, I know what's what.*

know what's what   Véase la entrada previa.

know which side one's bread is buttered on   saber lo que conviene a uno. (Es cliché.) □ *He'll do it if his boss tells him to. He knows which side his bread is buttered on.* □ *Since John knows which side his bread is buttered on, he'll be there on time.*

L

land-office business, do a Véase *do a land-office business.*

lap of luxury, in the Véase *in the lap of luxury.*

last but not least el último en una serie pero no en importancia. (Se usa mucho este cliché. Muchas veces se dice en las presentaciones.) □ *The speaker said, "And now, last but not least, I'd like to present Bill Smith, who will give us some final words." □ And last but not least, here is the loser of the race.*

last legs, on someone's or something's Véase *on someone's or something's last legs.*

last minute, at the Véase *at the last minute.*

laughing matter, no Véase *no laughing matter.*

laugh out of the other side of one's mouth cambiar rápidamente de la felicidad a la tristeza. (Es cliché.) → **quitarse las ganas de reírse.** □ *Now that you know the truth, you'll laugh out of the other side of your mouth. □ He was so proud that he won the election. He's laughing out of the other side of his mouth since they recounted the ballots and found out that he lost.*

laugh up one's sleeve reírse en secreto; reírse sin hacer ruido. □ *Jane looked very serious, but I knew she was laughing up her sleeve. □ I told Sally that her dress was darling, but I was laughing up my sleeve because her dress was too small.*

law unto oneself uno que decide en sus propias leyes o reglas; uno que decide en sus propios valores. → **hacer lo que le da la gana.** □ *You can't get Bill to follow the rules. He's a law unto himself. □ Jane is a law unto herself. She's totally unwilling to cooperate.*

lay a finger on someone or something   tocar a alguien o algo, aún ligeramente, con el dedo. (Normalmente se usa en el sentido negativo.) → **ponerle a alguien la mano encima.** ☐ *Don't you dare lay a finger on my pencil. Go get your own!* ☐ *If you lay a finger on me, I'll scream.*

lay an egg   hacer una interpretación o representación mala de algo. (Referente a las obras teatrales. También se usa literalmente, pero sólo con los pájaros.) → **meter la pata.** ☐ *The cast of the play really laid an egg last night.* ☐ *I hope I don't lay an egg when it's my turn to sing.*

lay down the law   **1.** plantear las reglas (de algo) firmemente. (Es cliché.) → **dar órdenes.** ☐ *Before the meeting, the boss laid down the law. We all knew exactly what to do.* ☐ *The way she laid down the law means that I'll remember her rules.* **2.** regañar a alguien por el mal comportamiento. ☐ *When the teacher caught us, he really laid down the law.* ☐ *Poor Bob. He really got it when his mother laid down the law.*

lay it on thick AND **pour it on thick; spread it on thick**   exagerar las alabanzas, las excusas, o la culpa. ☐ *Sally was laying it on thick when she said that Tom was the best singer she had ever heard.* ☐ *After Bob finished making his excuses, Sally said that he was pouring it on thick.* ☐ *Bob always spreads it on thick.*

lay one's cards on the table   Véase en *put one's cards on the table.*

lay something on the line   Véase en *put something on the line.*

lay something to waste AND **lay waste to something**   destruir o arrasar algo (literalmente o figuradamente). ☐ *The invaders laid the village to waste.* ☐ *The kids came in and laid waste to my clean house.*

lay waste to something   Véase la entrada previa.

lead a dog's life AND **live a dog's life**   llevar una vida miserable. → **tener una vida de perros.** ☐ *Poor Jane really leads a dog's life.* ☐ *I've been working so hard. I'm tired of living a dog's life.*

lead someone down the garden path   engañar a alguien. (Es cliché.) □ *Now, be honest with me. Don't lead me down the garden path.* □ *That cheater really led her down the garden path.*

lead someone on a merry chase   hacer que alguien participe en una caza sin propósito [de algo]. □ *What a waste of time. You really led me on a merry chase.* □ *Jane led Bill on a merry chase trying to find an antique lamp.*

lead the life of Riley   vivir en lujo. (No se sabe quién es Riley.) → **darse la gran vida; vivir a cuerpo de rey.** □ *If I had a million dollars, I could live the life of Riley.* □ *The treasurer took our money to Mexico, where he lived the life of Riley until the police caught him.*

leaps and bounds, by   Véase *by leaps and bounds.*

learn something from the bottom up   aprender algo a fondo, del principio; aprender todos los aspectos de algo. □ *I learned my business from the bottom up.* □ *I started out sweeping the floors and learned everything from the bottom up.*

leave a bad taste in someone's mouth   dejar [algo o alguien] una memoria mala o sentimiento malo con alguien. (También se usa literalmente.) → **dejarle a alguien mal sabor de boca.** □ *The whole business about the missing money left a bad taste in his mouth.* □ *It was a very nice party, but something about it left a bad taste in my mouth.* □ *I'm sorry that Bill was there. He always leaves a bad taste in my mouth.*

leave a sinking ship   Véase en *desert a sinking ship.*

leave no stone unturned   buscar algo en todos los sitios posibles. (Es cliché. Como si alguien encontrara algo debajo de una piedra.) → **remover Roma con Santiago.** □ *Don't worry. We'll find your stolen car. We'll leave no stone unturned.* □ *In searching for a nice place to live, we left no stone unturned.*

leave one to one's fate   dejar a uno a su destino, posiblemente a la muerte u otro suceso malo. □ *We couldn't rescue the miners, and we were forced to leave them to their fate.* □ *Please don't try to help. Just go away and leave me to my fate.*

leave someone for dead   abandonar a alguien porque se cree que está muerto. (Aunque la persona abandonada puede estar viva.) □ *He looked so bad that they almost left him for dead.* □ *As the soldiers turned—leaving the enemy captain for dead—the captain fired at them.*

leave someone high and dry   **1.** dejar a alguien sin apoyo ni ayuda; dejar indefenso a alguien. (Referente a un barco varado en la tierra o un arrecife.) → **dejar a alguien en la estacada; dejar a alguien tirado.** □ *All my workers quit and left me high and dry.* □ *All the children ran away and left Billy high and dry to take the blame for the broken window.* **2.** dejar a alguien sin ningún dinero. □ *Mrs. Franklin took all the money out of the bank and left Mr. Franklin high and dry.* □ *Paying the bills always leaves me high and dry.*

leave someone holding the bag   causar que alguien tenga que hacerse totalmente responsable de algo; causar que alguien parezca totalmente culpable. □ *They all ran off and left me holding the bag. It wasn't even my fault.* □ *It was the mayor's fault, but he wasn't left holding the bag.*

leave someone in peace   dejar de molestar a alguien. → **dejar a alguien en paz.** □ *Please go—leave me in peace.* □ *Can't you see that you're upsetting her? Leave her in peace.*

leave someone in the lurch   causar que alguien tenga que esperar o anticipar las acciones de uno. → **dejar a alguien en la estacada; dejar a alguien tirado.** □ *Where were you, John? You really left me in the lurch.* □ *I didn't mean to leave you in the lurch. I thought we had canceled our meeting.*

leave someone or something hanging in midair   dejar de trabajar con alguien o algo; dejar algo sin terminarlo. (También se usa literalmente.) □ *She left her sentence hanging in midair.* □ *She left us hanging in midair when she paused.* □ *Tell me the rest of the story. Don't leave me hanging in midair.* □ *Don't leave the story hanging in midair.* ALSO: **keep someone or something hanging in midair**   dejar de hacer algo con alguien; dejar de hacer algún proyecto que todavía requiere más trabajo. □ *Please don't keep us hanging in midair.*

left field, out in Véase *out in left field.*

leg to stand on, not have a Véase *not have a leg to stand on.*

lend an ear (to someone) escuchar a alguien; prestarle atención a alguien. □ *Lend an ear to John. Hear what he has to say.* □ *I'd be delighted to lend an ear. I find great wisdom in everything John has to say.*

lend oneself or itself to something ser [alguien] capaz de adaptarse; tener [algo] muchos usos; ser útil [alguien o algo] para algo. □ *This room doesn't lend itself to bright colors.* □ *John doesn't lend himself to casual conversation.*

less than no time, in Véase *in less than no time.*

Let bygones be bygones. un refrán significando que uno debe olvidarse de los problemas del pasado. (Es cliché.) → **El pasado, pasado está.** □ *Okay, Sally, let bygones be bygones. Let's forgive and forget.* □ *Jane was unwilling to let bygones be bygones. She still won't speak to me.*

let (the) grass grow under one's feet hacer nada; quedarse levantado de pie sin moverse. (Es cliché.) → **quedarse dormido.** □ *Mary doesn't let the grass grow under her feet. She's always busy.* □ *Bob is too lazy. He's letting grass grow under his feet.*

let off steam AND **blow off steam** soltar energía o ira de sobra. (También se usa literalmente.) → **dar rienda suelta a la indignación.** □ *Whenever John gets a little angry, he blows off steam.* □ *Don't worry about John. He's just letting off steam.*

let one's hair down AND **let down one's hair** ponerse más íntimo y empezar a hablar con franqueza. □ *Come on, Jane, let your hair down and tell me all about it.* □ *I have a problem. Do you mind if I let down my hair?*

Let sleeping dogs lie. un refrán significando que uno no debe buscar problemas, sino dejar las cosas como son. (Es cliché.) → **mejor no resolver el asunto; mejor es no menear.** □ *Don't mention that problem with Tom again. It's almost forgotten. Let* *sleeping dogs lie.* □ *You'll never be able to reform Bill. Leave him alone. Let sleeping dogs lie.*

let someone off (the hook)   liberar a alguien de alguna responsabilidad. □ *Please let me off the hook for Saturday. I have other plans.* □ *Okay, I'll let you off.*

let something slide   dejar de hacer algo; no cumplir con algo. → **dejar que las cosas se vengan abajo.** □ *John let his lessons slide.* □ *Jane doesn't let her work slide.*

let something slide by   Véase la entrada siguiente.

let something slip by AND **let something slide by**   1. olvidarse de o faltar a una fecha o cita importante. □ *I'm sorry I just let your birthday slip by.* □ *I let it slide by accidentally.* 2. malgastar algún período de tiempo. □ *You wasted the whole day by letting it slip by.* □ *We were having fun, and we let the time slide by.*

let the cat out of the bag AND **spill the beans**   revelar un secreto o una sorpresa sin querer hacerlo. (Las dos frases son clichés.) → **descubrir el pastel; levantar la liebre; levantar la perdiz.** □ *When Bill glanced at the door, he let the cat out of the bag. We knew then that he was expecting someone to arrive.* □ *We are planning a surprise party for Jane. Don't let the cat out of the bag.* □ *It's a secret. Try not to spill the beans.*

let the chance slip by   perder la oportunidad de hacer (algo). □ *When I was younger, I wanted to become a doctor, but I let the chance slip by.* □ *Don't let the chance slip by. Do it now!*

level, on the   Véase *on the level.*

lie through one's teeth   mentir con audacidad pero sin remordimiento. (Es cliché.) → **mentir descaradamente; mentir con toda la barba; mentir con todos los dientes.** □ *I knew she was lying through her teeth, but I didn't want to say so just then.* □ *I'm not lying through my teeth! I never do!*

life of the party   una persona muy animada que hace que una fiesta sea más divertida y emocionante. → **el alma de la fiesta.** □ *Bill is always the life of the party. Be sure to invite him.* □ *Bob isn't exactly the life of the party, but he's polite.*

light as a feather, (as)   Véase *(as) light as a feather.*

light, out like a   Véase *out like a light.*

like a bat out of hell   con mucha velocidad y mucho esfuerzo. (Es cliché. Tenga cuidado con la palabra *hell.*) → **como alma que lleva el diablo.** □ *Did you see her leave? She left like a bat out of hell.* □ *The car sped down the street like a bat out of hell.*

like a bolt out of the blue   de repente y sin aviso. (Es cliché. Referente al relámpago, que parece salir del cielo [azul].) □ *The news came to us like a bolt out of the blue.* □ *Like a bolt out of the blue, the boss came and fired us all.*

like a bump on a log   insensible; inmóvil. (Es cliché.) □ *I spoke to him, but he just sat there like a bump on a log.* □ *Don't stand there like a bump on a log. Give me a hand!*

like a fish out of water   desgarbado; en un ambiente ajeno a alguien o a que no está acostumbrado alguien. (Es cliché.) → **como gallina en corral ajeno; como sapo de otro pozo.** □ *At a formal dance, John is like a fish out of water.* □ *Mary was like a fish out of water at the bowling tournament.*

like a sitting duck AND **like sitting ducks**   desprevenido; confiado; inconsciente. (Es cliché. La segunda frase es la forma plural. Referente a los patos que están flotando en el agua en vez de volar por el aire.) □ *He was waiting there like a sitting duck— a perfect target for a mugger.* □ *The soldiers were standing at the top of the hill like sitting ducks. It's a wonder they weren't all killed.*

like a three-ring circus   caótico; emocionante y ocupado. (Es cliché.) □ *Our household is like a three-ring circus on Monday mornings.* □ *This meeting is like a three-ring circus. Quiet down and listen!*

like looking for a needle in a haystack   hacer una búsqueda inútil. (Es cliché.) → **como buscar una aguja en un pajar.** □ *Trying to find a white dog in the snow is like looking for a needle in a haystack.* □ *I tried to find my lost contact lens on the beach, but it was like looking for a needle in a haystack.*

likely as not, (as)   Véase *(as) likely as not.*

like water off a duck's back   fácilmente; sin mucho efecto. (Es cliché.) □ *Insults rolled off John like water off a duck's back.* □ *The bullets had no effect on the steel door. They fell away like water off a duck's back.*

limelight, in the   Véase *in the limelight.*

limit, go the   Véase *go the limit.*

line of duty, in the   Véase *in the line of duty.*

little bird told me, a   Véase *a little bird told me.*

little by little   lentamente; poco a poco. □ *Little by little, he began to understand what we were talking about.* □ *The snail crossed the stone little by little.*

little knowledge is a dangerous thing, A.   Véase *A little knowledge is a dangerous thing.*

live a dog's life   Véase en *lead a dog's life.*

live and let live   no entrometerse en los asuntos o preferencias de otras personas. (Es cliché.) □ *I don't care what they do! Live and let live, I always say.* □ *Your parents are strict. Mine just live and let live.*

live beyond one's means   gastar más dinero que tiene uno. → **llevar un tren de vida que no se puede costear; llevar un tren de vida que los ingresos no le permiten a uno.** □ *The Browns are deeply in debt because they are living beyond their means.* □ *I keep a budget so that I don't live beyond my means.*

live by one's wits   sobrevivir o tener éxito al ser astuto. → **vivir uno de su ingenio.** □ *When you're in the kind of business I'm in, you have to live by your wits.* □ *John was orphaned at the age of ten and grew up living by his wits.*

live from hand to mouth   vivir sin mucha comida; vivir en circunstancias pobres. → **vivir al día.** □ *When both my parents were out of work, we lived from hand to mouth.* □ *We lived from hand to mouth during the war. Things were very difficult.*

live in an ivory tower   no tener experiencia con las realidades de la vida. (Se puede usar varias expresiones que signifcan *dwell* o *spend time,* como se ve en los ejemplos. Muchas veces se dice que los académicos viven así.) □ *If you didn't spend so much time in your ivory tower, you'd know what people really think!* □ *Many professors are said to live in ivory towers. They don't know what the real world is like.*

live off the fat of the land   cultivar la tierra para obtener la comida; vivir de comida almacenada o abundante. (Es cliché.) □ *If I had a million dollars, I'd invest it and live off the fat of the land.* □ *I'll be happy to retire soon and live off the fat of the land.* □ *Many farmers live off the fat of the land.*

live out of a suitcase   vivir brevemente en algún sitio sin deshacer la maleta. □ *I hate living out of a suitcase. For my next vacation, I want to go to just one place and stay there the whole time.* □ *We were living out of suitcases in a motel while they repaired the damage the fire caused to our house.*

live within one's means   no gastar más dinero que tiene uno. □ *We have to struggle to live within our means, but we manage.* □ *John is unable to live within his means.*

lock horns (with someone)   tener una discusión con alguien. (Como los toros o los ciervos cuando se pelean.) □ *Let's settle this peacefully. I don't want to lock horns with the boss.* □ *The boss doesn't want to lock horns either.*

lock, stock, and barrel   todo. □ *We had to move everything out of the house—lock, stock, and barrel.* □ *We lost everything—lock, stock, and barrel—in the fire.*

loggerheads, at   Véase *at loggerheads.*

long for this world, not   Véase *not long for this world.*

long haul, over the   Véase *over the long haul.*

long run, in the   Véase *in the long run.*

Long time no see.   no haber visto a alguien desde hace mucho tiempo. □ *Hello, John. Long time no see.* □ *When John and Mary met on the street, they both said, "Long time no see."*

look as if butter wouldn't melt in one's mouth   parecer frío e insensible (a pesar de información al contrario). □ *Sally looks as if butter wouldn't melt in her mouth. She can be so cruel.* □ *What a sour face. He looks as if butter wouldn't melt in his mouth.*

look daggers at someone   darle una mirada mezquina a alguien. (Como si la mirada disparara dagas apuntadas a alguien.) □ *Tom must have been mad at Ann from the way he was looking daggers at her.* □ *Don't you dare look daggers at me. Don't even look cross-eyed at me!*

looking for a needle in a haystack, like   Véase *like looking for a needle in a haystack.*

look like a million dollars   estar muy guapo. (Es cliché.) □ *Oh, Sally, you look like a million dollars.* □ *Your new hairdo looks like a million dollars.*

look like the cat that swallowed the canary   parecer como si uno hubiera tenido mucho éxito. (Es cliché. Los gatos a veces tienen una cara de culpabilidad cuando hacen cosas malas.) □ *After the meeting John looked like the cat that swallowed the canary. I knew he must have been a success.* □ *What happened? You look like the cat that swallowed the canary.*

look the other way　no hacer caso de algo a propósito. (También se usa literalmente.) □ *John could have prevented the problem, but he looked the other way.* □ *By looking the other way, he actually made the problem worse.*

loose ends, at　Véase *at loose ends.*

lord it over someone　dominar a alguien; dirigir y controlar a alguien. □ *Mr. Smith seems to lord it over his wife.* □ *The boss lords it over everyone in the office.*

lose face　perder prestigio; perder respeto. □ *John is more afraid of losing face than losing money.* □ *Things will go better if you can explain to him where he was wrong without making him lose face.*

lose heart　perder el valor y la confianza. □ *Now, don't lose heart. Keep trying.* □ *What a disappointment! It's enough to make one lose heart.*

lose one's grip　**1.** perder el agarro (de algo). □ *I'm holding on to the rope as tightly as I can. I hope I don't lose my grip.* □ *This hammer is slippery. Try not to lose your grip.* **2.** perder control (de algo). □ *I can't seem to run things the way I used to. I'm losing my grip.* □ *They replaced the board of directors because it was losing its grip.*

lose one's temper　ponerse enfadado. □ *Please don't lose your temper. It's not good for you.* □ *I'm sorry that I lost my temper.*

lose one's train of thought　olvidarse de lo que estaba hablando o pensando uno. □ *Excuse me, I lost my train of thought. What was I talking about?* □ *You made the speaker lose her train of thought.*

lost in thought　preocupado con los pensamientos. □ *I'm sorry, I didn't hear what you said. I was lost in thought.* □ *Bill—lost in thought as always—went into the wrong room.*

lot going (for one), have a　Véase *have a lot going (for one).*

love at first sight　el amor que empieza cuando dos personas se ven por primera vez. (Es cliché.) → **amor a primera vista; un**

flechazo. □ *Bill was standing at the door when Ann opened it. It was love at first sight.* □ *It was love at first sight when they met, but it didn't last long.*

lovely weather for ducks   tiempo muy lluvioso. (Es cliché.) □ BOB: *Not very nice out today, is it?* BILL: *It's lovely weather for ducks.* □ *I don't like this weather, but it's lovely weather for ducks.*

low boiling point, have a   Véase *have a low boiling point.*

lower one's sights   fijar en metas menos difíciles. □ *Even though you get frustrated, don't lower your sights.* □ *I shouldn't lower my sights. If I work hard, I can do what I want.*

lower one's voice   hablar en voz más baja. □ *Please lower your voice, or you'll disturb the people who are working.* □ *He wouldn't lower his voice, so everyone heard what he said.*

lower the boom on someone   regañar o castigar a alguien severamente; tomar medidas severas contra alguien. (Originalmente una frase náutica.) □ *If Bob won't behave better, I'll have to lower the boom on him.* □ *The teacher lowered the boom on the whole class for misbehaving.*

low man on the totem pole   la persona de menor importancia. (Véase también *high man on the totem pole.*) □ *I was the last to find out because I'm low man on the totem pole.* □ *I can't be of any help. I'm low man on the totem pole.*

luck, out of   Véase *out of luck.*

luck would have it, as   Véase *as luck would have it.*

lunch, out to   Véase *out to lunch.*

M

mad as a hatter, (as) Véase *(as) mad as a hatter.*

mad as a hornet, (as) Véase *(as) mad as a hornet.*

mad as a March hare, (as) Véase *(as) mad as a March hare.*

mad as a wet hen, (as) Véase *(as) mad as a wet hen.*

mad rush, in a Véase *in a mad rush.*

make a beeline for someone or something ir o caminar directamente hacia alguien o algo. (También se usa literalmente para describir las abejas.) □ *Billy came into the kitchen and made a beeline for the cookies.* □ *After the game, we all made a beeline for John, who was serving cold drinks.*

make a clean breast of something confesar algo. □ *You'll feel better if you make a clean breast of it. Now tell us what happened.* □ *I was forced to make a clean breast of the whole affair.*

make a go of it hacer que alguna situación salga bien al fin. □ *It's a tough situation, but Ann is trying to make a go of it.* □ *We don't like living here, but we have to make a go of it.*

make a great show of something hacer que algo sea obvio; hacer algo de una manera ostentosa. □ *Ann made a great show of wiping up the drink that John spilled.* □ *Jane displayed her irritation at our late arrival by making a great show of serving the cold dinner.*

make a hit (with someone or something) agradar a alguien o algo. □ *The singer made a hit with the audience.* □ *She was afraid she wouldn't make a hit.* □ *John made a hit with my parents last evening.*

make a long story short   terminar el cuento. (Es cliché. Se usa para introducir un resumen de un cuento o un chiste.) □ *And—to make a long story short—I never got back the money that I lent him.* □ *If I can make a long story short, let me say that everything worked out fine.*

make a mountain out of a molehill   dar importancia a un asunto insignificante; exagerar la importancia de algo. (Es cliché.) □ *Come on, don't make a mountain out of a molehill. It's not that important.* □ *Mary is always making mountains out of molehills.*

make a nuisance of oneself   ser una molestia constante. □ *I'm sorry to make a nuisance of myself, but I do need an answer to my question.* □ *Stop making a nuisance of yourself and wait your turn.*

make a run for it   correr con rapidez para salir de o ir a algún lugar. □ *When the guard wasn't looking, the prisoner made a run for it.* □ *In the baseball game, the player on first base made a run for it, but he didn't make it to second base.*

make a silk purse out of a sow's ear   crear algo de valor de algo sin valor. (Es cliché. Muchas veces se usa en el sentido negativo.) □ *Don't bother trying to fix up this old bicycle. You can't make a silk purse out of a sow's ear.* □ *My mother made a lovely jacket out of an old coat. She succeeded in making a silk purse out of a sow's ear.*

make cracks (about someone or something)   ridiculizar a alguien o algo o hacer chistes sobre alguien o algo. □ *Please stop making cracks about my haircut. It's the new style.* □ *Some people can't help making cracks. They are just rude.*

make fast work of someone or something   Véase en *make short work of someone or something.*

make free with someone or something   Véase en *take liberties with someone or something.*

make good money   ganar mucho dinero. (*good* significa "abundante" en esta frase.) □ *Ann makes good money at her job.* □ *I don't know what she does, but she makes good money.*

Make hay while the sun is shining.   un refrán signficando que uno debe sacar el mayor partido de las épocas buenas de la vida. □ *There are lots of people here now. You should try to sell them soda pop. Make hay while the sun is shining.* □ *Go to school and get a good education while you're young. Make hay while the sun is shining.*

make life miserable for someone   hacer triste a alguien durante mucho tiempo. □ *My shoes are tight, and they are making life miserable for me.* □ *Jane's boss is making life miserable for her.*

make light of something   tratar algo como si fuera humorístico o sin importancia. □ *I wish you wouldn't make light of his problems. They're quite serious.* □ *I make light of my problems, and that makes me feel better.*

make oneself at home   ponerse cómodo, como si uno estuviera en su casa. □ *Please come in and make yourself at home.* □ *I'm glad you're here. During your visit, just make yourself at home.*

make short work of someone or something AND **make fast work of someone or something**   terminar con alguien o algo rápidamente. □ *I made short work of Tom so I could leave the office to play golf.* □ *Billy made fast work of his dinner so he could go out and play.*

make someone or something tick   causar que alguien o algo funcione o trabaje. (Normalmente dicha con *what*. Referente originalmente al reloj.) □ *I don't know what makes it tick.* □ *What makes John tick? I just don't understand him.* □ *I took apart the radio to find out what made it tick.*

make someone's blood boil   hacer que alguien se enfade. □ *It just makes my blood boil to think of the amount of food that gets wasted around here.* □ *Whenever I think of that dishonest mess, it makes my blood boil.*

make someone's blood run cold   asustar o horrorizar a alguien. □ *The terrible story in the newspaper made my blood run cold.* □ *I could tell you things about prisons that would make your blood run cold.*

make someone's hair stand on end   hacer que alguien esté asustado. □ *The horrible scream made my hair stand on end.* □ *The ghost story made our hair stand on end.*

make someone's head spin   Véase la entrada siguiente.

make someone's head swim AND **make someone's head spin**   **1.** hacer que alguien esté mareado o desorientado. □ *Riding in your car makes my head spin.* □ *Breathing the gas made my head swim.* **2.** confundir o abrumar a alguien. □ *All these numbers make my head swim.* □ *The physics lecture made my head spin.*

make someone's mouth water   hacer que alguien tenga hambre (para comer algo específico); causar salivar [alguien]. (También se usa literalmente.) □ *That beautiful salad makes my mouth water.* □ *Talking about food makes my mouth water.*

make someone the scapegoat for something   hacer responsable (alguien para algo). □ *They made Tom the scapegoat for the whole affair. It wasn't all his fault.* □ *Don't try to make me the scapegoat. I'll tell who really did it.*

make something from scratch   construir, cocinar, o hacer algo empezando con los ingredientes principales. □ *We made the cake from scratch, using no prepared ingredients.* □ *I didn't have a ladder, so I made one from scratch.*

make something up out of whole cloth AND **make up something out of whole cloth**   contar un cuento o una mentira sin incluir ni un hecho verdadero. (Es cliché.) □ *I don't believe you. I think you made that up out of whole cloth.* □ *Ann made up her explanation out of whole cloth. There was not a bit of truth in it.*

make the feathers fly   Véase la entrada siguiente.

make the fur fly AND **make the feathers fly**   provocar una lucha o una discusión. □ *When your mother gets home and sees what you've done, she'll really make the fur fly.* □ *When those two get together, they'll make the feathers fly. They hate each other.*

make the grade   estar satisfactorio; ser lo esperado. □ *I'm sorry, but your work doesn't exactly make the grade.* □ *This meal doesn't just make the grade. It is excellent.*

make up for lost time   hacer mucho; hacer algo muy rápidamente. □ *Because we took so long eating lunch, we have to drive faster to make up for lost time. Otherwise we won't arrive on time.* □ *At the age of sixty, Bill learned to play golf. Now he plays every day. He's making up for lost time.*

march to a different drummer   creer en los principios que son diferentes de los de otras personas. (Es cliché.) → **ir contra la corriente.** □ *John is marching to a different drummer, and he doesn't come to our parties anymore.* □ *Since Sally started marching to a different drummer, she has had a lot of great new ideas.*

market, on the   Véase *on the market.*

means, beyond one's   Véase *beyond one's means.*

meet one's end   morir. □ *The dog met his end under the wheels of a car.* □ *I don't intend to meet my end until I'm 100 years old.*

meet one's match   conocer a una persona muy parecida [en personalidad] a sí mismo. □ *John played tennis with Bill yesterday, and it looks as if John has finally met his match.* □ *Listen to Jane and Mary argue. I always thought that Jane was loud, but she has finally met her match.*

meet someone halfway   ofrecerle un acuerdo a alguien. □ *No, I won't give in, but I'll meet you halfway.* □ *They settled the argument by agreeing to meet each other halfway.*

melt in one's mouth   saber muy bien; estar muy rico y agradable. (Es cliché.) □ *This cake is so good it'll melt in your mouth.* □ *John said that the food didn't exactly melt in his mouth.*

mend (one's) fences   restablecer buenas relaciones con alguien. (También se usa literalmente.) □ *I think I had better get home and mend my fences. I had an argument with my daughter this morning.* □ *Sally called up her uncle to apologize and try to mend fences.*

mend, on the   Véase *on the mend*.

mention something in passing   mencionar algo de paso; mencionar algo mientras uno está hablando de otra cosa. □ *He just happened to mention in passing that the mayor had resigned.* □ *John mentioned in passing that he was nearly eighty years old.*

mill, been through the   Véase *been through the mill*.

millstone about one's neck   una carga o una desventaja continua. □ *This huge and expensive house is a millstone about my neck.* □ *Bill's inability to read is a millstone about his neck.*

mind one's own business   sólo prestar atención a las cosas acerca de uno. □ *Leave me alone, Bill. Mind your own business.* □ *I'd be fine if John would mind his own business.*

mind one's p's and q's   tener cuidado con el comportamiento; prestar atención a los detalles de la etiqueta. (De una frase antigua que advertía [a los niños o a los tipógrafos] de la diferencia entre la *p* y la *q*.) □ *When we go to the mayor's reception, please mind your p's and q's.* □ *I always mind my p's and q's when I eat at a restaurant with white tablecloths.*

mind, on one's   Véase *on one's mind*.

mind, out of one's   Véase *out of one's mind*.

mind's eye, in one's   Véase *in one's mind's eye*.

mint condition, in   Véase *in mint condition*.

Missouri, be from   Véase *be from Missouri*.

miss (something) by a mile   no dar en algo [como un blanco o objetivo] por distancia muy larga. (Es cliché.) □ *Ann shot the arrow and missed the target by a mile.* □ *"Good grief, you missed by a mile," shouted Sally.*

miss the point   no comprender la idea, el propósito, o la intención. → **no coger la idea.** □ *I'm afraid you missed the point. Let me explain it again.* □ *You keep explaining, and I keep missing the point.*

mixed feelings (about someone or something), have
Véase *have mixed feelings (about someone or something).*

Money burns a hole in someone's pocket.   un refrán significando que las personas siempre gastan el dinero que tienen. □ *Sally can't seem to save anything. Money burns a hole in her pocket.* □ *If money burns a hole in your pocket, you never have any for emergencies.*

money, in the   Véase *in the money.*

money is no object   el precio de algo no importa. □ *Please show me your finest automobile. Money is no object.* □ *I want the finest earrings you have. Don't worry about how much they cost because money is no object.*

Money is the root of all evil.   un refrán significando que el dinero es la raíz de todos los males. → **El dinero es el origen de todos los males.** □ *Why do you work so hard to make money? It will just cause you trouble. Money is the root of all evil.* □ *Any thief in prison can tell you that money is the root of all evil.*

money talks   el dinero le otorga poder e influencia a alguien para hacer las cosas como quiere. → **poderoso caballero es don Dinero.** □ *Don't worry. I have a way of getting things done. Money talks.* □ *I can't compete against rich old Mrs. Jones. She'll get her way because money talks.*

money to burn, have   Véase *have money to burn.*

mood to do something, in no   Véase *in no mood to do something.*

motions, go through the   Véase *go through the motions.*

mouth, down in the   Véase *down in the mouth.*

move heaven and earth to do something   hacer un esfuerzo fuerte para hacer algo. (Es cliché. No se usa literalmente.) → **remover el cielo y la tierra; remover Roma con Santiago.** □ *"I'll move heaven and earth to be with you, Mary," said Bill.* □ *I had to move heaven and earth to get there on time.*

move, on the   Véase *on the move.*

move up (in the world)   ascendarse y tener éxito. □ *The harder I work, the more I move up in the world.* □ *Keep your eye on John. He's really moving up.*

much ado about nothing   mucha emoción acerca de nada de importancia. (Es cliché. Es el título de una obra de Shakespeare. No se confuda entre *ado* y *adieu.*) → **mucho ruido y pocas nueces.** □ *All the commotion about the new tax law turned out to be much ado about nothing.* □ *Your promises always turn out to be much ado about nothing.*

N

name only, in   Véase *in name only*.

nape of the neck, by the   Véase *by the nape of the neck*.

neck and neck   exactamente iguales o empatados, especialmente en una carrera o concurso. → **a la par.** □ *John and Tom finished the race neck and neck.* □ *Mary and Ann were neck and neck in the spelling contest. Their scores were tied.*

neck (in something), up to one's   Véase *up to one's neck (in something)*.

neither fish nor fowl   ninguna cosa reconocible. (Es cliché.) □ *The car that they drove up in was neither fish nor fowl. It must have been made out of spare parts.* □ *This proposal is neither fish nor fowl. I can't tell what you're proposing.*

neither hide nor hair   ninguna señal o ningún indicio (de alguien o algo). (Es cliché.) → **no verle el pelo a alguien.** □ *We could find neither hide nor hair of him. I don't know where he is.* □ *There has been no one here—neither hide nor hair—for the last three days.*

nerve, of all the   Véase *of all the nerve*.

new lease on life   una actitud reavivada y resucitada hacia la vida; un comienzo nuevo de la vida. (Es cliché.) □ *Getting the job offer was a new lease on life.* □ *When I got out of the hospital, I felt as if I had a new lease on life.*

nick of time, in the   Véase *in the nick of time*.

nip and tuck   casi igual; casi empatado. □ *The horses ran nip and tuck for the first half of the race. Then my horse pulled ahead.* □ *In the football game last Saturday, both teams were nip and tuck throughout the game.*

nip something in the bud   poner fin a algo en una etapa incipiente. (Es cliché. Como si uno estuviera pellizcando el capullo de una planta irritante.) □ *John is getting into bad habits, and it's best to nip them in the bud.* □ *There was trouble in the classroom, but the teacher nipped it in the bud.*

no (ifs, ands, or) buts about it   ninguna discusión, disensión, ni duda acerca de algo. (Es cliché.) □ *I want you there exactly at eight, no ifs, ands, or buts about it.* □ *This is the best television set available for the money, no buts about it.*

no laughing matter   un asunto grave. (Es cliché.) □ *Be serious. This is no laughing matter.* □ *This disease is no laughing matter. It's quite deadly.*

none the worse for wear   no resulta mal a pesar del uso o del esfuerzo. □ *I lent my car to John. When I got it back, it was none the worse for wear.* □ *I had a hard day today, but I'm none the worse for wear.*

nosedive, go into a   Véase *go into a nosedive.*

nose in a book, have one's   Véase *have one's nose in a book.*

no skin off someone's nose   Véase la entrada siguiente.

no skin off someone's teeth AND **no skin off someone's nose**   sin ser una dificultad para alguien; sin ser una preocupación para alguien. (Es cliché.) □ *It's no skin off my nose if she wants to act that way.* □ *She said it was no skin off her teeth if we wanted to sell the house.*

no spring chicken   no ser joven. → **no ser ninguña niña; no ser ninguna nena.** □ *I don't get around very well anymore. I'm no spring chicken, you know.* □ *Even though John is no spring chicken, he still plays tennis twice a week.*

not able to see the forest for the trees permitir que muchos detalles de un problema oscurezcan el problema total. (Es cliché. Muchas veces se usa *can't* en vez de *not able to*.) □ *The solution is obvious. You missed it because you can't see the forest for the trees.* □ *She suddenly realized that she hadn't been able to see the forest for the trees.*

not born yesterday experimentado en algo; entendido de la vida. □ *I know what's going on. I wasn't born yesterday.* □ *Sally knows the score. She wasn't born yesterday.*

not have a leg to stand on no tener ningún apoyo [algún argumento o razón]. □ *You may think you're in the right, but you don't have a leg to stand on.* □ *My lawyer said I didn't have a leg to stand on, so I shouldn't sue the company.*

nothing but skin and bones AND **all skin and bones** muy delgado o fiaco. □ *Bill has lost so much weight. He's nothing but skin and bones.* □ *That old horse is all skin and bones. I won't ride it.*

nothing flat, in Véase *in nothing flat.*

Nothing ventured, nothing gained. un refrán o significando que no se puede tener éxito en algo si no se pone ningún esfuerzo. □ *Come on, John. Give it a try. Nothing ventured, nothing gained.* □ *I felt as if I had to take the chance. Nothing ventured, nothing gained.*

not hold water no tener sentido; ser ilógico. (Referente a las ideas o los argumentos, no a las personas.) □ *Your argument doesn't hold water.* □ *This scheme won't work because it won't hold water.*

not know enough to come in out of the rain ser muy estúpdio. (Es cliché.) □ *Bob is so stupid he doesn't know enough to come in out of the rain.* □ *You can't expect very much from somebody who doesn't know enough to come in out of the rain.*

not know someone from Adam no conocer a alguien. (Es cliché.) □ *I wouldn't recognize John if I saw him. I don't know him from Adam.* □ *What does she look like? I don't know her from Adam.*

not long for this world   ser a punto de morir. (Es cliché.) □ *Our dog is nearly twelve years old and not long for this world.* □ *I'm so tired. I think I'm not long for this world.*

not open one's mouth AND **not utter a word**   no decir nada; no contar nada (a ninguna persona). □ *Don't worry, I'll keep your secret. I won't even open my mouth.* □ *Have no fear. I won't utter a word.* □ *I don't know how they found out. I didn't even open my mouth.*

not set foot somewhere   no ir a ningún sitio. □ *I wouldn't set foot in John's room. I'm very angry with him.* □ *He never set foot here.*

not show one's face   no aparecer (en ningún sitio). □ *After what she said, she had better not show her face around here again.* □ *If I don't say I'm sorry, I'll never be able to show my face again.*

not sleep a wink   no dormir ni un momento. □ *I couldn't sleep a wink last night.* □ *Ann hasn't been able to sleep a wink for a week.*

not someone's cup of tea   no ser algo que prefiere uno. (Es cliché.) □ *Playing cards isn't her cup of tea.* □ *Sorry, that's not my cup of tea.*

not up to scratch AND **not up to snuff**   no aceptable. □ *Sorry, your paper isn't up to scratch. Please do it over again.* □ *The performance was not up to snuff.*

not up to snuff   Véase la entrada previa.

not utter a word   Véase en *not open one's mouth.*

O

odd man out una persona o cosa rara o atípica. □ *I'm odd man out because I'm not wearing a tie.* □ *You had better learn to work a computer unless you want to be odd man out.*

odds to be against one, for the Véase *for the odds to be against one.*

of all the nerve qué escandaloso; cómo se ha atrevido (alguien). (El hablador exclama, diciendo que alguien se está comportando de una manera descarada o grosera.) □ *How dare you talk to me that way! Of all the nerve!* □ *Imagine anyone coming to a formal dance in jeans. Of all the nerve!*

off base irrealizable; inexacto; equivocado. (También se usa literalmente en el béisbol.) □ *I'm afraid you're off base when you state that this problem will take care of itself.* □ *You're way off base!*

off-color 1. no del color que quiere uno. □ *The book cover used to be red, but now it's a little off-color.* □ *The wall was painted off-color. I think it was meant to be orange.* 2. grosero, vulgar, o maleducado. □ *That joke you told was off-color and embarrassed me.* □ *The nightclub act was a bit off-color.*

off duty no estar de turno. □ *I'm sorry, I can't talk to you until I'm off duty.* □ *The police officer couldn't help me because he was off duty.*

off the air no estar emitiendo (un programa de la radio o la televisión). □ *The radio audience won't hear what you say when you're off the air.* □ *When the performers were off the air, the director told them how well they had done.*

159

off the record   en confianza; extraoficialmente. □ *This is off the record, but I disagree with the mayor on this matter.* □ *Although her comments were off the record, the newspaper published them anyway.*

off the top of one's head   [decir algo] rápidamente sin pensarlo. □ *I can't think of the answer off the top of my head.* □ *Jane can tell you the correct amount off the top of her head.*

off to a running start   con un comienzo bueno y rápido, posiblemente con la ventaja. □ *I got off to a running start in math this year.* □ *The horses got off to a running start.*

of the first water   de la mejor calidad. (Esta frase originalmente describía la calidad de una perla.) □ *This is a very fine pearl—a pearl of the first water.* □ *Tom is of the first water—a true gentleman.*

on active duty   luchando en una batalla o dispuesto a luchar en una batalla. (Una frase militar.) □ *The soldier was on active duty for ten months.* □ *That was a long time to be on active duty.*

on all fours   sostenido en las manos y las rodillas. → **a gatas.** □ *I dropped a contact lens and spent an hour on all fours looking for it.* □ *The baby can walk, but is on all fours most of the time anyway.*

on a waiting list   puesto [el nombre de alguien] en una lista de personas que esperan la oportunidad de hacer algo. (Se puede usar *the* en vez de *a.*) □ *I couldn't get a seat on the plane, but I got on a waiting list.* □ *There is no room for you, but we can put your name on the waiting list.*

once in a blue moon   raras veces. (Es cliché.) □ *I seldom go to a movie—maybe once in a blue moon.* □ *I don't go into the city except once in a blue moon.*

on cloud nine   muy contento. □ *When I got my promotion, I was on cloud nine.* □ *When the check came, I was on cloud nine for days.*

on duty   de turno. □ *I can't help you now, but I'll be on duty in about an hour.* □ *Who is on duty here? I need some help.*

on earth AND **in creation; in the world**   ¡Qué increíble!; ¡Qué cosa más increíble! (Normalmente se usa para dar énfasis después de *who, what, when, where, how, which.*) ☐ *What on earth do you mean?* ☐ *How in creation do you expect me to do that?* ☐ *Who in the world do you think you are?* ☐ *When on earth do you expect me to do this?*

one ear and out the other, go in   Véase *go in one ear and out the other.*

one ear and out the other, in   Véase *in one ear and out the other.*

One good turn deserves another.   un refrán significando que se debe pagar una obra buena con otra. ☐ *If he does you a favor, you should do him a favor. One good turn deserves another.* ☐ *Glad to help you out. One good turn deserves another.*

one in a hundred   Véase en *one in a thousand.*

one in a million   Véase la entrada siguiente.

one in a thousand AND **one in a hundred; one in a million**   único; una de muy pocas personas o cosas. ☐ *He's a great guy. He's one in million.* ☐ *Mary's one in a hundred—such a hard worker.*

One man's meat is another man's poison.   un refrán significando que todas las personas no tienen las mismas preferencias. ☐ *John just loves his new fur hat, but I think it is horrible. Oh, well, one man's meat is another man's poison.* ☐ *The neighbors are very fond of their dog even though it's ugly, loud, and smelly. I guess one man's meat is another man's poison.*

One's bark is worse than one's bite.   un refrán significando que uno puede amenzar con hacer algo, pero no va a hacer mucho. ☐ *Don't worry about Bob. He won't hurt you. His bark is worse than his bite.* ☐ *She may scream and yell, but have no fear. Her bark is worse than her bite.*

one's better half el cónyuge de uno. (Normalmente referente a la esposa.) □ *I think we'd like to come for dinner, but I'll have to ask my better half.* □ *I have to go home now to my better half. We are going out tonight.*

one's days are numbered enfrentarse a la muerte o el despido de algún trabajo. (Es cliché.) □ *If I don't get this contract, my days are numbered at this company.* □ *Uncle Tom has a terminal disease. His days are numbered.*

one's desk, away from Véase *away from one's desk.*

one's eyes are bigger than one's stomach poner más comida en el plato que puede comer uno. □ *I can't eat all this. I'm afraid that my eyes were bigger than my stomach.* □ *Try to take less food. Your eyes are bigger than your stomach at every meal.* ALSO: **have eyes bigger than one's stomach** querer comer más comida que podría comer uno. □ *I know I have eyes bigger than my stomach, so I won't take a lot of food.*

one's heart is in one's mouth Véase en *have one's heart in one's mouth.*

one's heart is set on something Véase en *have one's heart set on something.*

one's number is up la hora de la muerte—o de sufrir—ha llegado. □ *John is worried. He thinks his number is up.* □ *When my number is up, I hope it all goes fast.*

one's song and dance about something, go into Véase *go into one's song and dance about something.*

one's tail is between one's legs Véase en *have one's tail between one's legs.*

one's words stick in one's throat Véase en *have one's words stick in one's throat.*

on one's feet **1.** levantado; levantado a pie. □ *Get on your feet. They are playing the national anthem.* □ *I've been on my feet all day, and they hurt.* **2.** sano, especialmente después de una enfermedad.

□ *I hope to be back on my feet next week.* □ *I can help out as soon as I'm back on my feet.*

on one's honor como juramento solemne de uno; compromiso sincero. □ *On my honor, I'll be there on time.* □ *He promised on his honor that he'd pay me back next week.*

on one's mind en los pensamientos; actualmente en los pensamientos. □ *You've been on my mind all day.* □ *Do you have something on your mind? You look so serious.*

on one's toes atento; despierto. □ *You have to be on your toes if you want to be in this business.* □ *My boss keeps me on my toes.*

on pins and needles preocupado; en vilo. (Es cliché.) □ *I've been on pins and needles all day, waiting for you to call with the news.* □ *We were on pins and needles until we heard that your plane landed safely.*

on second thought después de pensar más en algo; después de reconsiderar algo. □ *On second thought, maybe you should sell your house and move into an apartment.* □ *On second thought, let's not go to a movie.*

on someone's doorstep Véase en *at someone's doorstep.*

on someone's head en sí mismo. (Normalmente se usa con *blame.* Se puede usar *upon* en vez de *on.*) □ *All the blame fell on their heads.* □ *I don't think that all the criticism should be on my head.*

on someone's or something's last legs algo casi terminado. □ *This building is on its last legs. It should be torn down.* □ *I feel as if I'm on my last legs. I'm really tired.*

on someone's say-so con la autoridad de alguien; con el permiso de alguien. □ *I can't do it on your say-so. I'll have to get a written request.* □ BILL: *I canceled the contract with the A.B.C. Company.* BOB: *On whose say-so?*

on someone's shoulders en sí mismo. (Normalmente se usa con *responsibility.* Se puede usar *upon* en vez de *on.*) □ *Why should* *all the responsibility fall on my shoulders?* □ *She carries a tremendous amount of responsibility on her shoulders.*

on target   según el plan; según lo previsto. □ *Your estimate of the cost was right on target.* □ *My prediction was not on target.*

on the air   en el aire (un programa de la radio o de la televisión). □ *The radio station came back on the air shortly after the storm.* □ *We were on the air for two hours.*

on the average   normalmente. □ *On the average, you can expect about a 10 percent failure.* □ *This report looks okay, on the average.*

on the bench   **1.** estar dirigiendo una sesión del tribunal. (Se dice de un juez.) □ *I have to go to court tomorrow. Who's on the bench?* □ *It doesn't matter who's on the bench. You'll get a fair hearing.* **2.** estar sentado, esperando la oportunidad de entrar en algún juego. (Referente a los deportes, como el baloncesto, el fútbol, el fútbol americano, etc.) □ *Bill is on the bench now. I hope he gets to play.* □ *John played during the first quarter, but now he's on the bench.*

on the block   **1.** en la cuadra o la manzana de una ciudad. □ *John is the biggest kid on the block.* □ *We had a party on the block last weekend.* **2.** puesto a la venta en una subasta; sacado a subasta. □ *We couldn't afford to keep up the house, so it was put on the block to pay the taxes.* □ *That's the finest painting I've ever seen on the block.*

on the button   exactamente correcto; en el lugar adecuado; en el momento perfecto. □ *That's it! You're right on the button.* □ *He got here at one o'clock on the button.*

on the contrary   por otro lado. □ *I'm not ill. On the contrary, I'm very healthy.* □ *She's not in a bad mood. On the contrary, she's as happy as a lark.*

on the dot   en el momento adecuado. □ *I'll be there at noon on the dot.* □ *I expect to see you here at eight o'clock on the dot.*

on the go ocupado; estar moviéndose y con mucho que hacer. ☐ *I'm usually on the go all day long.* ☐ *I hate being on the go all the time.*

on the heels of something justamente después de algo. ☐ *There was a rainstorm on the heels of the windstorm.* ☐ *The team held a victory celebration on the heels of their winning season.*

on the horizon al punto de pasar. (También se usa literalmente.) ☐ *Do you know what's on the horizon?* ☐ *Who can tell what's on the horizon?*

on the horns of a dilemma indeciso entre dos cosas, personas, etc.; entre dos alternativas. ☐ *Mary found herself on the horns of a dilemma. She didn't know which to choose.* ☐ *I make up my mind easily. I'm not on the horns of a dilemma very often.*

on the hour cada hora; al comenzar la hora. ☐ *I have to take this medicine every hour on the hour.* ☐ *I expect to see you there on the hour, not one minute before and not one minute after.*

on the house una cosa gratis [dada por el comerciante de una tienda]. (También se usa literalmente.) ☐ *"Here," said the waiter, "have a cup of coffee on the house."* ☐ *I went to a restaurant last night. I was the ten thousandth customer, so my dinner was on the house.*

on the level honrado; justo. (También se usa con *strictly.*) ☐ *How can I be sure you're on the level?* ☐ *You can trust Sally. She's on the level.*

on the market puesto a la venta; disponible para la venta. ☐ *I had to put my car on the market.* ☐ *This is the finest home computer on the market.*

on the mend mejorada la salud de uno. ☐ *My cold was terrible, but I'm on the mend now.* ☐ *What you need is some hot chicken soup. Then you'll really be on the mend.*

on the move   con mucha prisa. □ *What a busy day. Things are really on the move at the store.* □ *When all the buffalo were on the move across the plains, it must have been very exciting.*

on the QT   calladamente; en secreto. □ *The company president was making payments to his wife on the QT.* □ *The mayor accepted a bribe on the QT.*

on the spot   1. en el lugar perfecto; en el momento perfecto. □ *It's noon, and I'm glad you're all here on the spot. Now we can begin.* □ *I expect you to be on the spot when and where trouble arises.* **2.** con problemas; en una situación difícil. □ *There is a problem in the department I manage, and I'm really on the spot.* □ *I hate to be on the spot when it's not my fault.*

on the spur of the moment   de repente; espontáneamente. □ *We decided to go on the spur of the moment.* □ *I had to leave town on the spur of the moment.*

on the tip of one's tongue   casi dicho; casi recordado. (Como si una palabra saliera de la punta de la lengua.) → **en la punta de la lengua.** □ *I have his name right on the tip of my tongue. I'll think of it in a second.* □ *John had the answer on the tip of his tongue, but Ann said it first.*

on the wagon   referente a una persona que ha dejado de tomar alcohol. (También se usa literalmente. Referente al carro que llevaba el agua de antaño.) □ *None for me, thanks. I'm on the wagon.* □ *Look at John. I don't think he's on the wagon anymore.*

on the wrong track   por el camino equivocado; [seguir] algunas suposiciones equivocadas. (También se usa literalmente para referirse a los trenes, los perrros de caza, etc.) □ *You'll never get the right answer. You're on the wrong track.* □ *They won't get it figured out because they are on the wrong track.*

on thin ice   en una situación peligrosa. □ *If you try that you'll really be on thin ice. That's too risky.* □ *If you don't want to find yourself on thin ice, you must be sure of your facts.* ALSO: **skate on thin ice**   estar en una situación peligrosa. (También se usa literalmente.) □ *I try to stay well informed so I don't end up skating on thin ice when the teacher asks me a question.*

on tiptoe levantado de puntillas o caminando en los pulpejos de los pies. (Se hace para parecer más alto o para caminar sin hacer ruido.) □ *I had to stand on tiptoe in order to see over the fence.* □ *I came in late and walked on tiptoe so I wouldn't wake anybody up.*

on top victorioso en algo; famoso o conocido por algo. □ *I have to study day and night to keep on top.* □ *Bill is on top in his field.*

on top of the world fenomenal, magnífico, o extático. (Es cliché.) □ *Wow, I feel on top of the world.* □ *Since he got a new job, he's on top of the world.*

on trial sometido al juicio. □ *My sister is on trial today, so I have to go to court.* □ *They placed the suspected thief on trial.*

on vacation de vacaciones. □ *Where are you going on vacation this year?* □ *I'll be away on vacation for three weeks.*

open a can of worms descubrir problemas con algo; crear complicaciones innecesarias. (*Can of worms* significa "lío." También se usa con *open up* y con variantes, por ejemplo, *new, whole, another,* como se ve en los ejemplos.) □ *Now you are opening a whole new can of worms.* □ *How about cleaning up this mess before you open up a new can of worms?*

open one's heart (to someone) revelarle los pensamientos más íntimos a alguien. □ *I always open my heart to my spouse when I have a problem.* □ *It's a good idea to open your heart every now and then.*

open one's mouth, not Véase *not open one's mouth.*

open Pandora's box descubrir muchos problemos no sospechados. (Es cliché.) □ *When I asked Jane about her problems, I didn't know I had opened Pandora's box.* □ *You should be cautious with people who are upset. You don't want to open Pandora's box.*

order, out of Véase *out of order.*

other side of the tracks　el barrio pobre de una ciudad o un pueblo, muchas veces (en los E.E.U.U.) cerca de las vías del tren. (Se usa especialmente con *from the* or *live on the*.) □ *Who cares if she's from the other side of the tracks?* □ *I came from a poor family—we lived on the other side of the tracks.*

ounce of prevention is worth a pound of cure, An.　Véase *An ounce of prevention is worth a pound of cure.*

out and about　capaz de salir de casa; bastante sano para salir de casa. □ *Beth has been ill, but now she's out and about.* □ *As soon as I feel better, I'll be able to get out and about.*

out cold AND **out like a light**　inconsciente. □ *I fell and hit my head. I was out cold for about a minute.* □ *Tom fainted! He's out like a light!*

out in left field　poco convencional; excéntrico. □ *Sally is a lot of fun, but she's sort of out in left field.* □ *What a strange idea. It's really out in left field.*

out like a light　Véase en *out cold.*

out of a clear blue sky AND **out of the blue**　de repente; sin aviso. (Es cliché.) □ *Then, out of a clear blue sky, he told me he was leaving.* □ *Mary appeared on my doorstep out of the blue.*

out of (all) proportion　totalmente desproporcionado; una proporción exagerada en comparación con otra cosa; desequilibrado (figuradamente). □ *This problem has grown out of all proportion.* □ *Yes, this thing is way out of proportion.* ALSO: **blow something out of all proportion**　hacer que algo sea totalmente desproporcionado con respecto a otra cosa. □ *The press has blown this issue out of all proportion.* □ *Let's be reasonable. Don't blow this thing out of proportion.*

out of circulation　**1.** no disponible para el uso o el préstamo. (Normalmente se dice de los libros de biblioteca.) □ *I'm sorry, but the book you want is temporarily out of circulation.* □ *How long will it be out of circulation?* **2.** no salir (socialmente) con otras personas. □ *I don't know what's happening because I've been out of circulation for a while.* □ *My cold has kept me out of circulation for a few weeks.*

out of commission   1. estar fuera de servicio [un buque]. □ *This vessel will remain out of commission for another month.* □ *The ship has been out of commission since repairs began.* 2. no estar funcionando; inoperable, o inutilizable. □ *My watch is out of commission and is running slowly.* □ *I can't run in the marathon because my knees are out of commission.*

out of gas   1. sin gasolina o petróleo (en un coche, camión, etc.) □ *We can't go any farther. We're out of gas.* □ *This car will be completely out of gas in a few more miles.* 2. cansado; agotado; ajado. □ *What a day! I've been working since morning, and I'm really out of gas.* □ *This electric clock is out of gas. I'll have to get a new one.* ALSO: **run out of gas** usar toda la gasolina (o petróleo) disponible. □ *I hope we don't run out of gas.*

out of hand   inmediatamente y sin hablar con nadie; sin demora. □ *I can't answer that out of hand. I'll check with the manager and call you back.* □ *The offer was so good that I accepted it out of hand.*

out of luck   sin buena suerte; con mala suerte. □ *If you wanted some ice-cream, you're out of luck.* □ *I was out of luck. I got there too late to get a seat.*

out of one's element   en una situación incómoda o poco natural. □ *When it comes to computers, I'm out of my element.* □ *Sally's out of her element in math.*

out of one's head   Véase la entrada siguiente.

out of one's mind AND **out of one's head; out of one's senses**   estúpido y sin sentido; loco; irracional. □ *Why did you do that? You must be out of your mind!* □ *Good grief, Tom! You have to be out of your head!* □ *She's acting as if she were out of her senses.*

out of one's senses   Véase la entrada previa.

out of order   1. no en el orden correcto. □ *This book is out of order. Please put it in the right place on the shelf.* □ *You're out of order, John. Please get in line after Jane.* 2. sin seguir los procedimientos correctos del tribunal. □ *I was declared out of order by the president.* □ *Ann inquired, "Isn't a motion to table the question out of order at this time?"*

out of practice   hacer algo mal a causa de la falta de práctica. □ *I used to be able to play the piano extremely well, but now I'm out of practice.* □ *The baseball players lost the game because they were out of practice.*

out of print   ya no disponible para la venta [un libro]; agotado. (Compárese a *in print.*) □ *The book you want is out of print, but perhaps I can find a used copy for you.* □ *It was published nearly ten years ago, so it's probably out of print.*

out of season   1. no disponible para la venta durante la estación o época actual. □ *Sorry, oysters are out of season. We don't have any.* □ *Watermelon is out of season in the winter.* 2. no poder cazar o coger con trampa bajo la ley. □ *Are salmon out of season?* □ *I caught a trout out of season and had to pay a fine.*

out of service   inoperable; no estar en funciona miento. □ *Both elevators are out of service, so I had to use the stairs.* □ *The washroom is temporarily out of service.*

Out of sight, out of mind.   un refrán significando que si uno no ve nada, no va a pensar en ello. □ *When I go home, I put my schoolbooks away so I won't worry about doing my homework. After all, out of sight, out of mind.* □ *Jane dented the fender on her car. It's on the right side, so she doesn't have to look at it. Like they say, out of sight, out of mind.*

out of sorts   gruñón; irritable. □ *I've been out of sorts for a day or two. I think I'm coming down with something.* □ *The baby is out of sorts. Maybe she's getting a tooth.*

out of the blue   Véase en *out of a clear blue sky.*

out of the corner of one's eye   [ver algo] de un vistazo; vislumbrar (algo). □ *I saw someone do it out of the corner of my eye. It might have been Jane who did it.* □ *I only saw the accident out of the corner of my eye. I don't know who is at fault.*

out of the frying pan into the fire   de una situación mala a una situación peor. (Es cliché. Una cosa que está caliente en la sartén está más caliente en el fuego.) □ *When I tried to argue about my fine for a traffic violation, the judge charged me with contempt of court. I really went out of the frying pan into the fire.* □ *I got deeply in debt. Then I really got out of the frying pan into the fire when I lost my job.*

out of the hole   sin deudas. (También se usa literalmente.) □ *I get paid next week, and then I can get out of the hole.* □ *I can't seem to get out of the hole. I keep spending more money than I earn.*

out of the question   imposible; no permitido. □ *I'm sorry, but it's out of the question.* □ *You can't go to Florida this spring. We can't afford it. It's out of the question.*

out of the red   sin deudas. □ *This year our firm is likely to get out of the red before fall.* □ *If we can cut down on expenses, we can get out of the red fairly soon.*

out of the running   ya no se considera; eliminado de un concurso. □ *After the first part of the diving meet, three members of our team were out of the running.* □ *After the scandal was made public, I was no longer in the running. I pulled out of the election.*

out of the woods   terminada la fase crítica □ *When the patient got out of the woods, everyone relaxed.* □ *I can give you a better prediction for your future health when you are out of the woods.*

out of thin air   de ningún lado; de la nada. □ *Suddenly—out of thin air—the messenger appeared.* □ *You just made that up out of thin air.*

out of this world   increíble; maravilloso. (Es cliché. También se usa literalmente.) □ *This pie is just out of this world.* □ *Look at you! How lovely you look—simply out of this world.*

out of tune (with someone or something)   **1.** no [estar] en armonía con alguien o algo. □ *The oboe is out of tune with the flute.* □ *The flute is out of tune with John.* □ *They are all out of tune.* **2.** no [estar] de acuerdo. □ *Your proposal is out of tune with my ideas of what we should be doing. Let's get all our efforts in tune.*

out of turn   no a la hora adecuada; sin orden adecuado. □ *We were permitted to be served out of turn, because we had to leave early.* □ *Bill tried to register out of turn and was sent away.*

out on a limb   en una posición peligrosa. □ *I don't want to go out on a limb, but I think I'd agree to your request.* □ *She really went out on a limb when she agreed.*

out on the town   [salir] de bar en bar o de lugar en lugar. □ *I'm really tired. I was out on the town until dawn.* □ *We went out on the town to celebrate our wedding anniversary.*

outside, at the   Véase *at the outside.*

out to lunch   [comer] afuera de la oficina donde trabaja uno. □ *I'm sorry, but Sally Jones is out to lunch. May I take a message?* □ *She's been out to lunch for nearly two hours. When will she be back?*

overboard, go   Véase *go overboard.*

over the hill   demasiado viejo para hacer algo. □ *Now that Mary's forty, she thinks she's over the hill.* □ *My grandfather was over eighty before he felt as if he was over the hill.*

over the hump   acabada la parte difícil. □ *This is a difficult project, but we're over the hump now.* □ *I'm halfway through—over the hump—and it looks as if I may get finished after all.*

over the long haul   a la larga; durante un período bastante largo. □ *Over the long haul, it might be better to invest in stocks.* □ *Over the long haul, everything will turn out all right.*

over the short haul   en el fututro inmediato; a corto plazo. □ *Over the short haul, you'd be better off to put your money in the bank.* □ *Over the short haul, you may wish you had done something different. But things will work out all right.*

over the top   [haber] logrado más de lo que intentaba lograr uno. □ *Our fund-raising campaign went over the top by $3,000.* □ *We didn't go over the top. We didn't even get half of what we set out to collect.*

P

packed (in) like sardines muy apretujados. (Es cliché. Observe algunas de las variaciones posibles en los ejemplos.) □ *It was terribly crowded there. We were packed in like sardines.* □ *The bus was full. The passengers were packed like sardines.* □ *They packed us in like sardines.*

paddle one's own canoe hacer algo solo; estar solo. (Es cliché. También se usa literalmente.) □ *I've been left to paddle my own canoe too many times.* □ *Sally isn't with us. She's off paddling her own canoe.*

pad the bill añadir cosas innecesarias a una factura (para recibir más dinero del cliente. □ *The plumber had padded the bill with things we didn't need.* □ *I was falsely accused of padding the bill.*

paint the town red ir de juerga. (No se usa literalmente.) □ *Let's all go out and paint the town red!* □ *Oh, do I feel awful. I was out all last night, painting the town red.*

pale, beyond the Véase *beyond the pale.*

part and parcel Véase en *bag and baggage.*

part someone's hair llegar [alguien o algo] muy cerca de uno. □ *That plane flew so low that it nearly parted my hair.* □ *He punched at me and missed. He only parted my hair.*

par, up to Véase *up to par.*

pass the buck echarle a alguien la culpa; darle a alguien la responsabilidad de algo. → **pasar la pelota.** □ *Don't try to pass the buck! It's your fault, and everybody knows it.* □ *Some people try to pass the buck whenever they can.*

pass the hat   intentar sacar dinero para algún proyecto de caridad.
□ *Bob is passing the hat to collect money to buy flowers for Ann.*
□ *He's always passing the hat for something.*

pay an arm and a leg (for something) AND **pay through the nose (for something)**   pagar demasiado para algo. → **costar un ojo de la cara.** □ *I hate to have to pay an arm and a leg for a tank of gas.* □ *If you shop around, you won't have to pay an arm and a leg.* □ *Why should you pay through the nose?* ALSO: **cost an arm and a leg**   costar demasiado. □ *It cost an arm and a leg, so I didn't buy it.*

pay one's debt (to society)   cumplir con una pena para un crimen, normalmente en la cárcel. □ *The judge said that Mr. Simpson had to pay his debt to society.* □ *Mr. Brown paid his debt in state prison.*

pay one's dues   1. pagar la cuota para hacerse socio de alguna organización. □ *If you haven't paid your dues, you can't come to the club picnic.* □ *How many people have paid their dues?* 2. ganar el derecho de hacer algo a causa del trabajo duro o el sufrimiento. □ *He worked hard to get to where he is today. He paid his dues and did what he was told.* □ *I have every right to be here. I paid my dues!*

pay the piper   aceptar los resultados de las acciones de sí mismo; recibir un castigo para algo. (Es cliché.) □ *You can put off paying your debts only so long. Eventually you'll have to pay the piper.* □ *You can't get away with that forever. You'll have to pay the piper someday.*

pay through the nose (for something)   Véase en *pay an arm and a leg (for something).*

penny saved is a penny earned, A.   Véase *A penny saved is a penny earned.*

penny-wise and pound-foolish   un refrán significando que es tonto perder mucho dinero para ahorrar poco. (Es cliché.) → **gastar a manos llenas y hacer economías en nimiedades.** □ *Sally shops very carefully to save a few cents on food, then charges the food to a charge card that costs a lot in annual interest. That's being* *penny-wise and pound-foolish.* □ *John drives thirty miles to buy gas for three cents a gallon less than it costs here. He's really penny-wise and pound-foolish.*

Perish the thought.   Ni tener algo en cuenta. (Es frase literaria.) □ *If you should become ill—perish the thought—I'd take care of you.* □ *I'm afraid that we need a new car. Perish the thought.*

pick up the tab   pagar la cuenta. (Recoger la cuenta de la mesa y pagarla.) □ *Whenever we go out, my father picks up the tab.* □ *Order whatever you want. The company is picking up the tab.*

pie in the sky   una recompensa por algo en el futuro, especialmente después de la muerte. (Es cliché. De una frase más amplia, "pie in the sky by and by when you die.") □ *Are you nice to people just because of pie in the sky, or do you really like them?* □ *Don't hold out for a big reward, you know—pie in the sky.*

pillar to post, from   Véase *from pillar to post.*

pink (of condition), in the   Véase *in the pink (of condition).*

pins and needles, on   Véase *on pins and needles.*

pitch in (and help)   ocuparse de ayudar (con algo). □ *Pick up a paintbrush and pitch in and help.* □ *Why don't some of you pitch in? We need all the help we can get.*

pitch someone a curve (ball)   sorprender a alguien con una acción o un suceso inesperado. (También se usa literalmente en el béisbol.) □ *You really pitched me a curve ball when you said I had done a poor job. I did my best.* □ *You asked Tom a hard question. You certainly pitched him a curve.*

plain as day, (as)   Véase *(as) plain as day.*

plain as the nose on one's face, (as)   Véase *(as) plain as the nose on one's face.*

play ball (with someone)   1. jugar a un juego de balón o de pelota (por ejemplo, el baloncesto o el béisbol) con alguien. (Observe el uso específico del béisbol en el segundo ejemplo.) □ *When* *will our team play ball with yours?* □ *Suddenly, the umpire shouted,* *"Play ball!" and the game began.* **2.** cooperar con alguien. □ *Look, friend, if you play ball with me, everything will work out all right.* □ *Things would go better for you if you'd learn to play ball.*

play both ends (against the middle)   intrigar para sembrar discordia entre dos personas o dos grupos (para beneficiarse). □ *I told my brother that Mary doesn't like him. Then I told Mary that my brother doesn't like her. They broke up, so now I can have the car this weekend. I succeeded in playing both ends against the middle.* □ *If you try to play both ends, you're likely to get in trouble with both sides.*

play by ear   Véase en *play something by ear.*

play cat and mouse (with someone)   capturar y luego liberar a alguien una y otra vez. (Se usa literalmente o figuradamente. Es cliché.) → **jugar al gato y al ratón con alguien.** □ *The police played cat and mouse with the suspect until they had sufficient evidence to make an arrest.* □ *Tom had been playing cat and mouse with Ann. Finally she got tired of it and broke up with him.*

play fast and loose (with someone or something) comportarse sin cuidado, consideración, o responsabilidad (con alguien o algo). □ *I'm tired of your playing fast and loose with me. Leave me alone.* □ *Bob got fired for playing fast and loose with the company's money.* □ *If you play fast and loose like that, you can get into a lot of trouble.*

play it safe   estar seguro; hacer algo de una manera segura. □ *You should play it safe and take your umbrella.* □ *If you have a cold or the flu, play it safe and go to bed.*

play one's cards close to one's vest   Véase la entrada siguiente.

play one's cards close to the chest AND **play one's cards close to one's vest**   trabajar o negociar de una manera secreta. (Referente a la acción de coger las cartas cerca de sí mismo para que nadie pueda verlas.) □ *It's hard to figure out what John is up to because he plays his cards close to his chest.* □ *Don't let them know what you're up to. Play your cards close to your vest.*

play second fiddle (to someone)   estar en una posición subordinada. □ *I'm tired of playing second fiddle to John.* □ *I'm better trained than he, and I have more experience. I shouldn't play second fiddle.*

play something by ear   1. poder tocar una pieza musical después de escucharla pocas veces, sin ver las notas o los acordes. □ *I can play "Stardust" by ear.* □ *Some people can play Chopin's music by ear.* 2. AND **play by ear**   tocar un instrumento muy bien, sin enseñanza formal. □ *John can play the piano by ear.* □ *If I could play by ear, I wouldn't have to take lessons—or practice!*

play the field   salir con muchas personas en vez de tener novio. □ *When Tom told Ann good-bye, he said he wanted to play the field.* □ *He said he wanted to play the field while he was still young.*

play to the gallery   interpretar algo con el fin de tener la aprobación del público; interpretar algo con el fin de tener la aprobación de las personas más bajas, o groseras, del público. □ *John is a competent actor, but he has a tendency to play to the gallery.* □ *When he made the rude remark, he was just playing to the gallery.*

play with fire   arriesgarse mucho. (También se usa literalmente.) □ *If you accuse her of stealing, you'll be playing with fire.* □ *I wouldn't try that if I were you—unless you like playing with fire.*

pocket, have someone in one's   Véase *have someone in one's pocket.*

poke fun (at someone)   burlarse de alguien. □ *Stop poking fun at me! It's not nice.* □ *Bob is always poking fun.*

poke one's nose in(to something) AND **stick one's nose in(to something)**   entrometerse en algo; ser fisgón (acerca de algo). (No se usa literalmente.) □ *I wish you'd stop poking your nose into my business.* □ *She was too upset for me to stick my nose in and ask what was wrong.*

poles apart, be   Véase *be poles apart.*

poor as a church mouse, (as)   Véase *(as) poor as a church mouse.*

poor taste, in Véase *in poor taste.*

pop the question pedir la mano de alguien. □ *I was surprised when he popped the question.* □ *I've been waiting for years for someone to pop the question.*

pot calling the kettle black, the Véase *the pot calling the kettle black.*

pot, go to Véase *go to pot.*

pound a beat rondar por una ruta específica. (Normalmente se dice de un policía en su patrulla.) □ *The patrolman pounded the same beat for years and years.* □ *Pounding a beat will wreck your feet.*

pound the pavement rondar por una ciudad buscando empleo; buscar empleo. □ *I spent two months pounding the pavement after the factory I worked for closed.* □ *Hey, Bob. You'd better get busy pounding those nails unless you want to be out pounding the pavement.*

pour cold water on something AND **dash cold water on something; throw cold water on something** disuadir a alguien de hacer algo; reducir el entusiasmo de uno para algo. (No se usa literalmente en este sentido.) □ *When my father said I couldn't have the car, he poured cold water on my plans.* □ *John threw cold water on the whole project by refusing to participate.*

pour it on thick Véase en *lay it on thick.*

pour money down the drain derrochar dinero. □ *What a waste! You're just pouring money down the drain.* □ *Don't buy any more of that low-quality merchandise. That's just throwing money down the drain.*

pour oil on troubled water calmar las cosas. (Es cliché. Si se echa el aceite al mar durante una tormenta, el agua volverá a ser más calmada, según las creencias populares.) □ *That was a good thing to say to John. It helped pour oil on troubled water. Now he looks happy.* □ *Bob is the kind of person who pours oil on troubled water.*

practice, out of   Véase *out of practice.*

practice what you preach   hacer lo que uno aconseja a otros. (Es cliché.) □ *If you'd practice what you preach, you'd be better off.* □ *You give good advice. Why not practice what you preach?*

premium, at a   Véase *at a premium.*

press one's luck   Véase en *push one's luck.*

press someone to the wall   Véase en *push someone to the wall.*

pretty as a picture, (as)   Véase *(as) pretty as a picture.*

Pretty is as pretty does.   uno debe hacer cosas agradables si quiere que se lo considere agradable. (Es cliché.) □ *Now, Sally. Let's be nice. Pretty is as pretty does.* □ *My great-aunt always used to say "pretty is as pretty does" to my sister.*

price on one's head, have a   Véase *have a price on one's head.*

prick up one's ears   escuchar más atentamente. □ *At the sound of my voice, my dog pricked up her ears.* □ *I pricked up my ears when I heard my name mentioned.*

prime, in one's or its   Véase *in one's or its prime.*

prime of life, in the   Véase *in the prime of life.*

print, in   Véase *in print.*

print, out of   Véase *out of print.*

promise the moon (to someone) AND **promise someone the moon**   hacer promesas muy extravagantes. □ *Bill will promise you the moon, but he won't live up to his promises.* □ *My boss promised the moon, but only paid the minimum wage.*

proportion, out of all   Véase *out of all proportion.*

proud as a peacock, (as)   Véase *(as) proud as a peacock.*

public eye, in the   Véase *in the public eye.*

pull oneself up (by one's own bootstraps)   lograr (algo) por el esfuerzo personal. (Es cliché.) □ *They simply don't have the resources to pull themselves up by their own bootstraps.* □ *If I could have pulled myself up, I'd have done it by now.*

pull someone's leg   tomarle el pelo a alguien; gastarle una broma a alguien. □ *You don't mean that. You're just pulling my leg.* □ *Don't believe him. He's just pulling your leg.*

pull someone's or something's teeth   disminuir el poder de alguien o algo. (También se usa literalmente.) □ *The mayor tried to pull the teeth of the new law.* □ *The city council pulled the teeth of the new mayor.*

pull something out of a hat AND **pull something out of thin air**   producir o presentar algo, como si fuera por magia. □ *This is a serious problem, and we just can't pull a solution out of a hat.* □ *I'm sorry, but I don't have a pen. What do you want me to do, pull one out of thin air?*

pull something out of thin air   Véase la entrada previa.

pull the rug out (from under someone)   causar que alguien ya no tenga poder. □ *The treasurer pulled the rug out from under the mayor.* □ *Things were going along fine until the treasurer pulled the rug out.*

pull the wool over someone's eyes   engañar a alguien. (Es cliché.) □ *You can't pull the wool over my eyes. I know what's going on.* □ *Don't try to pull the wool over her eyes. She's too smart.*

pull up stakes   mudarse de casa. (Como si uno estuviera desarraigando las estacas de una tienda de campaña.) □ *I've been here long enough. It's time to pull up stakes.* □ *I hate the thought of having to pull up stakes.*

push one's luck AND **press one's luck**   esperar una continuación de la buena suerte; esperar continuar escapándose de la mala suerte. □ *You're okay so far, but don't push your luck.* □ *Bob pressed his luck too much and got into a lot of trouble.*

push someone to the wall AND **press someone to the wall**   poner a alguien en una posición con una salida [figuradamente]; poner a alguien en una posición defensiva. (También se usa literalmente.) □ *There was little else I could do. They pushed me to the wall.* □ *When we pressed him to the wall, he told us where the cookies were hidden.*

put a bee in someone's bonnet   Véase en *have a bee in one's bonnet.*

put all one's eggs in one basket   arriesgar todo a la vez. (Es cliché. Muchas veces se usa en el sentido negativo. Si se deja caer la cesta, se va a romper todos los huevos.) □ *Don't put all your eggs in one basket. Then everything won't be lost if there is a catastrophe.* □ *John only applied to the one college he wanted to go to. He put all his eggs in one basket.*

put in a good word (for someone)   decirle algo a alguien para apoyar la posición de otra persona. □ *I hope you get the job. I'll put in a good word for you.* □ *Yes, I want the job. If you see the boss, please put in a good word.*

put in one's two cents (worth)   añadir la opinión personal (a algo). (La frase implica que la opinión no vale mucho necesariamente, pero es importante expresarla de todas formas.) □ *Can I put in my two cents worth?* □ *Sure, go ahead—put your two cents in.*

put on airs   comportarse con altanería. □ *Stop putting on airs. You're just human like the rest of us.* □ *Ann is always putting on airs. You'd think she was a queen.*

put one's best foot forward   comportarse lo mejor posible; intentar causar una buena impresión. (Es cliché.) □ *When you apply for a job, you should always put your best foot forward.* □ *I try to put my best foot forward whenever I meet someone for the first time.*

put one's cards on the table AND **lay one's cards on the table**   revelarlo todo; decir algo francamente. (Referente a los naipes, en que a veces se les muestran los naipes a los otros jugadores para ver lo que tienen todos.) □ *Come on, John, lay your* *cards on the table. Tell me what you really think.* □ *Why don't we both put our cards on the table?*

put one's dibs on something Véase en *have dibs on something.*

put one's foot in it Véase la entrada siguiente.

put one's foot in one's mouth AND **put one's foot in it; stick one's foot in one's mouth** decir algo que uno lamenta haber dicho; decir algo estúpido, insultante, o hiriente. □ *When I told Ann that her hair was more beautiful than I had ever seen it, I really put my foot in my mouth. It was a wig.* □ *I put my foot in it by telling John's secret.*

put one's hand to the plow empezar a hacer una tarea dura e importante; emprender una tarea importante. (Es cliché. Casi nunca se usa literalmente.) □ *If John would only put his hand to the plow, he could do an excellent job.* □ *You'll never accomplish anything if you don't put your hand to the plow.*

put one's nose to the grindstone ocuparse trabajando. (Nunca se usa literalmente. También se usa con *have* o *get,* como se ve en los ejemplos.) □ *The boss told me to put my nose to the grindstone.* □ *I've had my nose to the grindstone ever since I started working here.* □ *If the other people in this office would get their noses to the grindstone, more work would get done.* ALSO: **keep one's nose to the grindstone** trabajar mucho durante una época. □ *The manager told me to keep my nose to the grindstone or be fired.*

put one's oar in AND **put in one's oar** ayudar; entrometerse en algo con los consejos; añadir ayuda personal a un esfuerzo general. □ *You don't need to put your oar in. I don't need your advice.* □ *I'm sorry. I shouldn't have put in my oar.*

put one's shoulder to the wheel ponerse muy ocupado. (No se usa literalmente.) □ *You won't accomplish anything unless you put your shoulder to the wheel.* □ *I put my shoulder to the wheel and finished the job quickly.*

put one through one's paces   hacer que alguien muestre su capacidad de hacer algo; hacer que alguien haga su trabajo. □ *The boss really put me through my paces today. I'm tired.* □ *I tried out for a part in the play, and the director really put me through my paces.*

put on one's thinking cap   empezar a pensar de una manera seria. (Es cliché. No se usa literalmente. Normalmente se dice con respecto a los niños o referente a los niños.) □ *All right now, let's put on our thinking caps and do some arithmetic.* □ *It's time to put on our thinking caps, children.*

put someone or something out to pasture   jubilar a alguien o algo. (Referente a un caballo que ya no puede trabajar a causa de su vejez.) □ *Please don't put me out to pasture. I have lots of good years left.* □ *This car has reached the end of the line. It's time to put it out to pasture.*

put someone or something to bed   1. [con *someone*] acostar a alguien—normalmente un niño. □ *Come on, Billy, it's time for me to put you to bed.* □ *I want grandpa to put me to bed.* **2.** [con *something*] acabar con hacer algo; mandar algo al próximo paso de su producción o fabricación, especialmente en el campo editorial. □ *This edition is finished. Let's put it to bed.* □ *Finish the editing of this book and put it to bed.*

put someone or something to sleep   1. matar a alguien o algo. (Es eufemístico.) □ *We had to put our dog to sleep.* □ *The robber said he'd put us to sleep forever if we didn't cooperate.* **2.** causar que alguien duerma, posiblemente con las drogas o la anestesia. □ *The doctor put the patient to sleep before the operation.* □ *I put the cat to sleep by stroking its tummy.* **3.** [con *someone*] aburrir a alguien. (Se usa literalmente.) □ *That dull lecture put me to sleep.* □ *Her long story almost put me to sleep.*

put someone's nose out of joint   ofender a alguien; causar que alguien se sienta menospreciado u ofendido. (No se usa literalmente.) □ *I'm afraid I put his nose out of joint by not inviting him to the picnic.* □ *There is no reason to put your nose out of joint. I meant no harm.*

put someone through the wringer hacer que alguien tenga problemas o tenga que explicar sus acciones. (Referente a la dificultad de usar un rodillo para escurrir la ropa.) □ *They are really putting me through the wringer at school.* □ *The boss put Bob through the wringer over this contract.*

put someone to shame avergonzar a alguien; probar algo; hacer quedar mal. □ *Your excellent efforts put us all to shame.* □ *I put him to shame by telling everyone about his bad behavior.*

put someone to the test hacerle una prueba a alguien; ver lo que puede lograr alguien. □ *I think I can jump that far, but no one has ever put me to the test.* □ *I'm going to put you to the test right now!*

put something on ice AND **put something on the back burner** retrasar o aplazar algo; dejar de hacer algo durante un rato. (No se usan estas frases literalmente en estos sentidos.) □ *I'm afraid that we'll have to put your project on ice for a while.* □ *Just put your idea on ice and keep it there till we get some money.*

put something on paper escribir algo; escribir un acuerdo a máquina o a mano. □ *You have a great idea for a novel. Now put it on paper.* □ *I'm sorry, I can't discuss your offer until I see something in writing. Put it on paper, and then we'll talk.*

put something on the back burner Véase en *put something on ice.*

put something on the cuff comprar algo a crédito; añadir al dinero que debe uno. (Como si uno estuviera escribiendo el precio en el puño de la camisa.) □ *I'll take two of those, and please put them on the cuff.* □ *I'm sorry, Tom. We can't put anything more on the cuff.*

put something on the line AND **lay something on the line** hablar de algo con firmeza y franqueza. (Posiblemente referente a una línea militar.) → **no andarse con rodeos.** □ *She was very mad. She put it on the line, and we have no doubt about what she meant.* □ *All right, you kids! I'm going to lay it on the line. Don't ever do that again if you know what's good for you.*

put something through its paces　demostrar el funcionamiento buenísmo de algo; demostrar que se puede hacer algo. □ *I was down by the barn, watching Sally put her horse through its paces.* □ *This is an excellent can opener. Watch me put it through its paces.*

put the cart before the horse　tener las cosas en el orden equivocado; tener confusas las cosas. (Es cliché. También se usa con *have*.) □ *You're eating your dessert! You've put the cart before the horse.* □ *Slow down and get organized. Don't put the cart before the horse!* □ *John has the cart before the horse in most of his projects.*

put two and two together　entender algo de la información disponible. (Es cliché.) □ *Well, I put two and two together and came up with an idea of who did it.* □ *Don't worry. John won't figure it out. He can't put two and two together.*

put up a (brave) front　parecerse valiente (aún si uno no lo es). □ *Mary is frightened, but she's putting up a brave front.* □ *If she weren't putting up a front, I'd be more frightened than I am.*

put words into someone's mouth　hablar por otra persona sin su permiso. □ *Stop putting words into my mouth. I can speak for myself.* □ *The lawyer was scolded for putting words into the witness's mouth.*

Put your money where your mouth is!　un mandato que dice que uno debe dejar de hablar con apuestas grandes y apostar de una vez. (Es cliché. No se usa literalmente.) □ *I'm tired of your bragging about your skill at betting. Put your money where your mouth is!* □ *You talk about betting, but you don't bet. Put your money where your mouth is!*

q

QT, on the Véase *on the QT.*

quake in one's boots Véase en *shake in one's boots.*

question, out of the Véase *out of the question.*

quick as a wink, (as) Véase *(as) quick as a wink.*

quick on the draw Véase la entrada siguiente.

quick on the trigger AND **quick on the draw** **1.** sacar una pistola rápidamente y disparar. □ *Some of the old cowboys were known to be quick on the trigger.* □ *Wyatt Earp was particularly quick on the draw.* **2.** responder a cualquier cosa rápidamente. □ *John gets the right answer before anyone else. He's really quick on the trigger.* □ *Sally will probably win the quiz game. She's really quick on the draw.*

quick on the uptake comprender (algo) rápidamente. □ *Just because I'm not quick on the uptake, it doesn't mean I'm stupid.* □ *Mary understands jokes before anyone else because she's so quick on the uptake.*

quiet as a mouse, (as) Véase *(as) quiet as a mouse.*

R

rack and ruin, go to   Véase *go to rack and ruin.*

rack one's brain(s)   intentar mucho recordar algo. □ *I racked my brains all afternoon, but couldn't remember where I put the book.* □ *Don't waste any more time racking your brain. Go borrow the book from the library.*

rags, in   Véase *in rags.*

rags to riches, from   Véase *from rags to riches.*

rain cats and dogs   llover mucho. (Es cliché. No es literal.) → **llover a cántaros.** □ *It's raining cats and dogs. Look at it pour!* □ *I'm not going out in that storm. It's raining cats and dogs.*

rain or shine   no importa si llueve o si sale el sol. (Es cliché.) → **pase lo que pase.** □ *Don't worry. I'll be there rain or shine.* □ *We'll hold the picnic—rain or shine.*

rains but it pours, It never.   Véase *It never rains but it pours.*

raise one's sights   fijar en metas más elevadas para sí mismo. □ *When you're young, you tend to raise your sights too high.* □ *On the other hand, some people need to raise their sights.*

raise some eyebrows   asustar o sorprender a las personas (a causa de hacer o decir algo). (Se puede usar *a few, someone's, a lot of,* etc. en vez de *some.*) □ *What you just said may raise some eyebrows, but it shouldn't make anyone really angry.* □ *John's sudden marriage to Ann raised a few eyebrows.*

rake someone over the coals AND **haul someone over the coals**   regañar a alguien con severidad. □ *My mother hauled me over the coals for coming in late last night.* □ *The manager raked me over the coals for being late again.*

reach first base (with someone or something)   Véase en *get to first base (with someone or something).*

read between the lines   deducir algo (de algo); intentar comprender algo que no se puede leer con claridad o abiertamente. (Normalmente se usa figuradamente. No se refiere necesariamente a la información por escrito.) □ *After listening to what she said, if you read between the lines, you can begin to see what she really means.* □ *Don't believe everything you hear. Learn to read between the lines.*

read someone like a book   comprender a alguien muy bien. □ *I've got John figured out. I can read him like a book.* □ *Of course I understand you. I read you like a book.*

read someone the riot act   regañar a alguien con severidad. □ *The manager read me the riot act for coming in late.* □ *The teacher read the students the riot act for their failure to do their assignments.*

record, for the   Véase *for the record.*

record, off the   Véase *off the record.*

red, in the   Véase *in the red.*

red, out of the   Véase *out of the red.*

regular as clockwork, (as)   Véase *(as) regular as clockwork.*

return mail, by   Véase *by return mail.*

ride, go along for the   Véase *go along for the ride.*

ride roughshod over someone or something tratar a alguien o algo con desdén. ☐ *Tom seems to ride roughshod over his friends.* ☐ *You shouldn't have come into our town to ride roughshod over our laws and our traditions.*

ride the gravy train vivir en lujo. ☐ *If I had a million dollars, I sure could ride the gravy train.* ☐ *I wouldn't like loafing. I don't want to ride the gravy train.*

riding for a fall arriesgar con la posibilidad de sufrir un fracaso o un accidente, normalmente a causa de tener demasiada confianza. ☐ *Tom drives too fast, and he seems too sure of himself. He's riding for a fall.* ☐ *Bill needs to eat better and get more sleep. He's riding for a fall.*

right, in the Véase *in the right.*

right mind, in one's Véase *in one's right mind.*

right off the bat inmediatamente; lo primero. (Parece referirse a la pelota que sale del bate de béisbol, pero probablemente se refirió originalmente al bate de críquet. ☐ *When he was learning to ride a bicycle, he fell on his head right off the bat.* ☐ *The new manager demanded new office furniture right off the bat.*

right-of-way, have the Véase *have the right-of-way.*

ring in the New Year celebrar el comienzo del nuevo año el 31 de diciembre. (Como si tocaran las campanas de la iglesia esta noche.) ☐ *We are planning a big party to ring in the New Year.* ☐ *How did you ring in the New Year?*

risk one's neck (to do something) arriesgar el daño personal para lograr algo. ☐ *Look at that traffic! I refuse to risk my neck just to cross the street to buy a paper.* ☐ *I refuse to risk my neck at all.*

rob Peter to pay Paul tomar de una cosa para dar a otra. (Es cliché.) ☐ *Why borrow money to pay your bills? That's just robbing Peter to pay Paul.* ☐ *There's no point in robbing Peter to pay Paul. You still will be in debt.*

rob the cradle   casarse con o salir con alguien que es más joven que uno. (Como si uno estuviera asociándose con un niño.) □ *I hear that Bill is dating Ann. Isn't that sort of robbing the cradle? She's much younger than he is.* □ *Uncle Bill—who is nearly eighty— married a thirty-year-old woman. That is really robbing the cradle.*

rock and a hard place, between a   Véase *between a rock and a hard place.*

rock the boat   causar problemas; introducir problemas en una situación que es estable y satisfactoria por lo demás. (Muchas veces se usa en el sentido negativo.) □ *Look, Tom, everything is going fine here. Don't rock the boat!* □ *You can depend on Tom to mess things up by rocking the boat.*

rolling stone gathers no moss, A.   Véase *A rolling stone gathers no moss.*

roll out the red carpet for someone   Véase en *get the red-carpet treatment.*

Rome wasn't built in a day.   Las cosas importantes no se realizan rápidamente. (Es cliché.) □ *Don't expect a lot to happen right away. Rome wasn't built in a day, you know.* □ *Don't be anxious about how fast you are growing. Rome wasn't built in a day.*

roof, go through the   Véase *go through the roof.*

round figures, in   Véase *in round figures.*

round numbers, in   Véase *in round numbers.*

rub elbows with someone AND **rub shoulders with someone**   asociarse con alguien; trabajar mucho con alguien. □ *I don't care to rub elbows with someone who acts like that!* □ *I rub shoulders with John at work. We are good friends.*

rub shoulders with someone   Véase la entrada previa.

rub someone's fur the wrong way AND **rub someone the wrong way**   molestar a alguien. (Como si uno estuviera acariciando el pelaje de un animal, como de un gato, en la dirección equivocoda, con el resultado que molesta al animal. La segunda frase viene de la primera.) □ *I'm sorry I rubbed your fur the wrong way. I didn't mean to upset you.* □ *Don't rub her the wrong way!*

rub someone the wrong way   Véase la entrada previa.

rule the roost   ser el jefe, especialmente en casa. □ *Who rules the roost at your house?* □ *Our new office manager really rules the roost.*

run a fever AND **run a temperature**   tener fiebre. □ *I ran a fever when I had the flu.* □ *The baby is running a temperature and is grouchy.*

run (around) in circles   Véase la entrada siguiente.

run around like a chicken with its head cut off AND **run (around) in circles**   estar agitado, correr por todas partes frenéticamente y sin rumbo fijo; estar en un estado de caos. (Es cliché.) □ *I spent all afternoon running around like a chicken with its head cut off.* □ *If you run around in circles, you'll never get anything done.* □ *Get organized and stop running in circles.*

run a taut ship   Véase en *run a tight ship.*

run a temperature   Véase en *run a fever.*

run a tight ship AND **run a taut ship**   dirigir a los tripulantes de un buque o a los miembros de una organización de una manera ordenada y estricta. (*Taut* y *tight* significan la misma cosa. Se usa *taut* en el contexto náutico.) □ *The new office manager really runs a tight ship.* □ *Captain Jones is known for running a taut ship.*

run for one's life   correr para salvar la vida de sí mismo. □ *The dam has burst! Run for your life!* □ *The captain told us all to run for our lives.*

run in the family salir [una característica] en todos (o casi todos) los miembros de una familia. □ *My grandparents lived well into their nineties, and it runs in the family.* □ *My brothers and I have red hair. It runs in the family.*

run into a stone wall llegar a una barrera que dificulta el progreso. (También se usa literalmente.) □ *We've run into a stone wall in our investigation.* □ *Algebra was hard for Tom, but he really ran into a stone wall with geometry.*

running, out of the Véase *out of the running.*

running start, off to a Véase *off to a running start.*

run out of gas Véase en *out of gas.*

run someone ragged hacer que alguien permanezca muy ocupado. □ *This busy season is running us all ragged at the store.* □ *What a busy day. I ran myself ragged.*

run to seed AND **go to seed** ponerse [algo o alguien] gastado y descuidado. (Se dice especialmente del césped a que le falta el cuidado.) □ *Look at that lawn. The whole thing has run to seed.* □ *Pick things up around here. This place is going to seed. What a mess!*

S

safe and sound seguro y sano. (Es cliché.) → **sano y salvo.** ☐ *It was a rough trip, but we got there safe and sound.* ☐ *I'm glad to see you here safe and sound.*

same boat, in the Véase *in the same boat.*

same breath, in the Véase *in the same breath.*

same token, by the Véase *by the same token.*

save something for a rainy day ahorrar algo—normalmente el dinero—para alguna necesidad en el futuro. (Es cliché. También se usa literalmente. Se puede usar *put something aside, hold something back, keep something,* etc. en vez de *save something.*) ☐ *I've saved a little money for a rainy day.* ☐ *Keep some extra candy for a rainy day.*

save the day causar un resultado bueno cuando se espera un resultado malo. ☐ *The team was expected to lose, but Sally made many points and saved the day.* ☐ *Your excellent speech saved the day.*

say Jack Robinson, before you can Véase *before you can say Jack Robinson.*

say-so, on someone's Véase *on someone's say-so.*

scarce as hens' teeth, (as) Véase *(as) scarce as hens' teeth.*

scarcer than hens' teeth Véase en *(as) scarce as hens' teeth.*

scot-free, go Véase *go scot-free.*

scrape the bottom of the barrel   elegir algo de los peores; elegir de los restos. (Como uno estuviera tomando lo que quedaba al fondo de un barril.) □ *You've bought a bad-looking car. You really scraped the bottom of the barrel to get that one.* □ *The worker you sent over was the worst I've ever seen. Send me another—and don't scrape the bottom of the barrel.*

scrape (with someone or something), have a   Véase *have a scrape (with someone or something).*

scratch, not up to   Véase *not up to scratch.*

scratch the surface   apenas empezar a enterarse de algo; examinar sólo los aspectos superficiales de algo. □ *The investigation of the governor's staff revealed some suspicious dealing. It is thought that the investigators have just scratched the surface.* □ *We don't know how bad the problem is. We've only scratched the surface.*

scream bloody murder   Véase en *cry bloody murder.*

screw up one's courage   tratar de ponerse más valiente. □ *I guess I have to screw up my courage and go to the dentist.* □ *I spent all morning screwing up my courage to take my driver's test.*

sea (about something), at   Véase *at sea (about something).*

search something with a fine-tooth comb   Véase en *go over something with a fine-tooth comb.*

season, in   Véase *in season.*

season, out of   Véase *out of season.*

seat of one's pants, by the   Véase *by the seat of one's pants.*

second childhood, in one's   Véase *in one's second childhood.*

second nature to someone   fácil y natural para alguien. □ *Swimming is second nature to Jane.* □ *Driving is no problem for Bob. It's second nature to him.*

second thought, on   Véase *on second thought.*

seed, go to   Véase *go to seed.*

see eye-to-eye (about something) AND **see eye-to-eye on something**   estar de acuerdo con alguien (sobre algún tema). □ *John and Ann see eye-to-eye about the new law. Neither of them likes it.* □ *That's interesting because they rarely see eye-to-eye.*

see eye to eye on something   Véase la entrada previa.

see the forest for the trees, not able to   Véase *not able to see the forest for the trees.*

see the (hand)writing on the wall   saber con toda seguridad que algo va a pasar. (Es cliché.) □ *If you don't improve your performance, they'll fire you. Can't you see the writing on the wall?* □ *I know I'll get fired. I can see the handwriting on the wall.*

see the light (at the end of the tunnel)   prever un fin a los problemas de uno después de una época difícil. □ *I had been horribly ill for two months before I began to see the light at the end of the tunnel.* □ *I began to see the light one day in early spring. At that moment, I knew I'd get well.*

see the light, begin to   Véase *begin to see the light.*

see the light (of day)   llegar al fin de una época en que uno ha estado muy ocupado. □ *Finally, when the holiday season was over, we could see the light of day. We had been so busy!* □ *When business lets up for a while, we'll be able to see the light.*

sell like hot cakes   ser vendido muy rápidamente. □ *The delicious candy sold like hot cakes.* □ *The fancy new cars were selling like hot cakes.*

sell someone a bill of goods   hacer que alguien crea algo que no es verdadero; engañar a alguien. □ *Don't pay any attention to what John says. He's just trying to sell you a bill of goods.* □ *I'm not selling you a bill of goods. What I say is true.*

sell someone or something short   subestimar a alguien o algo; no ver las calidades buenas de alguien o algo. □ *This is a very good restaurant. Don't sell it short.* □ *When you say that John isn't interested in music, you're selling him short. Did you know he plays the violin quite well?*

send one about one's business   mandar a alguien que se vaya, normalmente de una manera poco amistosa. □ *Is that annoying man on the telephone again? Please send him about his business.* □ *Ann, I can't clean up the house with you running around. I'm going to have to send you about your business.*

send someone packing   mandar a alguien que se vaya; despedir a alguien, posiblemente con groserías. □ *I couldn't stand him anymore, so I sent him packing.* □ *The maid proved to be so incompetent that I had to send her packing.*

send someone to the showers   mandar a alguien [en un partido deportivo] que salga del partido. □ *John played so badly that the coach sent him to the showers after the third quarter.* □ *After the fistfight, the coaches sent both players to the showers.*

senses, out of one's   Véase *out of one's senses.*

separate the men from the boys   separar a los competentes de los menos competentes. □ *This is the kind of task that separates the men from the boys.* □ *This project requires a lot of thinking. It'll separate the men from the boys.*

separate the sheep from the goats   dividir a las personas en dos grupos. □ *Working in a place like this really separates the sheep from the goats.* □ *We can't go on with the game until we separate the sheep from the goats. Let's see who can jump the farthest.*

serve as a guinea pig   formar parte de un experimento médico o científico. (Es cliché.) □ *Try it on someone else! I don't want to serve as a guinea pig!* □ *Jane agreed to serve as a guinea pig. She'll be the one to try out the new flavor of ice-cream.*

serve someone right   castigar a alguien justamente [alguna acción o algún suceso]. □ *John copied off my test paper. It would serve him right if he fails the test.* □ *It'd serve John right if he got arrested.*

service, out of   Véase *out of service.*

set foot somewhere   ir a o entrar en algún sitio. (Muchas veces se usa en el sentido negativo.) □ *If I were you, I wouldn't set foot in that town.* □ *I wouldn't set foot in her house! Not after the way she spoke to me.*

set foot somewhere, not   Véase *not set foot somewhere.*

set great store by someone or something   tener muchas esperanzas buenas para alguien o algo. □ *I set great store by my computer and its ability to help me in my work.* □ *We set great store by John because of his quick mind.*

set one back on one's heels   sorprender, asustar, o aturdir a alguien. □ *Her sudden announcement set us all back on our heels.* □ *The manager scolded me, and that really set me back on my heels.*

set one's heart on something   Véase en *have one's heart set on something.*

set one's sights on something   elegir algo como meta para sí mismo. □ *I set my sights on a master's degree from the state university.* □ *Don't set your sights on something you cannot possibly do.*

set someone's teeth on edge   **1.** irritar a la boca [un sabor amargo o agrio] y hacer que se sienta rara. □ *Have you ever eaten a lemon? It'll set your teeth on edge.* □ *I can't stand food that sets my teeth on edge.* **2.** molestar a alguien [una persona o un ruido]. □ *Please don't scrape your fingernails on the blackboard! It sets my teeth on edge!* □ *Here comes Bob. He's so annoying. He really sets my teeth on edge.*

set the world on fire   hacer cosas emocionantes que llevan a la fama y la gloria. (No se usa literalmente. Muchas veces se usa en el sentido negativo.) □ *I'm not very ambitious. I don't want to set the world on fire.* □ *You don't have to set the world on fire. Just do a good job.*

seventh heaven, in   Véase *in seventh heaven.*

shake in one's boots AND **quake in one's boots**   tener miedo; sacudir a causa del miedo. □ *I was shaking in my boots because I had to go see the manager.* □ *Stop quaking in your boots, Bob. I'm not going to fire you.*

Shape up or ship out.   mejorar la ejecución de algo o dejar de hacerlo; mejorar el comportamiento o salir. (Es cliché.) □ *Okay, Tom. That's the end. Shape up or ship out!* □ *John was late again, so I told him to shape up or ship out.*

shed crocodile tears   fingir que uno está llorando. □ *The child wasn't hurt, but she shed crocodile tears anyway.* □ *He thought he could get his way if he shed crocodile tears.*

shoe fits, wear it, If the.   Véase *If the shoe fits, wear it.*

shoe is on the other foot, The.   Véase *The shoe is on the other foot.*

shoe on the other foot, have the   Véase *have the shoe on the other foot.*

shoot from the hip   1. disparar una pistola que está sostenida en la cadera. (El sostén en la cadera aumente la rapidez con que uno dispara.) □ *When I lived at home on the farm, my father taught me to shoot from the hip.* □ *I quickly shot the snake before it bit my horse. I'm glad I learned to shoot from the hip.* 2. hablar directa y francamente. □ *John has a tendency to shoot from the hip, but he generally speaks the truth.* □ *Don't pay any attention to John. He means no harm. It's just his nature to shoot from the hip.*

short haul, over the   Véase *over the short haul.*

short order, in   Véase *in short order.*

short supply, in Véase *in short supply.*

shot in the arm un estímulo; algo que le anima a alguien. □ *Thank you for cheering me up. It was a real shot in the arm.* □ *Your friendly greeting card was just what I needed—a real shot in the arm.*

shoulders, on someone's Véase *on someone's shoulders.*

should have stood in bed deber haber quedado en la cama durante el día. (No tiene nada que ver con estar de pie.) □ *What a horrible day! I should have stood in bed.* □ *The minute I got up and heard the news this morning, I knew I should have stood in bed.*

show one's face, not Véase *not show one's face.*

show one's (true) colors mostrar o revelar qué tipo de persona es uno o lo que piensa uno. □ *Whose side are you on, John? Come on. Show your colors.* □ *It's hard to tell what Mary is thinking. She never shows her true colors.*

show someone the ropes Véase en *know the ropes.*

sick as a dog, (as) Véase *(as) sick as a dog.*

sight, out of mind, Out of. Véase *Out of sight, out of mind.*

signed, sealed, and delivered firmado formal y legalmente; otorgar [un documento]. (Es cliché.) □ *Here is the deed to the property—signed, sealed, and delivered.* □ *I can't begin work on this project until I have the contract signed, sealed, and delivered.*

sign one's own death warrant firmar alguna orden de ejecución de uno (figuradamente). (Es cliché.) □ *I wouldn't ever gamble a large sum of money. That would be signing my own death warrant.* □ *The killer signed his own death warrant when he walked into the police station and gave himself up.*

sign on the dotted line firmar un contrato u otro documento importante. (Es cliché.) □ *This agreement isn't properly concluded* *until we both sign on the dotted line.* ☐ *Here are the papers for the purchase of your car. As soon as you sign on the dotted line, that beautiful, shiny automobile will be all yours!*

sink one's teeth into something (Es cliché.) **1.** comer alguna clase de comida por mordiscos, normalmente una comida especial. ☐ *I can't wait to sink my teeth into a nice juicy steak.* ☐ *Look at that chocolate cake! Don't you want to sink your teeth into that?* **2.** tener la oportunidad de hacer, aprender, o controlar algo. ☐ *That appears to be a very challenging assignment. I can't wait to sink my teeth into it.* ☐ *Being the manager of this department is a big task. I'm very eager to sink my teeth into it.*

sink or swim fracasar o tener éxito. (Es cliché.) ☐ *After I've studied and learned all I can, I have to take the test and sink or swim.* ☐ *It's too late to help John now. It's sink or swim for him.*

sit on one's hands hacer nada; no ayudar con nada. (No se usa literalmente.) ☐ *When we needed help from Mary, she just sat on her hands.* ☐ *We need the cooperation of everyone. You can't sit on your hands!* ALSO: **sit on its hands** no querer aplaudir [el público de una obra de teatro o de una interpretación musical]. (No se usa literalmente.) ☐ *We saw a very poor performance of the play. The audience sat on its hands for the entire play.*

sit tight esperar; esperar con paciencia. (No se refiere necesariamente al sentarse.) ☐ *Just relax and sit tight. I'll be right with you.* ☐ *We were waiting in line for the gates to open when someone came out and told us to sit tight because it wouldn't be much longer before we could go in.*

sitting duck, like a Véase *like a sitting duck.*

sitting on a powder keg en una situación peligrosa o posible-mente explosiva; en una situación en que las cosas se pueden poner graves o peligrosas de un momento. (No se usa literalmente. *Powder keg* es barrilete de pólvora.) ☐ *Things are very tense at work. The whole office is sitting on a powder keg.* ☐ *The fire at the oil field seems to be under control for now, but all the workers there are sitting on a powder keg.*

sit up and take notice despertarse y prestar atención. □ *A loud noise from the front of the room caused everyone to sit up and take notice.* □ *The company wouldn't pay any attention to my complaints. When I had my lawyer write them a letter, they sat up and took notice.*

sixes and sevens, at Véase *at sixes and sevens.*

six of one and half a dozen of the other igual de un modo u otro. (Es cliché.) □ *It doesn't matter to me which way you do it. It's six of one and half a dozen of the other.* □ *What difference does it make? They're both the same—six of one and half a dozen of the other.*

skate on thin ice Véase en *on thin ice.*

skeleton in the closet un secreto oculto y escandaloso; un hecho secreto que tiene que ver con uno mismo. (Muchas veces se usa en la forma plural. Como si uno hubiera escondido los resultados espeluznantes de un asesinato en el armario.) □ *You can ask anyone about how reliable I am. I don't mind. I don't have any skeletons in the closet.* □ *My uncle was in jail for a day once. That's our family's skeleton in the closet.*

skin off someone's nose, no Véase *no skin off someone's nose.*

skin off someone's teeth, no Véase *no skin off someone's teeth.*

skin of one's teeth, by the Véase *by the skin of one's teeth.*

sleep a wink, not Véase *not sleep a wink.*

sleep like a log dormir muy profundamente. (Es cliché. No es literal.) □ *Nothing can wake me up. I usually sleep like a log.* □ *Everyone in our family sleeps like a log, so no one heard the fire engines in the middle of the night.*

sleep on something pensar en algo hasta la mañana; pensar en alguna decisión hasta la mañana. □ *I don't know whether I agree* *to do it. Let me sleep on it.* □ *I slept on it, and I've decided to accept your offer.*

slip of the tongue   un error que hace uno cuando está hablando, posiblemente en la pronunciación. (Como si la lengua hubiera causado el error.) → **un lapsus.** □ *I didn't mean to tell her that. It was a slip of the tongue.* □ *I failed to understand the instructions because the speaker made a slip of the tongue at an important point.*

slip one's mind   olvidarse de algo que debería de haber recordado. (Como si el pensamiento se haya caído de la mente.) □ *I meant to go to the grocery store on the way home, but it slipped my mind.* □ *My birthday slipped my mind. I guess I wanted to forget it.*

slippery as an eel, (as)   Véase *(as) slippery as an eel.*

slip through someone's fingers   escapar de alguien; perder la pista de alguien o algo; perder algo. □ *I had a copy of the book you want, but somehow it slipped through my fingers.* □ *There was a detective following me, but I managed to slip through his fingers.*

Slow and steady wins the race.   un refrán signficando que la determinación llevará al éxito, o (literalmente) con el paso lento y continuo uno ganará la carrera. □ *I worked my way through college in six years. Now I know what they mean when they say, "Slow and steady wins the race."* □ *Ann won the race because she started off slowly and established a good pace. The other runners tried to sprint the whole distance, and they tired out before the final lap. Ann's trainer said, "You see! I told you! Slow and steady wins the race."*

smack-dab in the middle   exactamente en el medio de algo. □ *I want a big helping of mashed potatoes with a glob of butter smack-dab in the middle.* □ *Tom and Sally were having a terrible argument, and I was trapped—smack-dab in the middle.*

smart as a fox, (as)   Véase *(as) smart as a fox.*

smoke, go up in   Véase *go up in smoke.*

snail's pace, at a   Véase *at a snail's pace.*

snuff, not up to   Véase *not up to snuff.*

snug as a bug in a rug, (as)   Véase *(as) snug as a bug in a rug.*

sober as a judge, (as)   Véase *(as) sober as a judge.*

soft as a baby's bottom, (as)   Véase *(as) soft as a baby's bottom.*

soft spot in one's heart for someone or something, have a   Véase *have a soft spot in one's heart for someone or something.*

soil one's hands   Véase en *get one's hands dirty.*

soon as possible, (as)   Véase *(as) soon as possible.*

so quiet you could hear a pin drop   Véase *so still you could hear a pin drop.*

sorts, out of   Véase *out of sorts.*

so still you could hear a pin drop AND **so quiet you could hear a pin drop**   muy callado. (Es cliché. También se usa con *can.*) □ *When I came into the room, it was so still you could hear a pin drop. Then everyone shouted, "Happy birthday!"* □ *Please be quiet. Be so quiet you can hear a pin drop.*

sow one's wild oats   hacer cosas locas o imprudentes durante la juventud. (Se piensa muchas veces que la frase tiene algún sentido sexual, y que *wild oats* es referente al semen de un hombre joven.) □ *Dale was out sowing his wild oats last night, and he's in jail this morning.* □ *Mrs. Smith told Mr. Smith that he was too old to be sowing his wild oats.*

spare, have something to   Véase *have something to spare.*

spare time, in one's   Véase *in one's spare time.*

speak of the devil   dicha cuando una persona cuyo nombre ha sido mencionado hace un momento aparece, llama, o escribe. (Es cliché.) □ *Well, speak of the devil! Hello, Tom. We were just talking*

about you. □ I had just mentioned Sally when—speak of the devil—
she walked in the door.

spill the beans   Véase en *let the cat out of the bag.*

spit and image of someone, be the   Véase *be the spit and*
image of someone.

spitting image of someone, be the   Véase *be the spit and*
image of someone.

split the difference   dividir la diferencia [en algún asunto de
dinero] con otra persona. □ *You want to sell for $120, and I want*
to buy for $100. Let's split the difference and close the deal at $110.
□ *I don't want to split the difference. I want $120.*

spot, in a (tight)   Véase *in a (tight) spot.*

spotlight, in the   Véase *in the spotlight.*

spot, on the   Véase *on the spot.*

spread it on thick   Véase en *lay it on thick.*

spread like wildfire   propagar o difundir rápidamente y sin
control. (Es cliché.) □ *The epidemic is spreading like wildfire.*
Everyone is getting sick. □ *John told a joke that was so funny it*
spread like wildfire.

spread oneself too thin   hacer tantas cosas que no se puede
hacer ni una bien. □ *It's a good idea to get involved in a lot of*
activities, but don't spread yourself too thin. □ *I'm too busy these*
days. I'm afraid I've spread myself too thin.

spring chicken, no   Véase *no spring chicken.*

spur of the moment, on the   Véase *on the spur of the moment.*

square peg in a round hole   un inadaptado. (Es cliché.) □ *John*
can't seem to get along with the people he works with. He's just a
square peg in a round hole. □ *I'm not a square peg in a round hole.*
It's just that no one understands me.

squeak by (someone or something)   apenas poder hacer algo; apenas hacer algo. □ *The guard was almost asleep, so I squeaked by him.* □ *I wasn't very well prepared for the test, and I just squeaked by.*

stab someone in the back   traicionar a alguien. (También se usa literalmente.) □ *I thought we were friends! Why did you stab me in the back?* □ *You don't expect a person whom you trust to stab you in the back.*

stage (of the game), at this   Véase *at this stage (of the game).*

stag, go   Véase *go stag.*

stand one's ground AND **hold one's ground**   salir en defensa de los derechos de sí mismo; resistir a un ataque. □ *The lawyer tried to confuse me when I was giving testimony, but I managed to stand my ground.* □ *Some people were trying to crowd us off the beach, but we held our ground.*

stand on one's own two feet   ser independiente y autosuficiente en vez de que otra persona lo mantiene. □ *I'll be glad when I have a good job and can stand on my own two feet.* □ *When Jane gets out of debt, she'll be able to stand on her own two feet again.*

stand up and be counted   declarar el apoyo (por alguien o algo); declararse a favor de alguien o algo. □ *If you believe in more government help for farmers, write your representative—stand up and be counted.* □ *I'm generally in favor of what you propose, but not enough to stand up and be counted.*

start from scratch   empezar desde el principio; empezar de la nada. → **hacer algo partiendo desde el principio.** □ *Whenever I bake a cake, I start from scratch. I never use a cake mix in a box.* □ *I built every bit of my own house. I started from scratch and did everything with my own hands.*

start (off) with a clean slate   empezar de nuevo; intentar olvidarse del pasado y empezar de nuevo. □ *I plowed under all last year's flowers so I could start with a clean slate next spring.* □ *If I start off with a clean slate, then I'll know exactly what each plant is.*

start to finish, from Véase *from start to finish.*

steal a base pasar de una base a otra a escondidas en el béisbol. □ *The runner stole second base, but he nearly got put out on the way.* □ *Tom runs so slowly that he never tries to steal a base.*

steal a march (on someone) llegar a tener alguna ventaja sobre alguien sin que se la vea. □ *I got the contract because I was able to steal a march on my competitor.* □ *You have to be clever and fast—not dishonest—to steal a march.*

steal someone's thunder disminuir la fuerza o la autoridad de alguien. (No se usa literalmente.) □ *What do you mean by coming in here and stealing my thunder? I'm in charge here!* □ *Someone stole my thunder by leaking my announcement to the press.*

steal the show Véase la entrada siguiente.

steal the spotlight AND **steal the show** hacer la mejor interpretación, representación, o presentación de un espectáculo, obra de teatro, u otro suceso; llamarle la atención a sí mismo. □ *The lead in the play was very good, but the butler stole the show.* □ *Ann always tries to steal the spotlight when she and I make a presentation.*

steam, under one's own Véase *under one's own steam.*

stem to stern, from Véase *from stem to stern.*

step on it Véase en *step on the gas.*

step on someone's toes AND **tread on someone's toes** entrometerse en los asuntos de alguien; ofender a alguien. (También se usa literalmente. Observe los ejemplos con *anyone.*) □ *When you're in public office, you have to avoid stepping on anyone's toes.* □ *Ann trod on someone's toes during the last campaign and lost the election.*

step on the gas AND **step on it** apresurarse. □ *I'm in a hurry, driver. Step on it!* □ *I can't step on the gas, mister. There's too much traffic.*

step out of line   1. salir durante un momento de la cola. (Se usa literalmente.) □ *I stepped out of line for a minute and lost my place.* □ *It's better not to step out of line if you aren't sure you can get back in again.* 2. comportarse mal; hacer algo que puede ofender a alguien. → **saltarse (de) las reglas.** □ *I'm terribly sorry. I hope I didn't step out of line.* □ *John is a lot of fun to go out with, but he has a tendency to step out of line.*

stew in one's own juice   quedarse solo hasta que pase la ira o la decepción. □ *John has such a terrible temper. When he got mad at us, we just let him go away and stew in his own juice.* □ *After John stewed in his own juice for a while, he decided to come back and apologize to us.*

stick one's foot in one's mouth   Véase en *put one's foot in one's mouth.*

stick one's neck out   arriesgarse. → **jugarse el tipo.** □ *Why should I stick my neck out to do something for her? What's she ever done for me?* □ *He made a risky investment. He stuck his neck out because he thought he could make some money.*

stick one's nose in(to something)   Véase en *poke one's nose in(to something).*

stick to one's guns   mantenerse las creencias fuertes; salir en defensa de los derechos de sí mismo. → **mantenerse en sus trece.** □ *I'll stick to my guns on this matter. I'm sure I'm right.* □ *Bob can be persuaded to do it our way. He probably won't stick to his guns on this point.*

Still waters run deep.   un refrán significando que una persona callada probablemente esté pensando en cosas profundas o importantes. □ *Jane is so quiet. She's probably thinking. Still waters run deep, you know.* □ *It's true that still waters run deep, but I think that Jane is really half asleep.*

stir up a hornet's nest   producir problemas o dificultades. → **sembrar cizaña** □ *What a mess you have made of things. You've really stirred up a hornet's nest.* □ *Bill stirred up a hornet's nest when he discovered the theft.*

stock, have something in   Véase *have something in stock.*

stock, in   Véase *in stock.*

stone's throw away, a   Véase *a stone's throw away.*

straight from the horse's mouth   de alguna fuente fiable o de autoridad. (Es cliché. No se usa literalmente.) □ *I know it's true! I heard it straight from the horse's mouth!* □ *This comes straight from the horse's mouth, so it has to be believed.*

straight from the shoulder   sinceramente; francamente; sin dejar de decir algo. (Es cliché.) □ *Sally always speaks straight from the shoulder. You never have to guess what she really means.* □ *Bill gave a good presentation—straight from the shoulder and brief.*

strike a happy medium AND **hit a happy medium**   llegar a un acuerdo; llegar a un acuerdo a la mitad de dos extremos inaceptables. □ *Ann likes very spicy food, but Bob doesn't care for spicy food at all. We are trying to find a restaurant that strikes a happy medium.* □ *Tom is either very happy or very sad. He can't seem to hit a happy medium.*

strike a match   encender una cerilla. □ *Mary struck a match and lit a candle.* □ *When Sally struck a match to light a cigarette, Jane said quickly, "No smoking, please."*

strike a sour note AND **hit a sour note**   significar algo desagradable. □ *Jane's sad announcement struck a sour note at the annual banquet.* □ *News of the crime hit a sour note in our holiday celebration.*

strike, go (out) on   Véase *go (out) on strike.*

strike it rich   adquirir mucho dinero de repente. □ *If I could strike it rich, I wouldn't have to work anymore.* □ *Sally ordered a dozen oysters and found a huge pearl in one of them. She struck it rich!*

strike someone funny   divertir a alguien; ser humorístico. □ *Sally has a great sense of humor. Everything she says strikes me funny.* □ *Why are you laughing? Did something I said strike you funny?*

strike someone's fancy   atraer a alguien. ☐ *I'll have some ice-cream, please. Chocolate strikes my fancy right now.* ☐ *Why don't you go to the store and buy a record album that strikes your fancy?*

strike up a friendship   hacerse amigos (con alguien). ☐ *I struck up a friendship with John while we were on a business trip together.* ☐ *If you're lonely, you should go out and try to strike up a friendship with someone you like.*

strike while the iron is hot   hacer algo en el momento oportuno. (Es cliché.) ☐ *He was in a good mood, so I asked for a loan of $200. I thought I'd better strike while the iron was hot.* ☐ *Please go to the bank and settle this matter now! They are willing to be reasonable. You've got to strike while the iron is hot.*

strings attached, with no   Véase *with no strings attached.*

strings attached, without any   Véase *without any strings attached.*

strong as an ox, (as)   Véase *(as) strong as an ox.*

stubborn as a mule, (as)   Véase *(as) stubborn as a mule.*

stuff and nonsense   tonterías. ☐ *Come on! Don't give me all that stuff and nonsense!* ☐ *I don't understand this book. It's all stuff and nonsense as far as I am concerned.*

stuff the ballot box   meter votos fraudulentos en la urna; estafar en el recuento de los votos durante una elección. ☐ *The election judge was caught stuffing the ballot box in the election yesterday.* ☐ *Election officials are supposed to guard against stuffing the ballot box.*

suit someone to a T AND **fit someone to a T**   ser muy adecuado para alguien; venir de molde. ☐ *This kind of job suits me to a T.* ☐ *This is Sally's kind of house. It fits her to a T.*

sweat of one's brow, by the   Véase *by the sweat of one's brow.*

sweet tooth, have a Véase *have a sweet tooth.*

swim against the current Véase la entrada siguiente.

swim against the tide AND **swim against the current**
hacer lo opuesto de lo que hace todo el mundo. → **ir contra corriente.** □ *Bob tends to do what everybody else does. He isn't likely to swim against the tide.* □ *Mary always swims against the current. She's a very contrary person.*

T

table, under the   Véase *under the table*.

tail between one's legs, have one's   Véase *have one's tail between one's legs*.

tailspin, go into a   Véase *go into a tailspin*.

tail wagging the dog   una situación en que una parte pequeña de algo lo controla todo. □ *John was just hired yesterday, and today he's bossing everyone around. It's a case of the tail wagging the dog.* □ *Why is this small matter so important? Now the tail is wagging the dog!*

take a backseat (to someone)   delegar a alguien; darle el control a alguien. → **dejarse relegar a un segundo plano.** □ *I decided to take a backseat to Mary and let her manage the project.* □ *I had done the best I could, but it was time to take a backseat and let someone else run things.*

take a leaf out of someone's book   comportarse como se comportaría otra persona; hacer algo como lo haría otra persona. (*Leaf* significa "hoja.") → **seguir el ejemplo de alguien.** □ *When you act like that, you're taking a leaf out of your sister's book, and I don't like it!* □ *You had better do it your way. Don't take a leaf out of my book. I don't do it well.*

take a load off one's feet   Véase en *get a load off one's feet*.

take a nosedive   Véase en *go into a nosedive*.

take cold   Véase en *catch cold*.

take forty winks   pasar un rato durmiendo; dormirse. → **echarse una siesta; dar una cabezadita.** □ *I think I'll go to bed and take forty winks. See you in the morning.* □ *Why don't you go take forty winks and call me in about an hour?*

take it or leave it   aceptar algo como es o dejarlo. □ *This is my last offer. Take it or leave it.* □ *It's not much, but it's the only food we have. You can take it or leave it.*

take liberties with someone or something AND **make free with someone or something**   utilizar a alguien o algo; abusar de alguien o algo. → **tomarse libertades con alguien; tomarse confianzas con alguien.** □ *You are overly familiar with me, Mr. Jones. One might think you were taking liberties with me.* □ *I don't like it when you make free with my lawn mower. You should at least ask when you want to borrow it.*

take one's death of cold   Véase en *catch one's death (of cold).*

take one's medicine   aceptar el castigo o la mala suerte que merece uno. (También se usa literalmente.) → **apechugar con las consecuencias de algo (sin chistar).** □ *I know I did wrong, and I know I have to take my medicine.* □ *Billy knew he was going to get spanked, and he didn't want to take his medicine.*

take someone or something by storm   abrumar a alguien o algo; atraer mucha atención de alguien o algo. (Es cliché.) → **cautivar a alguien o algo.** □ *Jane is madly in love with Tom. He took her by storm at the office party, and they've been together ever since.* □ *The singer took the world of opera by storm with her performance in* La Boheme.

take someone or something for granted   tratar de alguien o algo bueno sin gratitud, como si fuera lo normal. → **dar algo por sentado; dar algo por descontado.** □ *We tend to take a lot of things for granted.* □ *Mrs. Franklin complained that Mr. Franklin takes her for granted.*

take someone's breath away   **1.** causar que alguien se quede sin respiración a causa del asombro o del esfuerzo físico. □ *Walking* *this fast takes my breath away.* □ *Mary frightened me and took my breath away.* **2.** aturdir a alguien con la belleza o el esplendor. → **dejar a alguien sin habla.** □ *The magnificent painting took my breath away.* □ *Ann looked so beautiful that she took my breath away.*

take someone under one's wing(s)   cuidar a alguien. → **hacerse cargo de alguien.** □ *John wasn't doing well in geometry until the teacher took him under her wing.* □ *I took the new workers under my wings, and they learned the job in no time.*

take something at face value   aceptar algo como ha sido presentado. □ *John said he wanted to come to the party, and I took that at face value. I'm sure he'll arrive soon.* □ *He made us a promise, and we took his word at face value.*

take something in stride   aceptar algo como natural o esperado. → **tomarse algo con calma.** □ *The argument surprised him, but he took it in stride.* □ *It was a very rude remark, but Mary took it in stride.*

take something lying down   aguantar o tolerar algo desa-gradable sin luchar. □ *He insulted me publicly. You don't expect me to take that lying down, do you?* □ *I'm not the kind of person who'll take something like that lying down.*

take something on faith   aceptar algo o creer en algo a base de poca o ninguna prueba. □ *Please try to believe what I'm telling you. Just take it on faith.* □ *Surely you can't expect me to take a story like that on faith.*

take something on the chin   experimentar o aguantar un golpe (figurada o literalmente). → **encajar bien un golpe.** □ *The bad news was a real shock, and John took it on the chin.* □ *The worst luck comes my way, and I always end up taking it on the chin.*

take something with a pinch of salt AND **take something with a grain of salt**   escuchar a un cuento o una explicación con dudas. → **no creerse algo al pie de la letra; tomar algo con pinzas.** □ *You must take anything she says with a grain* *of salt. She doesn't always tell the truth.* □ *They took my explanation with a pinch of salt. I was sure they didn't believe me.*

take the bitter with the sweet   aceptar los sucesos malos junto con los buenos. (Es cliché.) □ *We all have disappointments. You have to learn to take the bitter with the sweet.* □ *There are good days and bad days, but every day you take the bitter with the sweet. That's life.*

take the bull by the horns   enfrentarse directamente con un reto. (Es cliché.) → **agarrar (o coger) al toro por los cuernos (o las astas).** □ *If we are going to solve this problem, someone is going to have to take the bull by the horns.* □ *This threat isn't going to go away by itself. We are going to take the bull by the horns and settle this matter once and for all.*

take the law into one's own hands   intentar administrar la ley; hacer el papel del juez y jurado con una persona que ha hecho algo malo. → **tomarse la justicia por su propia mano.** □ *Citizens don't have the right to take the law into their own hands.* □ *The shopkeeper took the law into his own hands when he tried to arrest the thief.*

take the stand   ir al estrado como testigo en el tribunal. → **subir al estrado.** □ *I was in court all day, waiting to take the stand.* □ *The lawyer asked the witness to take the stand.*

take the words out of one's mouth   decir alguien lo que iba a decir uno. (También se usa con *right,* como se ve en los ejemplos.) □ *John said exactly what I was going to say. He took the words out of my mouth.* □ *I agree with you, and I wanted to say the same thing. You took the words right out of my mouth.*

take to one's heels   salir corriendo. → **salir pitando; poner pies en polvorosa.** □ *The little boy said hello and then took to his heels.* □ *The man took to his heels to try to get to the bus stop before the bus left.*

take up one's abode somewhere   echar raíces y vivir en algún sitio. (Literaria.) □ *I took up my abode downtown near my office.* □ *We decided to take up our abode in a warmer climate.*

talk a blue streak   decir mucho y hablar muy rápidamente. □ *Billy didn't talk until he was six, and then he started talking a blue streak.* □ *I can't understand anything Bob says. He talks a blue streak, and I can't follow his thinking.*

talk in circles   hablar con rodeos. □ *I couldn't understand a thing he said. All he did was talk in circles.* □ *We argued for a long time and finally decided that we were talking in circles.*

talk shop   hablar de los asuntos de negocios en una fiesta u otra ocasión social (donde no se debe hablar de estos asuntos.) □ *All right, everyone, we're not here to talk shop. Let's have a good time.* □ *Mary and Jane stood by the punch bowl, talking shop.*

talk through one's hat   decir tonterías; fanfarronear. → **hablar sin ton ni son.** □ *John isn't really as good as he says. He's just talking through his hat.* □ *Stop talking through your hat and start being sincere!*

talk until one is blue in the face   hablar hasta cansarse. □ *I talked until I was blue in the face, but I couldn't change her mind.* □ *She had to talk until she was blue in the face in order to convince him.*

target, on   Véase *on target.*

teacher's pet, be the   Véase *be the teacher's pet.*

tear one's hair   estar preocupado, descontento, o enojado (No se usa literalmente.) → **subirse por las paredes.** □ *I was so nervous, I was about to tear my hair.* □ *I had better get home. My parents will be tearing their hair.*

tell one to one's face   decirle algo directamente a la cara de alguien. □ *I'm sorry that Sally feels that way about me. I wish she had told me to my face.* □ *I won't tell Tom that you're mad at him. You should tell him to his face.*

tell tales out of school   contar secretos o hacer correr rumores. □ *I wish that John would keep quiet. He's telling tales out of school* *again.* □ *If you tell tales out of school a lot, people won't know when to believe you.*

tempest in a teapot   un tumulto que origina en algo de poca importancia. (Es cliché.) → **una tormenta en un vaso de agua.** □ *This isn't a serious problem—just a tempest in a teapot.* □ *Even a tempest in a teapot can take a lot of time to get settled.*

thank one's lucky stars   dar gracias uno por la buena suerte que tiene. (Es cliché.) → **dar gracias al cielo.** □ *You can thank your lucky stars that I was there to help you.* □ *I thank my lucky stars that I studied the right things for the test.*

That's the last straw. AND **That's the straw that broke the camel's back.**   Es la última cosa que uno puede aguantar. (Es cliché.) → **Es el colmo; Es la gota que colmó el vaso; Es la gota que derramó al vino.** □ *Now it's raining! That's the last straw. The picnic is canceled!* □ *When Sally came down sick, that was the straw that broke the camel's back.*

That's the straw that broke the camel's back.   Véase la entrada previa.

That's the ticket.   Es exactamente lo necesario. (Es cliché.) → **Esto viene como anillo al dedo.** □ *That's the ticket, John. You're doing it just the way it should be done.* □ *That's the ticket! I knew you could do it.*

That takes care of that.   Está decidido. (Es cliché.) □ *That takes care of that, and I'm glad it's over.* □ *I spent all morning dealing with this matter, and that takes care of that.*

The coast is clear.   Ya no hay peligro visible. → **No hay moros en la costa.** □ *I'm going to stay hidden here until the coast is clear.* □ *You can come out of your hiding place now. The coast is clear.*

The early bird gets the worm.   un refrán significando que la persona que se levanta temprano o que llega más temprano sale ganando al fin. → **El que madruga, Dios lo ayuda.** □ *Don't be late again! Don't you know that the early bird gets the worm?* □ *I'll be there before the sun is up. After all, the early bird gets the worm.*

The fat is in the fire.   un refrán significando que ya hay muchos problemas. → **Se va a armar la gorda; La cosa está que arde.** □ *Now that Mary is leaving, the fat is in the fire. How can we get along without her?* □ *The fat's in the fire! There's $3,000 missing from the office safe.*

The honeymoon is over.   El comienzo agradable de algo ha terminado. (Es cliché.) □ *Okay, the honeymoon is over. It's time to settle down and do some hard work.* □ *I knew the honeymoon was over when they started yelling at me to work faster.*

the pot calling the kettle black   cuando una persona con alguna falta dice que otro no debe tener la misma falta. (Es cliché.) → **Dijo la sartén al cazo: retírate que me tiznas.** □ *Ann is always late, but she was rude enough to tell everyone when I was late. Now that's the pot calling the kettle black!* □ *You're calling me thoughtless? That's really a case of the pot calling the kettle black.*

There are plenty of other fish in the sea   Hay muchas elecciones. (Es cliché. Referente a las personas) → **Hay mucho más donde elegir.** □ *When John broke up with Ann, I told her not to worry. There are plenty of other fish in the sea.* □ *It's too bad that your secretary quit, but there are plenty of other fish in the sea.*

There's more than one way to skin a cat.   un refrán significando que hay más de una manera de hacer algo. □ *If that way won't work, try another way. There's more than one way to skin a cat.* □ *Don't worry, I'll figure out a way to get it done. There's more than one way to skin a cat.*

There's no accounting for taste.   un refrán significando que uno no puede explicar las preferencias diferentes de las personas. □ *Look at that purple and orange car! There's no accounting for taste.* □ *Some people seemed to like the music, although I thought it was worse than noise. There's no accounting for taste.*

There will be the devil to pay.   Va a haber muchos problemas. □ *If you damage my car, there will be the devil to pay.* □ *Bill broke a window, and now there will be the devil to pay.*

The shoe is on the other foot. un refrán significando que uno está experimentado las mismas cosas que ha causado que otro experimente. (Observe las variaciones en los ejemplos.) → **Se ha dado vuelta la tortilla.** □ *The teacher is taking a course in summer school and is finding out what it's like when the shoe is on the other foot.* □ *When the policeman was arrested, he learned what it was like to have the shoe on the other foot.*

thick and thin, through Véase *through thick and thin.*

thick as pea soup, (as) Véase *(as) thick as pea soup.*

thick as thieves, (as) Véase *(as) thick as thieves.*

thin air, out of Véase *out of thin air.*

thin ice, on Véase *on thin ice.*

think on one's feet pensar uno mientras que está hablando. □ *If you want to be a successful teacher, you must be able to think on your feet.* □ *I have to write out everything I'm going to say, because I can't think on my feet too well.*

thorn in someone's side, be a Véase *be a thorn in someone's side.*

three-ring circus, like a Véase *like a three-ring circus.*

through thick and thin durante las épocas buenas y malas de la vida. (Es cliché.) → **por las buenas y las malas; contra viento y marea; contigo pan y cebolla.** □ *We've been together through thick and thin and we won't desert each other now.* □ *Over the years, we went through thick and thin and enjoyed every minute of it.*

throw a monkey wrench in the works causar problemas en los planes de uno. → **fastidiarlo todo.** □ *I don't want to throw a monkey wrench in the works, but have you checked your plans with a lawyer?* □ *When John refused to help us, he really threw a monkey wrench in the works.*

throw caution to the wind   ponerse muy descuidado. (Es cliché.) □ *Jane, who is usually cautious, threw caution to the wind and went windsurfing.* □ *I don't mind taking a little chance now and then, but I'm not the type of person who throws caution to the wind.*

throw cold water on something   Véase en *pour cold water on something.*

throw down the gauntlet   desafiar a alguien que disenta algo. → **arrrojar el guante.** □ *When Bob challenged my conclusions, he threw down the gauntlet. I was ready for an argument.* □ *Frowning at Bob is the same as throwing down the gauntlet. He loves to get into a fight about something.*

throw good money after bad   gastar más dinero en algo después de gastar dinero en la misma cosa al principio. (Es cliché.) → **seguir tirando dinero a la basura.** □ *I bought a used car and then had to spend $300 on repairs. That was throwing good money after bad.* □ *The Browns are always throwing good money after bad. They bought an acre of land that turned out to be swamp, and then had to pay to have it filled in.*

throw in the sponge   Véase la entrada siguiente.

throw in the towel AND **throw in the sponge**   dejar de hacer algo. → **tirar la esponja; tirar la toalla.** □ *When John could stand no more of Mary's bad temper, he threw in the towel and left.* □ *Don't give up now! It's too soon to throw in the sponge.*

throw oneself at someone's feet   acercarse a alguien con humildad. □ *Do I have to throw myself at your feet in order to convince you that I'm sorry?* □ *I love you sincerely, Jane. I'll throw myself at your feet and await your command. I'm your slave!*

throw oneself on the mercy of the court AND **throw oneself at the mercy of the court**   pedir clemencia al juez en el tribunal. □ *Your honor, please believe me, I didn't do it on purpose. I throw myself on the mercy of the court and beg for a light sentence.* □ *Jane threw herself at the mercy of the court and hoped for the best.*

throw someone a curve 1. lanzar una pelota en forma de curva en el béisbol. □ *The pitcher threw John a curve, and John swung wildly against thin air.* □ *During that game, the pitcher threw everyone a curve at least once.* 2. confundir a alguien haciendo algo inesperado. → **agarrar a alguien desprevenido; coger a alguien desprevenido.** □ *When you said* house *you threw me a curve. The password was supposed to be home.* □ *John threw me a curve when we were making our presentation, and I forgot my speech.*

throw someone for a loop AND **knock someone for a loop** confundir o asustar a alguien. → **dejar a alguien helado; dejar a alguien de piedra.** □ *When Bill heard the news, it threw him for a loop.* □ *The manager knocked Bob for a loop by firing him on the spot.*

throw someone to the wolves sacrificar a alguien (figuradamente). (Es cliché. No se usa literalmente.) □ *The press was demanding an explanation, so the mayor blamed the mess on John and threw him to the wolves.* □ *I wouldn't let them throw me to the wolves! I did nothing wrong, and I won't take the blame for their errors.*

throw something into the bargain añadir algo a algún trato. □ *To encourage me to buy a new car, the car dealer threw a free radio into the bargain.* □ *If you purchase three pounds of chocolates, I'll throw one pound of salted nuts into the bargain.*

thumb a ride AND **hitch a ride** ir coche de algún desconocido; hacer una señal con el pulgar que indica a los chóferes que uno quiere ir en su coche. → **hacer dedo; hacer autostop; ir de aventón.** □ *My car broke down on the highway, and I had to thumb a ride to get back to town.* □ *Sometimes it's dangerous to hitch a ride with a stranger.*

thumb one's nose at someone or something hacer un gesto grosero de repugnancia con el pulgar y la nariz (literal o figuradamente). □ *The tramp thumbed his nose at the lady and walked away.* □ *You can't just thumb your nose at people who give you trouble. You've got to learn to get along.*

tickle someone's fancy   interesar a alguien; poner a alguien interesado en algo. □ *I have an interesting problem here that I think will tickle your fancy.* □ *This doesn't tickle my fancy at all. This is dull and boring.*

tied to one's mother's apron strings   dominado por la madre; dependiente de la madre. → **estar pegado a las faldas de la madre.** □ *Tom is still tied to his mother's apron strings.* □ *Isn't he a little old to be tied to his mother's apron strings?*

tie someone in knots   ponerse preocupado o inquieto. □ *John tied himself in knots worrying about his wife during the operation.* □ *This waiting and worrying really ties me in knots.*

tie someone's hands   impedir que alguien haga algo. (También se usa literalmente.) □ *I'd like to help you, but my boss has tied my hands.* □ *Please don't tie my hands with unnecessary restrictions. I'd like the freedom to do whatever is necessary.*

tie the knot   casarse. □ *Well, I hear that you and John are going to tie the knot.* □ *My parents tied the knot almost forty years ago.*

tight as a tick, (as)   Véase *(as) tight as a tick.*

tight as Dick's hatband, (as)   Véase *(as) tight as Dick's hatband.*

tighten one's belt   gastar menos dinero; ahorrar. □ *Things are beginning to cost more and more. It looks like we'll all have to tighten our belts.* □ *Times are hard, and prices are high. I can tighten my belt for only so long.*

tilt at windmills   luchar (figuradamente) con los enemigos imaginarios; luchar (figuradamente) contra enemigos o asuntos poco importantes. (Como el personaje Don Quijote, quien atacó a los molinos de viento como si fueran enemigos.) → **luchar contra molinos de viento.** □ *Aren't you too smart to go around tilting at windmills?* □ *I'm not going to fight this issue. I've wasted too much of my life tilting at windmills.*

Time hangs heavy on someone's hands. El tiempo pasa lentamente cuando uno no tiene mucho que hacer. (No se usa literalmente. Observe las variaciones en los ejemplos.) □ *I don't like it when time hangs so heavily on my hands.* □ *John looks so bored. Time hangs heavy on his hands.*

Time is money. El tiempo mío vale mucho, así que no lo derroche Ud. → **El tiempo es oro.** □ *I can't afford to spend a lot of time standing here talking. Time is money, you know!* □ *People who keep saying time is money may be working too hard.*

time of one's life, have the Véase *have the time of one's life.*

tip of one's tongue, on the Véase *on the tip of one's tongue.*

tip the scales at something pesar alguien cierta cantidad importante. □ *Tom tips the scales at nearly 200 pounds.* □ *I'll be glad when I tip the scales at a few pounds less.*

tiptoe, on Véase *on tiptoe.*

toes, on one's Véase *on one's toes.*

toe the line Véase la entrada siguiente.

toe the mark AND **toe the line** hacer lo esperado; seguir las reglas. → **acatar la disciplina.** □ *You'll get ahead, Sally. Don't worry. Just toe the mark, and everything will be okay.* □ *John finally got fired. He just couldn't learn to toe the line.*

tongue-in-cheek poco sincero; de broma. □ *Ann made a tongue-in-cheek remark to John, and he got mad because he thought she was serious.* □ *The play seemed very serious at first, but then everyone saw that it was tongue-in-cheek, and they began laughing.*

too good to be true casi increíble; tan bueno que no puede ser la verdad. (Es cliché.) □ *The news was too good to be true.* □ *When I finally got a big raise, it was too good to be true.*

Too many cooks spoil the broth. Véase la entrada siguiente.

Too many cooks spoil the stew. AND **Too many cooks spoil the broth.**   un refrán significando que cuando demasiadas personas trabajan en hacer algo sencillo lo estropean o lo destruyen. □ *Let's decide who is in charge around here. Too many cooks spoil the stew.* □ *Everyone is giving orders, but no one is following them! Too many cooks spoil the broth.*

too many irons in the fire, have   Véase *have too many irons in the fire.*

to one's heart's content   tanto como quiere uno. □ *John wanted a week's vacation so he could go to the lake and fish to his heart's content.* □ *I just sat there, eating chocolate to my heart's content.*

toot one's own horn AND **blow one's own horn**   vangloriarse (de sí mismo). □ *Tom is always tooting his own horn. Is he really as good as he says he is?* □ *I find it hard to blow my own horn, but I manage.*

top of one's head, off the   Véase *off the top of one's head.*

top of one's lungs, at the   Véase *at the top of one's lungs.*

top of one's voice, at the   Véase *at the top of one's voice.*

top of the world, on   Véase *on top of the world.*

top, on   Véase *on top.*

top, over the   Véase *over the top.*

top to bottom, from   Véase *from top to bottom.*

toss one's hat into the ring   declarar que uno va a presentarse como candidato en una elección. → **estar en la contienda; entrar en liga; lanzarse al ruedo.** □ *Jane wanted to run for treasurer, so she tossed her hat into the ring.* □ *The mayor never tossed his hat into the ring. Instead he announced his retirement.*

to the ends of the earth   hasta las partes más remotas e inaccesibles de la tierra. → **hasta el fin del mundo; hasta los confines de la tierra.** □ *I'll pursue him to the ends of the earth.* □ *We've almost explored the whole world. We've traveled to the ends of the earth trying to learn about our world.*

To the victors belong the spoils.   un refrán significando que los ganadores pueden apoderarse de las personas y la propriedad. □ *The mayor took office and immediately fired many workers and hired new ones. Everyone said, "To the victors belong the spoils."* □ *The office of president includes the right to live in the White House and at Camp David. To the victors belong the spoils.*

tough act to follow   una presentación o representación difícil de seguir. (Es cliché.) □ *Bill's speech was excellent. It was a tough act to follow, but my speech was good also.* □ *In spite of the fact that I had a tough act to follow, I did my best.*

tough row to hoe   una tarea difícil de emprender. (Es cliché.) □ *It was a tough row to hoe, but I finally got a college degree.* □ *Getting the contract signed is going to be a tough row to hoe, but I'm sure I can do it.*

town, go to   Véase *go to town.*

town, out on the   Véase *out on the town.*

tread on someone's toes   Véase en *step on someone's toes.*

trial, on   Véase *on trial.*

true to one's word   cumplir con una promesa; hacer tal como promete uno. □ *True to his word, Tom showed up at exactly eight o'clock.* □ *We'll soon know if Jane is true to her word. We'll see if she does what she promised.*

try one's wings (out) AND **try out one's wings**   intentar hacer algo que últimamente se ha puesto calificado para hacer (como hace un pájaro joven con las alas). → **alzar el vuelo; levantar el vuelo.** □ *John just got his driver's license and wants* *to borrow the car to try out his wings.* □ *I learned to skin dive, and I want to go to the seaside to try out my wings.* □ *You've read about it enough. It's time to try your wings.*

try someone's patience   hacer algo que puede fastidiar a alguien; causar que una persona se fastidie. □ *Stop whistling. You're trying my patience. Very soon I'm going to lose my temper.* □ *Some students think it's fun to try the teacher's patience.*

tune (with someone or something), out of   Véase *out of tune (with someone or something).*

turn a blind eye to someone or something   pasar algo por alto y fingir que no lo ve. → **hacer la vista gorda frente a algo.** □ *The usher turned a blind eye to the little boy who sneaked into the theater.* □ *How can you turn a blind eye to all those starving children?*

turn a deaf ear (to something)   hacer caso omiso de lo que dice alguien; hacer caso omiso de un ruego. → **hacer oídos sordos a alguien o algo.** □ *How can you just turn a deaf ear to their cries for food and shelter?* □ *The government has turned a deaf ear.*

turn on a dime   dar una vuelta en poco espacio. → **ser maniobrable.** □ *This car handles very well. It can turn on a dime.* □ *The speeding car turned on a dime and headed in the other direction.*

turn one's nose up at someone or something AND **turn up one's nose at someone or something**   adoptar un aire despreciativo en cuanto a algo; rechazar a alguien o algo. → **hacerle ascos a alguien o algo.** □ *John turned his nose up at Ann, and that hurt her feelings.* □ *I never turn up my nose at dessert, no matter what it is.*

turn, out of   Véase *out of turn.*

turn over a new leaf   empezar algo de nuevo con el propósito de hacerlo mejor; empezar de nuevo, no pensando en los errores del pasado. (Es cliché.) → **hacer borrón y cuenta nueva.** □ *Tom promised to turn over a new leaf and do better from now on.* □ *After* *a minor accident, Sally decided to turn over a new leaf and drive more carefully.*

turn over in one's grave estar escandalizado [un muerto]. (Es cliché. Claro que no se usa literalmente.) □ *If Beethoven heard Mary play one of his sonatas, he'd turn over in his grave.* □ *If Aunt Jane knew what you were doing with her favorite chair, she would turn over in her grave.*

turn someone's stomach hacer que alguien se ponga enfermo (literal o figuradamente). □ *This milk is spoiled. The smell of it turns my stomach.* □ *The play was so bad that it turned my stomach.*

turn something to one's advantage sacar ventaja de algo que podría haber sido desventaja. □ *Sally found a way to turn the problem to her advantage.* □ *The ice-cream store manager was able to turn the hot weather to her advantage.*

turn the other cheek pasar por alto los abusos o los insultos. (Es referencia bíblica.) □ *When Bob got mad at Mary and yelled at her, she just turned the other cheek.* □ *Usually I turn the other cheek when someone is rude to me.*

turn the tide causar un cambio completo en alguna tendencia; causar un cambio completo de la opinión pública acerca de algo. □ *It looked as if the team was going to lose, but near the end of the game, our star player turned the tide.* □ *At first, people were opposed to our plan. After a lot of discussion, we were able to turn the tide.*

twiddle one's thumbs pasar el tiempo jugando con los dedos. □ *What am I supposed to do while waiting for you? Sit here and twiddle my thumbs?* □ *Don't sit around twiddling your thumbs. Get busy!*

twinkling of an eye, in the Véase *in the twinkling of an eye.*

twist someone around one's little finger manipular y controlar a alguien. (Es cliché.) □ *Bob really fell for Jane. She can twist him around her little finger.* □ *Billy's mother has twisted him around her little finger. He's very dependent on her.*

twist someone's arm   forzar o persuadir a alguien de hacer algo.
□ *At first she refused, but after I twisted her arm a little, she agreed to help.* □ *I didn't want to run for mayor, but everyone twisted my arm.*

two shakes of a lamb's tail, in   Véase *in two shakes of a lamb's tail.*

U

under a cloud (of suspicion)   ser sospechado dc hacer algo. □ *Someone stole some money at work, and now everyone is under a cloud of suspicion.* □ *Even the manager is under a cloud.*

under construction   en obras. □ *We cannot travel on this road because it's under construction.* □ *Our new home has been under construction all summer. We hope to move in next month.*

under fire   durante un ataque. □ *There was a scandal in city hall, and the mayor was forced to resign under fire.* □ *John is a good lawyer because he can think under fire.*

under one's own steam   a causa del poder o del esfuerzo de uno. □ *I missed my ride to class, so I had to get there under my own steam.* □ *John will need some help with this project. He can't do it under his own steam.*

under the counter   ilegalmente o en secreto [la venta o la compra de algo]. (También se usa literalmente.) □ *The drugstore owner was arrested for selling liquor under the counter.* □ *This owner was also selling dirty books under the counter.*

under the table   algo hecho en secreto, como el ofrecimiento de un soborno. (También se usa literalmente.) □ *The mayor had been paying money to the construction company under the table.* □ *Tom transferred the deed to the property to his wife under the table.*

under the weather   enfermo. □ *I'm a bit under the weather today, so I can't go to the office.* □ *My head is aching, and I feel a little under the weather.*

under the wire   apenas a tiempo o justamente a tiempo. ☐ *I turned in my report just under the wire.* ☐ *Bill was the last person to get in the door. He got in under the wire.*

up a blind alley   en un callejón sin salida (literal o figuradamente). ☐ *I have been trying to find out something about my ancestors, but I'm up a blind alley. I can't find anything.* ☐ *The police are up a blind alley in their investigation of the crime.*

up in arms   alzarse en armas; muy enojado. → **poner el grito en el cielo; estar que subirse por las paredes.** ☐ *My father was really up in arms when he got his tax bill this year.* ☐ *The citizens were up in arms, pounding on the gates of the palace, demanding justice.*

up in the air   pendiente; no resuelto. (También se usa literalmente.) ☐ *I don't know what Sally plans to do. Things were sort of up in the air the last time we talked.* ☐ *Let's leave this question up in the air until next week.*

upset the apple cart   estropear o arruinar algo. ☐ *Tom really upset the apple cart by telling Mary the truth about Jane.* ☐ *I always knew he'd upset the apple cart.*

up to one's ears (in something)   Véase la entrada siguiente.

up to one's neck (in something) AND **up to one's ears (in something)**   muy envuelto en algo. → **metido hasta el cuello.** ☐ *I can't come to the meeting. I'm up to my neck in these reports.* ☐ *Mary is up to her ears in her work.*

up to par   tan bueno como la norma o el promedio. ☐ *I'm just not feeling up to par today. I must be coming down with something.* ☐ *The manager said that the report was not up to par and gave it back to Mary to do over again.*

use every trick in the book   intentar por todos los modos posibles hacer o conseguir algo. ☐ *I used every trick in the book, but I still couldn't manage to get a ticket to the game Saturday.* ☐ *Bob tried to use every trick in the book, but he still failed.*

utter a word, not   Véase *not utter a word.*

V

vacation, on Véase *on vacation.*

vanish into thin air desaparecer sin dejar huellas. □ *My money gets spent so fast. It seems to vanish into thin air.* □ *When I came back, my car was gone. I had locked it, and it couldn't have vanished into thin air!*

Variety is the spice of life. un refrán significando que con mucho cambio la vida es más interesante. □ *Mary reads all kinds of books. She says variety is the spice of life.* □ *The Franklins travel all over the world so they can learn how different people live. After all, variety is the spice of life.*

vicious circle, in a Véase *in a vicious circle.*

victors belong the spoils, To the. Véase *To the victors belong the spoils.*

virtue of something, by Véase *by virtue of something.*

vote a straight ticket llenar la papeleta de votación con todos los miembros del mismo partido político. □ *I'm not a member of any political party, so I never vote a straight ticket.* □ *I usually vote a straight ticket because I believe in the principles of one party and not in the other's.*

wagon, on the Véase *on the wagon.*

wait-and-see attitude una actitud escéptica; una actidud con la cual uno va a esperar a ver lo que pasa antes de decidir algo. □ *John thought that Mary couldn't do it, but he took a wait-and-see attitude.* □ *His wait-and-see attitude didn't influence me at all.*

waiting list, on a Véase *on a waiting list.*

wait on someone hand and foot cuidar a alguien muy bien. □ *I don't mind bringing you your coffee, but I don't intend to wait on you hand and foot.* □ *I don't want anyone to wait on me hand and foot. I can take care of myself.*

walk a tightrope estar en una situación posiblemente peligrosa. (También se usa literalmente.) □ *I've been walking a tightrope all day. I need to relax.* □ *Our business is about to fail. We've been walking a tightrope for three months.*

walk on air estar muy contento; estar eufórico. (Nunca se usa literalmente.) □ *Ann was walking on air when she got the job.* □ *On the last day of school, all the children are walking on air.*

walk on eggs estar muy cauteloso. (Nunca se usa literalmente.) □ *The manager is very hard to deal with. You really have to walk on eggs.* □ *I've been walking on eggs ever since I started working here.*

walk the floor caminar de arriba para abajo mientras uno espera algo. □ *While Bill waited for news of the operation, he walked the floor for hours on end.* □ *Walking the floor won't help. You might as well sit down and relax.*

wall, go to the Véase *go to the wall.*

walls have ears   posiblemente otros nos oigan. (Es cliché.) □ *Let's not discuss this matter here. Walls have ears, you know.* □ *Shhh. Walls have ears. Someone may be listening.*

warm the bench   no jugar durante un partido [un atleta], sentado en el banquillo. □ *John spent the whole game warming the bench.* □ *Mary never warms the bench. She plays from the beginning to the end.*

warm the cockles of someone's heart   hacer que alguien esté muy contento. (Es cliché.) □ *It warms the cockles of my heart to hear you say that.* □ *Hearing that old song again warmed the cockles of her heart.*

wash one's hands of someone or something   dejar de asociarse con alguien o algo. □ *I washed my hands of Tom. I wanted no more to do with him.* □ *That car was a real headache. I washed my hands of it long ago.*

waste one's breath   perder el tiempo hablando; hablar en balde. □ *Don't waste your breath talking to her. She won't listen.* □ *You can't persuade me. You're just wasting your breath.*

watched pot never boils, A.   Véase *A watched pot never boils.*

water off a duck's back, like   Véase *like water off a duck's back.*

water under the bridge   pasado y olvidado. (Es cliché.) □ *Please don't worry about it anymore. It's all water under the bridge.* □ *I can't change the past. It's water under the bridge.*

weak as a kitten, (as)   Véase *(as) weak as a kitten.*

weakness for someone or something, have a   Véase *have a weakness for someone or something.*

wear more than one hat   tener varias responsabilidades; tener más de un cargo. □ *The mayor is also the police chief. She wears more than one hat.* □ *I have too much to do to wear more than one hat.*

wear out one's welcome   quedarse más allá de lo esperado (como invitado); visitar a algún lugar durante demasiado tiempo. (Es cliché.) □ *Tom visited the Smiths so often that he wore out his welcome.* □ *At about midnight, I decided that I had worn out my welcome, so I went home.*

weather, under the   Véase *under the weather.*

well-fixed   Véase la entrada siguiente.

well-heeled AND **well-fixed; well-off**   rico; con bastante dinero. □ *My uncle can afford a new car. He's well-heeled.* □ *Everyone in his family is well-off.*

well-off   Véase la entrada previa.

well-to-do   rico y con buena posición social. (Muchas veces se usa con *quite,* como en los ejemplos.) □ *The Jones family is quite well-to-do.* □ *There is a gentleman waiting for you at the door. He appears quite well-to-do.*

were, as it   Véase *as it were.*

wet behind the ears   joven y sin experiencia. □ *John's too young to take on a job like this! He's still wet behind the ears!* □ *He may be wet behind the ears, but he's well trained and totally competent.*

What is sauce for the goose is sauce for the gander.   un refrán significando que lo que es sirve para una persona sirve para otra. □ *If John gets a new coat, I should get one, too. After all, what is sauce for the goose is sauce for the gander.* □ *If I get punished for breaking the window, so should Mary. What is sauce for the goose is sauce for the gander.*

what makes someone tick   lo que motiva a alguien; lo que causa que alguien se comporte de alguna manera. □ *William is sort of strange. I don't know what makes him tick.* □ *When you get to know people, you find out what makes them tick.*

When in Rome, do as the Romans do.   un refrán significando que las personas se deben comportar en un sitio como los que viven allí. → **Donde fueres haz como vieres.** □ *I don't usually eat lamb, but I did when I went to Australia. When in Rome, do as the Romans do.* □ *I always carry an umbrella when I visit London. When in Rome, do as the Romans do.*

When the cat's away the mice will play.   Algunas personas hacen travesuras cuando nadie las mira. (Es cliché.) → **Cuando el gato duerme, bailan los ratones.** □ *The students behaved very badly for the substitute teacher. When the cat's away the mice will play.* □ *John had a wild party at his house when his parents were out of town. When the cat's away the mice will play.*

when the time is ripe   en el momento preciso. □ *I'll tell her the good news when the time is ripe.* □ *When the time is ripe, I'll bring up the subject again.*

Where there's a will there's a way.   un refrán significando que una persona puede llegar a hacer algo si de veras quiere hacerlo. □ *Don't give up, Ann. You can do it. Where there's a will there's a way.* □ *They told John he'd never walk again after his accident. He worked at it, and he was able to walk again! Where there's a will there's a way.*

Where there's smoke there's fire.   un refrán significando que los indicios de un problema probablemente indican que hay un problema. □ *There is a lot of noise coming from the classroom. There is probably something wrong. Where there's smoke there's fire.* □ *I think there is something wrong at the house on the corner. The police are there again. Where there's smoke there's fire.*

whisker, by a   Véase *by a whisker.*

white as the driven snow, (as)   Véase *(as) white as the driven snow.*

wide of the mark   **1.** lejos del blanco. □ *Tom's shot was wide of the mark.* □ *The pitch was quite fast, but wide of the mark.* **2.** inepto;

sin darse en lo requerido o esperado. □ *Jane's efforts were sincere, but wide of the mark.* □ *He failed the course because everything he did was wide of the mark.*

wild-goose chase   una caza en vano. □ *I wasted all afternoon on a wild-goose chase.* □ *John was angry because he was sent out on a wild-goose chase.*

win by a nose   ganar por una diferencia muy escasa. (Como en las carreras de caballos.) □ *I ran the fastest race I could, but I only won by a nose.* □ *Sally won the race, but she only won by a nose.*

wind, in the   Véase *in the wind.*

wire, down to the   Véase *down to the wire.*

wire, under the   Véase *under the wire.*

wise as an owl, (as)   Véase *(as) wise as an owl.*

with all one's heart and soul   muy sinceramente. (Es cliché.) □ *Oh, Bill, I love you with all my heart and soul, and I always will!* □ *She thanked us with all her heart and soul for the gift.*

with both hands tied behind one's back   Véase en *with one hand tied behind one's back.*

wither on the vine AND **die on the vine**   disminuir o irse apagando algo en una etapa temprana de su desarrollo. (También se usa literalmente para referirse a las uvas u otras frutas.) □ *You have a great plan, Tom. Let's keep it alive. Don't let it wither on the vine.* □ *The whole project died on the vine when the contract was canceled.*

with every (other) breath   repitada y continuamente [diciendo algo]. □ *Bob was out in the yard, raking leaves and cursing with every other breath.* □ *The child was so grateful that she was thanking me with every breath.*

with flying colors   fácilmente y por excelencia. □ *John passed his geometry test with flying colors.* □ *Sally qualified for the race with flying colors.*

within an inch of one's life   muy cercano a la muerte. (Es cliché.) □ *The accident frightened me within an inch of my life.* □ *When Mary was seriously ill in the hospital, she came within an inch of her life.*

with no strings attached AND **without any strings attached**   sin condiciones ni obligaciones. □ *My parents gave me a computer without any strings attached.* □ *I want this only if it comes with no strings attached.*

with one hand tied behind one's back AND **with both hands tied behind one's back**   con desventaja; fácilmente. (Es cliché.) □ *I could put an end to this argument with one hand tied behind my back.* □ *John could do this job with both hands tied behind his back.*

without any strings attached   Véase en *with no strings attached.*

without batting an eye   sin mostrar preocupación ni reacción. (Es cliché.) □ *I knew I had insulted her, but she turned to me and asked me to leave without batting an eye.* □ *Right in the middle of the speech—without batting an eye—the speaker walked off the stage.*

without further ado   sin hablar más. (Es cliché. Se usa muchas veces en los anuncios.) □ *And without further ado, I would like to introduce Mr. Bill Franklin!* □ *The time has come to leave, so without further ado, good evening and good-bye.*

wit's end, at one's   Véase *at one's wit's end.*

wolf in sheep's clothing   algo amenazante disfrazado de algo bueno. (Es cliché.) → **un lobo disfrazado de cordero.** □ *Beware of the police chief. He seems polite, but he's a wolf in sheep's clothing.* □ *This proposal seems harmless enough, but I think it's a wolf in sheep's clothing.*

woods, out of the   Véase *out of the woods.*

word, go back on one's   Véase *go back on one's word.*

word go, from the   Véase *from the word go.*

word of mouth, by   Véase *by word of mouth.*

words stick in one's throat, have one's   Véase *have one's words stick in one's throat.*

work like a horse   trabajar muy asiduamente. (Es cliché.) □ *I've been working like a horse all day, and I'm tired.* □ *I'm too old to work like a horse. I'd prefer to relax more.*

work one's fingers to the bone   trabajar muy duro. (Es cliché.) → **deslomarse trabajando.** □ *I worked my fingers to the bone so you children could have everything you needed. Now look at the way you treat me!* □ *I spent the day working my fingers to the bone, and now I want to relax.*

work out for the best   terminar lo más bien posible. □ *Don't worry. Things will work out for the best.* □ *It seems bad now, but it'll work out for the best.*

world, in the   Véase *in the world.*

world of one's own, in a   Véase *in a world of one's own.*

world, out of this   Véase *out of this world.*

worst comes to worst, if   Véase *if worst comes to worst.*

worth its weight in gold   de mucho valor. (Es cliché.) □ *This book is worth its weight in gold.* □ *Oh, Bill. You're wonderful. You're worth your weight in gold.*

worth one's salt   merecer el sueldo que cobra uno. (Es cliché.) □ *Tom doesn't work very hard, and he's just barely worth his salt, but he's very easy to get along with.* □ *I think he's more than worth his salt. He's a good worker.*

wrack and ruin, go to   Véase *go to wrack and ruin.*

wrong, in the   Véase *in the wrong.*

wrong track, on the   Véase *on the wrong track.*

X

X marks the spot Es el lugar preciso. (Es cliché. También se puede usar literalmente cuando alguien dibuja una ["X"] en un sitio para marcarlo.) □ *This is where the rock struck my car—X marks the spot.* □ *Now, please move that table over here. Yes, right here— X marks the spot.*

Y

year in, year out todo el año; año tras año. □ *I seem to have hay fever year in, year out. I never get over it.* □ *John wears the same old suit, year in, year out.*

You can say that again! AND **You said it!** Es la verdad; Tiene Ud. la razón. (*That* tiene el énfasis.) □ MARY: *It sure is hot today.* JANE: *You can say that again!* □ BILL: *This cake is yummy!* BOB: *You said it!*

You can't take it with you. Se debe gozar del dinero ahora, porque no se va a poder hacerlo después de la muerte. (Es cliché.) □ *My uncle is a wealthy miser. I keep telling him, "You can't take it with you."* □ *If you have money, you should make out a will. You can't take it with you, you know!*

You can't teach an old dog new tricks. un refrán significando que las personas viejas no pueden aprender cosas nuevas. (También se usa literalmente referente a los perros.) → **Loro viejo no aprende a hablar.** □ *"Of course I can learn," bellowed uncle John. "Who says you can't teach an old dog new tricks?"* □ *I'm sorry. I can't seem to learn to do it right. Oh, well. You can't teach an old dog new tricks.*

Your guess is as good as mine. Su respuesta tiene la misma probabildad de ser correcta como la mía. □ *I don't know where the scissors are. Your guess is as good as mine.* □ *Your guess is as good as mine as to when the train will arrive.*

You said it! Véase en *You can say that again!*

Z

zero in on something concentrarse en algo; enfocar en algo. □ *"Now," said Mr. Smith, "I would like to zero in on another important point."* □ *Mary is very good about zeroing in on the most important and helpful ideas.*

Index of Spanish Phrases

a buen santo te encomiendas   Véase *bark up the wrong tree.*

A caballo regalado no hay que mirarle el diente   Véase *Beggars can't be choosers.*

a empezar de nuevo   Véase *back to the drawing board.*

a estas alturas   Véase *at this stage (of the game).*

a gatas   Véase *on all fours.*

a grandes pasos   Véase *by leaps and bounds.*

a grito pelado   Véase *at the top of one's voice.*

a la par   Véase *neck and neck.*

a las puertas de la muerte   Véase *at death's door.*

A los tontos no les dura el dinero   Véase *A fool and his money are soon parted.*

a lo sumo   Véase *at the outside.*

a mano   Véase *close at hand.*

a media asta   Véase *at half-mast.*

a paso de tortuga   Véase *at a snail's pace.*

A quien madruga, Dios le ayuda   Véase *Early to bed, early to rise, (makes a man healthy, wealthy, and wise).*

a tiro de piedra   Véase *a stone's throw away.*

a última hora   Véase *at the eleventh hour; at the last minute.*

a un paso   Véase *a stone's throw away.*

a voz en cuello   Véase *at the top of one's voice.*

a voz en grito   Véase *at the top of one's voice.*

a vuelo de pájaro   Véase *as the crow flies.*

a vuelta de correo   Véase *by return mail.*

abrir los ojos   Véase *begin to see the light.*

abrir nuevas fronteras   Véase *break new ground.*

acatar la disciplina   Véase *toe the mark.*

agarrar a alguien desprevenido   Véase *throw someone a curve.*

agarrar al toro por las astas   Véase *beard the lion in his den.*

agarrar (o coger) al toro por los cuernos (o las astas)   Véase *take the bull by the horns.*

al chas chas   Véase *cash-and-carry.*

al final todo se arreglará   Véase *come out in the wash.*

al pan, pan y al vino, vino   Véase *call a spade a spade.*

alzar el vuelo   Véase *try one's wings (out).*

amor a primera vista   Véase *love at first sight.*

andar escaso de algo   Véase *caught short.*

andarse con rodeos   Véase *beat around the bush.*

andarse por las ramas   Véase *beat around the bush.*

apechugar con las consecuencias de algo (sin chistar)   Véase *take one's medicine.*

apuntarse al carro   Véase *climb on the bandwagon.*

arrimarse al que lleva la batuta   Véase *climb on the bandwagon.*

arrrojar el guante   Véase *throw down the gauntlet.*

asediar a alguien   Véase *beat a path to someone's door.*

beben agua del mismo jarrito   Véase *(as) thick as thieves.*

brillar uno por su ausencia   Véase *conspicuous by one's absence.*

buscarse problemas   Véase *ask for trouble.*

cada mochuelo a su olivo   Véase *back to the salt mines.*

cada pago aguante su vela   Véase *bear one's cross.*

callejón sin salida   Véase *in a vicious circle.*

caso pertinente   Véase *case in point.*

cautivar a alguien o algo   Véase *take someone or something by storm.*

cerrar las filas   Véase *close ranks.*

ciego como un topo   Véase *(as) blind as a bat.*

coger a alguien desprevenido   Véase *throw someone a curve.*

coger al toro por los cuernos   Véase *beard the lion in his den.*

coger catarro   Véase *catch cold.*

coger un resfriado   Véase *catch cold.*

como alma que lleva el diablo   Véase *like a bat out of hell.*

como arar en el mar   Véase *beat a dead horse.*

como buscar una aguja en un pajar   Véase *like looking for a needle in a haystack.*

como Dios manda   Véase *according to Hoyle.*

como gallina en corral ajeno   Véase *like a fish out of water.*

como machacar en hierro frío   Véase *beat a dead horse.*

como sapo de otro pozo   Véase *like a fish out of water.*

como un reloj   Véase *(as) regular as clockwork.*

como unas pascuas   Véase *(as) happy as a lark.*

comprar algo por cuatro cuartos   Véase *buy something for a song.*

comprar algo por poca cosa   Véase *buy something for a song.*

comprender las cosas   Véase *begin to see the light.*

con el sudor de la frente   Véase *by the sweat of one's brow.*

confiarse en algo   Véase *bank on something.*

contigo pan y cebolla   Véase *through thick and thin.*

contra viento y marea   Véase *come what may; through thick and thin.*

costar un ojo de la cara   Véase *cost a pretty penny; pay an arm and a leg (for something).*

Cuando el gato duerme, bailan los ratones   Véase *When the cat's away the mice will play.*

cuanto antes   Véase *(as) soon as possible.*

cuento chino   Véase *cock-and-bull story.*

dar algo por descontado   Véase *take someone or something for granted.*

dar algo por sentado   Véase *take someone or something for granted.*

dar el primer paso   Véase *break the ice.*

dar en el blanco   Véase *hit the bull's-eye.*

dar gracias al cielo   Véase *thank one's lucky stars.*

dar la noticia   Véase *break the news (to someone).*

dar órdenes   Véase *lay down the law.*

dar por acabado   Véase *call it a day.*

dar rienda suelta a la indignación   Véase *let off steam.*

dar una cabezadita   Véase *take forty winks.*

dar vueltas de cabeza   Véase *boggle someone's mind.*

darle la lata a alguien   Véase *bend someone's ear.*

darse la gran vida   Véase *lead the life of Riley.*

darse un batacazo   Véase *come a cropper.*

de bracete   Véase *arm-in-arm.*

de esto ni palabra a nadie   Véase *keep something under one's hat.*

de palabra   Véase *by word of mouth.*

de tal palo, tal astilla   Véase *a chip off the old block.*

de un tirón   Véase *at one fell swoop.*

de una sola vez   Véase *at one fell swoop.*

de viva voz   Véase *by word of mouth.*

dejar a alguien de piedra   Véase *throw someone for a loop.*

dejar a alguien en la estacada   Véase *leave someone high and dry.*

dejar a alguien en la estacada   Véase *leave someone in the lurch.*

dejar a alguien en paz   Véase *leave someone in peace.*

dejar a alguien helado   Véase *throw someone for a loop.*

dejar a alguien sin habla   Véase *take someone's breath away.*

dejar a alguien tirado   Véase *leave someone high and dry; leave someone in the lurch.*

dejar que las cosas se vengan abajo   Véase *let something slide.*

dejarle a alguien mal sabor de boca   Véase *leave a bad taste in someone's mouth.*

dejarse de cuentos   Véase *come to the point.*

dejarse relegar a un segundo plano   Véase *take a backseat (to someone).*

descubrir el pastel   Véase *let the cat out of the bag.*

desde abajo   Véase *at the bottom of the ladder.*

deslomarse   Véase *break one's neck (to do something).*

deslomarse trabajando   Véase *work one's fingers to the bone.*

Dijo la sartén al cazo: retírate que me tiznas   Véase *the pot calling the kettle black.*

Dios los cría y ellos se juntan   Véase *Birds of a feather flock together.*

Donde fueres haz como vieres   Véase *When in Rome, do as the Romans do.*

dormir como un tronco   Véase *dead to the world.*

echar leña al fuego   Véase *add fuel to the fire.*

echarse una siesta   Véase *take forty winks.*

ejemplo claro   Véase *case in point.*

el alma de la fiesta   Véase *life of the party.*

El dinero es el origen de todos los males   Véase *Money is the root of all evil.*

El movimiento se demuestra andando   Véase *Actions speak louder than words.*

El pasado, pasado está   Véase *Let bygones be bygones.*

el que espera, desespera   Véase *A watched pot never boils.*

El que madruga, Dios lo ayuda   Véase *The early bird gets the worm.*

El tiempo es oro   Véase *Time is money.*

en cualquier momento   Véase *at the drop of a hat.*

en la flor de la vida [referente a personas]   Véase *in one's or its prime.*

en la flor de la vida [referente a personas]   Véase *in the prime of life.*

en la punta de la lengua   Véase *on the tip of one's tongue.*

En las malas se conoce a los amigos   Véase *A friend in need is a friend indeed.*

en las últimas   Véase *at the end of one's rope.*

en sesión continua   Véase *back-to-back.*

en un abrir y cerrar de ojos   Véase *(as) quick as a wink.*

en virtud de algo   Véase *by virtue of something.*

encajar bien un golpe   Véase *take something on the chin.*

encontrarse en seguida en su salsa con algo   Véase *as a duck takes to water.*

entrar en liga   Véase *toss one's hat into the ring.*

entrar en razón   Véase *come to one's senses.*

entre la espada y la pared   Véase *between a rock and a hard place.*

envainar la espada   Véase *bury the hatchet.*

equivocarse de medio a medio   Véase *bark up the wrong tree.*

errar la marcha   Véase *bring up the rear.*

Es el colmo   Véase *That's the last straw.*

Es la gota que colmó el vaso   Véase *That's the last straw.*

Es la gota que derramó al vino   Véase *That's the last straw.*

escurridizo como una anguila   Véase *(as) slippery as an eel.*

espalda con espalda   Véase *back-to-back.*

estancarse Véase *come to a standstill.*

estar a partir un piñon Véase *(as) thick as thieves.*

estar a tope Véase *burst at the seams.*

estar como una cabra Véase *(as) mad as a hatter.*

estar desesperado Véase *at one's wit's end.*

estar en circulación Véase *back in circulation.*

estar en desacuerdo Véase *at loggerheads.*

estar en la contienda Véase *toss one's hat into the ring.*

estar en la gloria Véase *(as) snug as a bug in a rug.*

estar en pugna con Véase *at loggerheads.*

estar encima de alguien Véase *breathe down someone's neck.*

estar hasta atrás Véase *(as) high as a kite.*

estar hecho un lío Véase *at sixes and sevens.*

estar más visto que el tebeo Véase *be old hat.*

estar muy cotizado Véase *at a premium.*

estar muy embrollado Véase *at sixes and sevens.*

estar pegado a las faldas de la madre Véase *tied to one's mother's apron strings.*

estar que subirse por las paredes Véase *up in arms.*

estar resentido Véase *have a chip on one's shoulder.*

estar totalmente colocado Véase *(as) high as a kite.*

estar totalmente drogado Véase *(as) high as a kite.*

estar totalmente perdido Véase *babe in the woods.*

estar uña y carne Véase *(as) thick as thieves.*

Esto viene como anillo al dedo Véase *That's the ticket.*

exhalar el último suspiro Véase *breathe one's last.*

fastidiarlo todo Véase *throw a monkey wrench in the works.*

fuerte como un roble Véase *(as) strong as an ox.*

fuerte como un toro Véase *(as) strong as an ox.*

gastar a manos llenas y hacer economías en nimiedades   Véase *penny-wise and pound-foolish.*

habérselas con algo   Véase *come to grips with something.*

hablar sin ton ni son   Véase *talk through one's hat.*

hacer algo partiendo desde el principio   Véase *start from scratch.*

hacer antesala larga   Véase *cool one's heels.*

hacer autostop   Véase *thumb a ride.*

hacer borrón y cuenta nueva   Véase *turn over a new leaf.*

hacer dedo   Véase *thumb a ride.*

hacer la vista gorda frente a algo   Véase *turn a blind eye to someone or something.*

hacer las paces   Véase *bury the hatchet.*

hacer lo que le da la gana   Véase *law unto oneself.*

hacer oídos sordos a alguien o algo   Véase *turn a deaf ear (to something).*

hacerle ascos a alguien o algo   Véase *turn one's nose up at someone or something.*

hacerse cargo de alguien   Véase *take someone under one's wing(s).*

hacerse mayor de edad   Véase *come of age.*

hasta el fin del mundo   Véase *to the ends of the earth.*

hasta los confines de la tierra   Véase *to the ends of the earth.*

Hay mucho más donde elegir   Véase *There are plenty of other fish in the sea.*

hoyo en uno   Véase *hole in one.*

ir a contrapelo   Véase *go against the grain.*

ir a vendimiar y llevar uvas de postre   Véase *carry coals to Newcastle.*

ir al grano   Véase *come to the point.*

ir contra corriente   Véase *swim against the tide.*

llegar a un callejón sin salida   Véase *come to a dead end.*

llegar a un punto muerto   Véase *come to a standstill.*

llevar leña al monte   Véase *carry coals to Newcastle.*

llevar un tren de vida que los ingresos no le permiten a uno   Véase *live beyond one's means.*

llevar un tren de vida que no se puede costear   Véase *live beyond one's means.*

llover a cántaros   Véase *rain cats and dogs.*

lo más pronto posible   Véase *(as) soon as possible.*

Loro viejo no aprende a hablar   Véase *You can't teach an old dog new tricks.*

luchar contra molinos de viento   Véase *tilt at windmills.*

malograrle los planes a uno   Véase *cook someone's goose.*

mandarle unas letras a alguien   Véase *drop someone a line.*

mantener a alguien al tanto   Véase *keep someone posted.*

mantenerse en sus trece   Véase *stick to one's guns.*

manzana de la discordia   Véase *bone of contention.*

más bueno que el pan   Véase *(as) good as gold.*

más fresco que una lechuga   Véase *(as) cool as a cucumber.*

más pobre que las ratas   Véase *(as) poor as a church mouse.*

más terco que una mula   Véase *(as) stubborn as a mule.*

Más vale pájaro en mano que ciento [o buitre] volando   Véase *A bird in the hand is worth two in the bush.*

matar dos pájaros de un tiro   Véase *kill two birds with one stone.*

mejor es no menear   Véase *Let sleeping dogs lie.*

mejor no resolver el asunto   Véase *Let sleeping dogs lie.*

mentir con toda la barba   Véase *lie through one's teeth.*

mentir con todos los dientes   Véase *lie through one's teeth.*

mentir descaradamente   Véase *lie through one's teeth.*

meter la pata   Véase *lay an egg.*

metido hasta el cuello   Véase *up to one's neck (in something).*

morder el polvo [persona]   Véase *bite the dust.*

mucho ruido y pocas nueces   Véase *much ado about nothing.*

no andar sobrado de algo   Véase *caught short.*

no andarse con rodeos   Véase *put something on the line.*

no coger la idea   Véase *miss the point.*

no creerse algo al pie de la letra   Véase *take something with a pinch of salt.*

no encontrar ni pies ni cabeza a alguien o algo   Véase *can't make heads or tails (out) of someone or something.*

No es oro todo lo que reluce   Véase *All that glitters is not gold.*

no hacer pie   Véase *beyond one's depth.*

No hay moros en la costa   Véase *The coast is clear.*

no llegar ni a la suela del zapato de alguien   Véase *can't hold a candle to someone.*

no meterse donde no te llaman   Véase *go about one's business.*

no poder cantar afinado   Véase *can't carry a tune.*

no saber más qué hacer   Véase *at one's wit's end.*

no se puede estar en la misa y picando   Véase *have one's cake and eat it too.*

no ser ninguna nena   Véase *no spring chicken.*

no ser ninguña niña   Véase *no spring chicken.*

no tocar el fondo   Véase *beyond one's depth.*

no verle el pelo a alguien   Véase *neither hide nor hair.*

Obras son amores y no buenas razones   Véase *Actions speak louder than words.*

para colmo   Véase *add insult to injury.*

para más inri   Véase *add insult to injury.*

pararse   Véase *come to a standstill.*

romper el hielo   Véase *break the ice.*

romper (partir) el corazón a alguien   Véase *break someone's heart.*

sacar a luz   Véase *bring something to light.*

sacar partido de algo   Véase *cash in (on something).*

salir a la luz   Véase *come out of the closet; come to light.*

salir ganando   Véase *come out ahead.*

salir pitando   Véase *take to one's heels.*

saltarse (de) las reglas   Véase *step out of line.*

sano como una manzana   Véase *(as) fit as a fiddle.*

sano y salvo   Véase *safe and sound.*

Se ha dado vuelta la tortilla   Véase *The shoe is on the other foot.*

Se va a armar la gorda   Véase *The fat is in the fire.*

seguir el ejemplo de alguien   Véase *take a leaf out of someone's book.*

seguir tirando dinero a la basura   Véase *throw good money after bad.*

seguro que la gente murmurará   Véase *cause (some) tongues to wag.*

sembrar cizaña   Véase *stir up a hornet's nest.*

ser copión   Véase *be a copycat.*

ser de influencia   Véase *carry weight (with someone).*

ser de peso   Véase *carry weight (with someone).*

ser de postal   Véase *(as) pretty as a picture.*

ser el favorito del profesor   Véase *be the teacher's pet.*

ser el vivo retrato de alguien   Véase *be the spit and image of someone.*

ser la viva imagen de alguien   Véase *be the spit and image of someone.*

ser maniobrable   Véase *turn on a dime.*

tomarse la justicia por su propia mano   Véase *take the law into one's own hands.*

tomarse libertades con alguien   Véase *take liberties with someone or something.*

un fin en sí mismo   Véase *end in itself.*

un flechazo   Véase *love at first sight.*

un lapsus   Véase *slip of the tongue.*

un lobo disfrazado de cordero   Véase *wolf in sheep's clothing*

un tren de vida que no se puede costear   Véase *beyond one's means.*

un tren de vida que sus ingresos no se la permiten   Véase *beyond one's means.*

una tormenta en un vaso de agua   Véase *tempest in a teapot.*

venir a menos   Véase *come down in the world.*

vérselas negras   Véase *been through the mill.*

vislumbrar el final   Véase *begin to see daylight.*

vivir a cuerpo de rey   Véase *lead the life of Riley.*

vivir al día   Véase *live from hand to mouth.*

vivir una vida muy agitada   Véase *burn the candle at both ends.*

vivir uno de su ingenio   Véase *live by one's wits.*

vuelta a empezar   Véase *back to the drawing board.*